DATE DUE

OC 18 '99			
4-53			
6-26			
AP 25 '00			
DE 18 02			
MY 19 '03			

DEMCO 38-296

Shakespeare's
Sweet Thunder

Shakespeare's Sweet Thunder

Essays on the Early Comedies

Edited by

Michael J. Collins

DELAWARE

Newark: University of Delaware Press
London: Associated University Presses

© 1997 by Associated University Presses, Inc.

ɔn to photocopy items for internal or personal
use of specific clients, is granted by the copy-
ɪe fee of $10.00, plus eight cents per page, per
ɪyright Clearance Center, 222 Rosewood Drive,
23. [0-87413-582-6/97 $10.00 + 8¢ pp, pc.]

Associated University Presses
440 Forsgate Drive
Cranbury, NJ 08512

Associated University Presses
16 Barter Street
London WC1A 2AH, England

Associated University Presses
P.O. Box 338, Port Credit
Mississauga, Ontario
Canada L5G 4L8

The paper used in this publication meets the requirements
of the American National Standard for Permanence of Paper
for Printed Library Materials Z39.48–1984.

Library of Congress Cataloging-in-Publication Data

Shakespeare's sweet thunder : essays on the early comedies / edited by
Michael J. Collins.
    p.   cm.
Includes bibliographical references and index.
ISBN 0-87413-582-6 (alk. paper)
    1. Shakespeare, William, 1564–1616—Comedies. 2. Comedy.
I. Collins, Michael J., 1941–
PR2981.S435 1997
822.3'3—dc20   96-5747
                                                  CIP

PRINTED IN THE UNITED STATES OF AMERICA

CONTENTS

Contributors

CAROL J. CARLISLE is Professor Emerita of English at the University of South Carolina. She has written extensively on Shakespeare and the theater and is currently co-editor of *The Two Gentlemen of Verona* for the New Shakespeare Variorum. The annual Carol Jones Carlisle Research Award was established in her honor at the University of South Carolina in 1989.

RALPH ALAN COHEN, Professor of English at James Madison University, is Executive Director and cofounder of the Shenandoah Shakespeare Express, for which he has directed several productions. A winner of Virginia's Outstanding Faculty Award, he has twice been a guest editor of *Shakespeare Quarterly* for issues devoted to teaching Shakespeare and has written a book on the subject.

MICHAEL J. COLLINS is adjunct Professor of English and Dean of the School for Summer and Continuing Education at Georgetown University.

PATTY S. DERRICK is Assistant Professor of English at the University of Pittsburgh at Johnstown, where she teaches Renaissance Literature and Shakespeare to students of theater and literature. She is assistant editor of *The Two Gentlemen of Verona* for the New Shakespeare Variorum. She has written on the theatrical interpretation of Shakespeare, especially by actresses.

ALAN C. DESSEN, Peter G. Phialas Professor of English at the University of North Carolina at Chapel Hill, is the Director of ACTER (A Center for Theatre, Education, and Research) and the editor of the section on Shakespeare Performed in *Shakespeare Quarterly*. He has written six books on Shakespeare and Elizabethan drama including, most recently, *Recovering Shakespeare's Theatrical Vocabulary*.

MIRIAM GILBERT, Professor of English at the University of Iowa, has focused her work on performance criticism and performance-

7

related approaches in the classroom. She has taught seven NEH seminars on "Shakespeare: Text and Theatre," some of which have been held in Stratford-upon-Avon, where she has a second home. Her most recent book is *Shakespeare in Performance: "Love's Labor's Lost."*

JAY L. HALIO is Professor of English at the University of Delaware. He has recently edited *King Lear* for the New Cambridge Shakespeare and written a book on *A Midsummer Night's Dream* in performance.

ROBERT S. MIOLA is Professor of English at Loyola College in Baltimore, Maryland. His interest in the classical sources of Shakespeare's plays has resulted in two of his books, *Shakespeare's Rome* and *Shakespeare and Classical Tragedy: the Influence of Seneca.*

JEANNE ADDISON ROBERTS is Professor *Emerita* of Literature at The American University in Washington, D.C. She has taught in Bangkok, Thailand and Beirut, Lebanon and has served as a scholar in residence for the Teaching Shakespeare Institute at the Folger Shakespeare Library. Her most recent book is *The Shakespearean Wild: Geography, Genus, and Gender.*

CAROL RUTTER lectures at the University of Warwick. She is author of *Documents of the Rose Playhouse* and *Clamorous Voices: Shakespeare's Women Today.* She is currently writing about the representation of women's death in Shakespeare's theater and on the contemporary stage.

BRUCE R. SMITH is Professor of English at Georgetown University and has served as Director of Graduate Studies. He has been guest curator of "Roasting the Swan," an exhibition at the Folger Shakespeare Library, and President of the Shakespeare Association of America (1994–95). His most recent book is *Homosexual Desire in Shakespeare's England: A Cultural Poetics.*

HOMER SWANDER, Professor *Emeritus* of English at the University of California at Santa Barbara, has written frequently on Shakespeare in performance and has directed more than fifteen productions of the plays. He founded ACTER (A Center for Theatre, Education, and Research) in 1975 and served as its director for twenty years.

ANN THOMPSON is Professor of English and Head of the English Department at Roehampton Institute in London. She has edited *The Taming of the Shrew* for the New Cambridge Shakespeare, is general editor of a series of books on feminist criticism of Shakespeare for Routledge, and is one of the general editors of the Arden Shakespeare, third series, for which she is co-editing *Hamlet* with Neil Taylor.

Shakespeare's
Sweet Thunder

Introduction: The Afterlife of Shakespeare's Early Comedies

MICHAEL J. COLLINS

I

SHAKESPEARE'S early comedies have had, to borrow a word from Jonathan Miller, an "afterlife" that might seem, on reflection, surprisingly long.[1] They first appeared on the stage in London some four hundred years ago, in a time and place very different from our own. Yet for all the differences between our world and Shakespeare's, all of the early comedies were in production, either in Stratford or London, at one time or another in 1993, each one making clear the openness of Shakespeare's four-hundred-year-old scripts to subsequent theatrical interpretation that both reflects its own time and speaks in a variety of ways to it.

Ian Judge's 1990 production for the Royal Shakespeare Company of *The Comedy of Errors*, in a Christmas revival at the Barbican, turned the play into a brightly colored, fast moving, superbly timed farce: the set contained nine doors, and Desmond Barrit, wearing a red or orange blazer to distinguish them, played the two Antipholi. At the same time, the Canadian director Robert Lepage, drawing in part on Jan Kott's reading of the play, staged *A Midsummer Night's Dream* at the Royal National Theatre as "a watery dream, a dark dream,"[2] with a pool of mud on the stage for the lovers to crawl through. David Thacker's production of *The Two Gentlemen of Verona* at the Haymarket Theatre in London, originally staged at the Swan Theatre in Stratford in 1991, set the play in the 1930s: the men wore striped blazers, the women cotton dresses of the period, and an eight-piece band and a singer remained upstage throughout the evening, performing songs by Cole Porter and Irving Berlin between the scenes. Incorporating the Sly material from *A Shrew* into the Folio text and transforming the Lord and his huntsmen into five contemporary young aristocrats apparently hunting some amusement on the quiet streets of Stratford, Bill Alexander's production of *The Taming of the Shrew* for the Royal Shakespeare Company at the Barbican explored, in a generous and often deeply moving way, the shifting relationships among characters, audience, actors, and the world outside the theater. Finally, in a production of *Love's Labor's Lost* that opened in Stratford in October, Ian Judge moved the play from Navarre to an Oxbridge college in Edwardian England and, following Berowne's dismay at the delay of twelve months, ended the play with the noise of gunfire and shells and an image of a battlefield in France during the First World War. While such freewheeling transformations inevitably failed to please everyone, Shakespeare's early comedies, as these productions suggest, remain, after four hundred years, open to theatrical interpretations that address the interests of their own time and place.

The recent theatrical history of *A Midsummer Night's Dream* reflects the openness of all the early comedies to interpretation and the varied afterlives all these plays have had in our own time. The example of two productions makes clear, in broad terms, the larger interpretive possibilities of the script. In 1989, John Caird staged *Dream* at the Royal Shakespeare Theatre in Stratford as a genial, generous, consistently hilarious play that let no comic possibility go by. The transformed Bottom looked like a child's stuffed animal with furry ears, large eyes, and long, fluttering lashes. Parodying Max Reinhardt's classic version of the play, the fairies, dressed as ballerinas but with black hightop shoes, moved gawkily over the stage. John Carlisle's Oberon was kind, gentle, deeply troubled by his estrangement from Titania, and Puck, played by Richard McCabe as a mischievous schoolboy in cap, jacket, striped tie, and short pants, had to be comforted by Oberon after he had frightened himself with his description of the damned spirits who walk at night (3.2.378–95).[3] Although the lovers were at first incorrectly (but happily) paired as they walked off the stage, they at the last moment recognized their mistake and quickly switched partners, walking hand in hand back to Athens. The restored Titania gave one comic shriek when she saw Bottom in her bed and then, putting her arms around Oberon, laughed at the joke he had played on her. As the audience left the theater, listening to the music of two small orchestras on either side of the stage, it seemed asked to believe that, as the lovers in the play, all its dreams could also come true.

In the fall of the same year, Liviu Ciulei directed (for at least the third time) an entirely different *Dream* at the Arena Stage in Washington, D.C., one along the lines of John Lepage's a few years later. It began with what seemed a scene from an internment camp: Hippolyta was stripped of her fatigue uniform and forced to wear a long, elaborate dress and train. Stanley Anderson's Bottom was a lustful ass who fondled Titania and repulsed her fairies with his stench. Unlike the lovers in Caird's production, Ciulei's copulated interchangeably beneath a tent of long silk scarves, and when they left the stage for Athens, they seemed uneasy, walking off individually, separated from one another by their own troubled thoughts. When she saw his ass-shaped shadow on the floor of the stage, the restored Titania, frightened and horrified by her memory of the night, had to be comforted by a now-repentant Oberon. As the production came to a close, Theseus and Hippolyta stood alone on the stage. Hippolyta began her exit, leaving Theseus standing behind her. At the very last moment, just as she was about to move offstage, she stopped and, without looking back at him, extended her hand behind her. Moving quickly across the stage, Theseus embraced her, and they went off hand in hand. A moment later, however, Bottom and his friends entered dancing, only to find their generous patron, Theseus, had forgotten them. The audiences that left Liviu Ciulei's production at the Arena Stage had thus seen a version of *A Midsummer Night's Dream* that, by making apparent the darker implications of the play, had diluted its comic vision.

Although Shakespeare and the company of actors who worked with him four hundred years ago in London could probably never have imagined either of these productions, they both grew out of what seemed an honest response to the script and an imaginative reach for theatrical metaphors to articulate that response on the stage. If together they stand roughly as poles to mark the characteristic range of interpretations the play has recently been given on the stage, they did not by any means, as John Lepage's *Dream* soon made clear, exhaust all the local possibilities of the script. Rather, they suggested the enduring openness of Shakespeare's early comedies to imaginative, thoughtful, provocative, energetic interpretation that, while simultaneously suppressing some dimensions of the script, nonetheless gives the play an afterlife that allows audiences to discover in it something of themselves and their own time and place, an interpretation that, as Jonathan Miller puts it, assimilates an object of the past into the interests of the present.[4]

II

The essays that follow are all, in one way or another, not only concerned with the afterlife of Shakespeare's early comedies, but are also themselves examples of it. Since production provides the plays their natural afterlife, most of the essays focus, to a greater or lesser degree, on performance, discussing its history and meaning and the impact of particular historic moments upon it. But performance is not the only way by which the early comedies find an afterlife. Literary critics, as some of the essays suggest, give the plays another kind of afterlife in the books and essays they write, thus assimilating them in a different way into the interests of the present. Then, like all of Shakespeare's plays, the early comedies, particularly *The Taming of the Shrew* and *A Midsummer Night's Dream*, have yet a third afterlife, different from the one either the director or the literary critic gives them. The early comedies, for better or worse, live today in our class-rooms and have an afterlife in the talking and writing and acting they occasion among teachers and students. That encounter with Shakespeare's early comedies, distinct from either performance or literary criticism, yet often closely linked to both, may be the most common way in which the plays find an afterlife in our own time and become assimilated into the interests of the present.

The essays seek then both to explore the afterlife of Shakespeare's early comedies some four hundred years after their first appearances on the stage and, by looking at them from the perspective of our own time, to enlarge it as well. Robert S. Miola begins the process by examining one dimension of the afterlife that scholars have given the plays, their relationship to their sources. Tracing the influence of New Comedy on *The Comedy of Errors* and *The Taming of the Shrew*, his essay not only suggests what Shakespeare's variations and transformations might reveal about the two plays, but also illustrates a relatively new sense of intertextuality among literary scholars and their recent broadened understanding of what constitutes a source.

The next two essays, by Alan C. Dessen and Homer Swander, explore a more troubled afterlife, a more ambiguous intertextuality, the relationship between versions of the same play and its implications for performance. Dessen compares *The Taming of a Shrew* (the Quarto version of 1594) with *The Taming of the Shrew* (the Folio version of 1623) to suggest the difference the precedence of one or the other might "make to interpretation today on the page or the stage." Swander's essay on *Love's Labor's Lost* examines the afterlife of the Quarto of 1598 and proposes that a history of editorial interventions has created a new play that, while more rational and symmetrical, has less theatrical vitality. While neither Dessen nor Swander will say which version reflects more precisely what we might call Shakespeare's script, nor which version forms part of the afterlife of Shakespeare's play, Swander, trusting his experience of directing *Love's Labor's Lost*, stops just short of making his answer explicit.

The second group of essays begins with another exploration of intertextuality, Jeanne Addison Roberts's study of the relationship of *Love's Labor's Lost* to *The Convent of Pleasure*, a play by Margaret Cavendish, published in 1668, that seems to have been inspired by Shakespeare's. Marking the unconventional qualities of the two plays, Roberts finds "some signs of incipient feminism" in both of them and thus introduces "a plane of interest or meaning"[5] in the early comedies that has come into particularly sharp focus today—their concern with issues of gender and the relationships it brings about. Both Ann Thompson and Bruce R. Smith, in the two essays that follow, turn their attention to these issues. Assimilating objects of the past into the interests of the present, Ann Thompson, noting that "most feminist critics have simply ignored *The Comedy of Errors* and *Love's Labor's Lost*," surveys "such work as has been done so far" and considers "lines of investigation that might be undertaken in the future." Bruce R. Smith, using the methods of the new historicism, discusses *The Comedy of Errors* from the viewpoint of men's studies, describing the social context of its first performance and proposing that the play "offers itself as a particularly revealing document about what it meant to be male—for one privileged group of men, at least—in early modern England."

As Smith's essay implies, Shakespeare's plays find their natural afterlife in the productions that turn scripts into performances. The next group of essays, then, appropriately the largest in the collection, explores the afterlife of Shakespeare's early comedies on the stage. Carol J. Carlisle and Patty S. Derrick examine how both theatrical conventions and social and political attitudes have influenced productions of *The Two Gentlemen of Verona*, shaping both the representation of its characters and the overall interpretation of the play. Miriam Gilbert then explores some of the same influences on performance as she recounts the history of *Love's Labor's Lost* on the stage. In an essay that recalls Homer Swander's reflections on the play, she explains the disappearance of *Love's Labor's Lost* from the stage in the eighteenth century, traces its subsequent return in the nineteenth, and finds, in its dark and unconventional ending, the reason for its continued popularity on the stage in our own time.

The next essay, which looks back to Alan C. Dessen's examination of the Quarto and Folio versions of the play, deals with recent productions of *The Taming of the Shrew*. As it makes clear, *The Shrew* has been assimilated, probably more explicitly than any of the other early comedies, into the interests of the present, and its highly controversial afterlife in our own time accounts for the degree of continued attention it receives today from both critics and directors. In a long essay on the play, Carol Rutter first deciphers what she calls the "secret" *Shrew*, Shakespeare's "anti-play that is an Elizabethan subversion of the conventional shrew-taming story." Then, finding that "the performance of Kate's submission speech challenges the orthodoxy of its content while occupying a theater space that allows both the conservative and the revolutionary to resonate simultaneously," she turns her attention to the playing of the woman's part in recent productions of *The Shrew*, discussing first Fiona Shaw's understanding of Kate in Jonathan Miller's production for the Royal Shakespeare Company in 1987, then the role of Bianca as Rebecca Saire acted it in Bill Alexander's production for the Royal Shakespeare Company in 1992, and finally the work and observations of Emily Watson and Catherine Mears, who portrayed two of the aristocrats Alexander kept on the stage to watch and eventually take part in the performance of the play. This large group of essays, all centered on performance, concludes with Jay L. Halio's examination of John Lepage's controversial production of *A Midsummer Night's Dream* at the Royal National Theatre in 1992.

The last essay in the collection, drawing on both criticism and performance, suggests how the insights and observations of the preceding essays might come to make Shakespeare's early comedies more enjoyable and ultimately more meaningful to students. With a series of specific exercises for teaching them, Ralph Alan Cohen offers ways in which the afterlife that Shakespeare's early comedies inevitably find in the classroom can become more resonant and rewarding for the teachers and students who together create it.

These diverse essays grow to something of constancy then in their efforts to enlarge and bring some new vitality to the afterlife of Shakespeare's early comedies, to suggest how these four-hundred-year-old objects of the past have been and might continue to be, in the study, on the stage, and in the classroom, assimilated to the interests of the present, to the interests of the men and women who encounter them in the last years of the twentieth century. As the essays themselves suggest, that encounter seems most appropriate and indeed most rewarding in the theater, where the scripts of the early comedies are given their most telling and powerful afterlife through the collaboration of actors, directors, and designers.

III

The great power of the early comedies in performance recently became clear once again in Bill Alexander's production of The Taming of the Shrew, the one Carol Rutter describes and comments upon. In keeping Sly and the young aristocrats on the stage throughout the evening, in giving the aristocrats roles to play, in twice allowing Sly to break the boundary between his world and the play's, the production not only blurred the distinction between theatrical illusion and reality, but also put one of the play's climactic moments at risk. As Tranio, Biondello, and the Pedant ran off the stage (5.1 in the Folio), Sly, holding the neck of a shattered bottle, moved downstage and said, "Nobody's going to prison." The play stopped. Wary of the bottle's jagged edge, the actors shifted out of their roles, and the one playing Petruchio told Sly, "It's all right. It's only a play." Convinced nobody would go to prison, Sly returned to his seat upstage. The actors, resuming their places, at Petruchio's orchestration ran some lines a second time, and the play continued.

Some forty lines later, Kate and Petruchio kissed at center stage, a kiss that seemed Kate's first. Initially, her arms were straight out behind him, but then, as she apparently got the knack of it, they folded slowly around him. While they held their kiss, the lights came down, and they remained motionless, in silhouette, embracing one another at the edge of the stage. The performance had taken hold again: what, only forty lines earlier, had been explicitly revealed as play, as illusion, now made a powerful and convincing impact on both its audiences. The couples upstage moved together. Sly reached out to hold the hand of the man dressed as his recalcitrant wife, and she at last allowed him to do so. But more importantly, the long embrace of Kate and Petruchio seemed as deeply moving in the house as it was on the stage, for at that moment the production brought its audience to feel the quiet joy that love between people sometimes makes possible. In such moving moments of theater, Shakespeare's early comedies enjoy their most significant and powerful afterlife, making felt their connection to our world, even though that world seems often very different from their own. The essays that follow, then, themselves part of the afterlife of Shakespeare's early comedies, are meant finally to suggest not just their meanings for our own time, but their enduring power to make felt in the theater their complex vision of human life, to make heard Shakespeare's sweet thunder.

NOTES

1. In *Subsequent Performances*, Jonathan Miller explains that "this term and idea [i.e., the "afterlife"] applies not only to plays but to other works of art that survive the period in which they were conceived and first realized." (London: Faber and Faber, 1986), 23.

2. Robert Lepage in an interview by Charles Spencer in *The Daily Telegraph* on 6 July 1992. Quoted by George L. Geckle, review of *A Midsummer Night's Dream* in *Shakespeare Bulletin* 11, no. 2 (Spring, 1993): 27.

3. All citations of Shakespeare's plays, here and in the essays that follow, unless otherwise indicated, are from *The Riverside Shakespeare*, G. Blakemore Evans and others, eds. (Boston: Houghton Mifflin, 1974).

4. In an interview by Ralph Berry, Miller says "the job of the artist in the theatre is illumination and reconstruction, and the endless task of assimilating the objects of the past into the interests of the present." Ralph Berry, *On Directing Shakespeare: Interviews with Contemporary Directors* (London: Hamish Hamilton, 1989), 40.

5. As Jonathan Miller sees it, "each generation tends to regard certain lines as the crucial ones, but that is because that generation has decided to focus upon a particular plane of interest or meaning within the play and within that plane certain lines obviously assume a dazzling precedence. Another generation will focus on another plane within which a different set of lines will assume a precedence." Ibid, 39.

The Influence of New Comedy on *The Comedy of Errors* and *The Taming of the Shrew*

Robert S. Miola

The critical conception of Shakespeare's sources has undergone great change since the first productions of his plays some four hundred years ago. Today, critics are much more interested in Shakespeare's creative use of sources, his tendency to revise radically and contrarily, and his habit of eclectically mixing various texts and traditions into new creations. Recent advances in Renaissance intertextuality have also broadened our conception of influence to include various manifestations, nonverbal as well as verbal—"transformed convention, rhetorical or structural format, scenic rhythm, ideational or imagistic concatenation, thematic articulation."[1] Moreover, these advances have attuned criticism to the reality of mediated or collateral influence; in the age of imitation, one text always leads into and out toward many others. Thus many new texts and traditions now qualify as sources for Shakespeare.

Examination of two of the plays treated in this volume, *The Comedy of Errors* and *The Taming of the Shrew*, well illustrate these changes.[2] *The Comedy of Errors*, of course, has long-recognized sources in Plautus' *Menaechmi* and *Amphitruo*, Gower's *Confessio Amantis*, and Paul's Epistles; *The Taming of the Shrew* is indebted to various folk traditions as well as to the *The Taming of a Shrew* and Gascoigne's *Supposes*. This essay will illustrate the present attitudes toward sources by examining the influence of New Comedy on both plays. In *The Comedy of Errors*, we shall observe how Shakespeare uses his sources, specifically how he adapts Plautus to meet new theatrical and

I am indebted to Oxford University Press for permission to reprint some material in this essay.

21

moral concerns. In *The Taming of the Shrew*, we shall discern
the presence of New Comedy, specifically *Eunuchus* and *Captivi*,
in mediated form, as deep sources of structure, design, and
meaning.

Shakespeare's obvious indebtedness to *Menaechmi* in *The
Comedy of Errors* originally became a focal point in the "Small
Latine" debate of the eighteenth century. As Brian Vickers notes,
Langbaine's erroneous assertion that Shakespeare used Warner's
translation echoed in the judgments of Rowe, Gildon, Dennis,
Pope, Mrs. Lennox, and Johnson.[3] Dennis, in fact, asserted that
he could "never believe" Shakespeare capable of reading Plautus
"without Pain and Difficulty" and speculated about the assistance of a "Stranger" or "some learned Friend." Richard Farmer,
influential debunker of Shakespeare's classical attainments,
jeered at two other instances of direct influence, both alleged by
George Colman (1765). Farmer observed that the disguise plot of
The Taming of the Shrew derives from Gascoigne's *Supposes*,
not Plautus's *Trinummus*, and that Shakespeare's altered quotation of a line from Terence derives from Lily's grammar rather
than the source in *Eunuchus*. In effect, early critics of these plays
denied rather than discerned the influence of New Comedy on
Shakespeare.

Since T. W. Baldwin's monumental labors settled many major
points in the debate about Shakespeare's classical learning, commentators can freely analyze Shakespeare's use of New Comedy
in this play. Though Shakespeare follows *Menaechmi* more
closely than he does any other classical model, comedy or tragedy, he, with Italianate brio, doubles the number of identical
twins and increases the incidents of error from seventeen to fifty.[4]
The eristic impulse, the urge to outdo, to overgo the classical
model is endemic to the age, evident also in neoclassical plays
like the anonymous *The Birth of Hercules*, which adds a second
servant to the *Amphitruo* story and develops the minuscule part
of Thessala.[5] Lyly's *Mother Bombie* (1594) likewise exceeds Roman models by presenting two pairs of changeling children, four
old men, four servants, and three pairs of lovers. Apparent also
in *The Comedy of Errors* is Shakespeare's focus on love affairs:
the merely functional Wife becomes the complicated Adriana,
whose marriage to the citizen twin will be a center of attention;
the irascible and opportunistic Menaechmus of Syracuse becomes the bewildered lover, Antipholus, conveniently provided
for by the invented Luciana.

Shakespeare, of course, changes the setting from Epidamnus

to Ephesus, a place that at first seems equally inhospitable. Ephesus, however, threatens not only one's wallet but also one's self and soul:

> They say this town is full of cozenage:
> As nimble jugglers that deceive the eye,
> Dark-working sorcerers that change the mind,
> Soul-killing witches that deform the body,
> Disguised cheaters, prating mountebanks,
> And many such-like liberties of sin.
>
> (1.2.97–102)

Emphasizing witchcraft instead of Plautine thievery (see also 4.3.71 ff.), Shakespeare probably follows the lead of St. Paul and his depiction of Ephesian sorcery. In so doing, the playwright restores the emphasis found in ancient folktales of this type, wherein a witch commonly lures the husband, but winds up with the traveling twin, who outwits her.[6] Of course, Adriana is neither witch nor courtesan, but wife, and Shakespeare's expansion of the *matrona* [wife] here is a signal feature of Renaissance *imitatio*. Bullough notes similar expansion in Italian adaptations of *Menaechmi* by Firenzuola, Trissino, and Cecchi.[7] And other English plays—*Jack Juggler* and Chapman's *All Fools*, for example—likewise feature wives expanded from their classical models.

In her opening dialogue with Luciana (2.1), Adriana exhibits jealousy, a theme hinted at in the original (110 ff.; 787 ff.) but developed here like a courtly debate. The touch is lighter than many have recognized: their conversation switches into rhymed couplets (10); Adriana wryly punctures Luciana's philosophical paean to male dominance, "This servitude makes you to keep unwed" (26); the scene ends with Adriana's misinterpretation and her foolish display of jealousy and self-pity. Thus it sets up the subsequent confrontation with the traveling twin, a comic error that Adriana's earnestness only heightens. Still, the poetry of her complaint, insisting on a union "undividable, incorporate," sometimes betokens more than merely comic exasperation:

> How comes it now, my husband, O, how comes it,
> That thou art then estranged from thyself?
> Thyself I call it, being strange to me,
> That, undividable, incorporate,
> Am better than thy dear self's better part.
>
> (2.2.119–23)

Shakespeare turns the Plautine predation into a scene that briefly touches on the mystery of identity from another angle, that of two selves becoming one in marriage. We hear echoes of Portia's memorable conversation with Brutus and, perhaps, the Anglican wedding service. And echoes of Plautus too, as Adriana continues:

> For know, my love, as easy mayst thou fall
> A drop of water in the breaking gulf
> And take unmingled thence that drop again,
> Without addition or diminishing,
> As take from me thyself and not me too.
>
> (2.2.125–9)

The speech recalls Antipholus of Syracuse:

> He that commends me to mine own content
> Commends me to the thing I cannot get.
> I to the world am like a drop of water
> That in the ocean seeks another drop,
> Who, falling there to find his fellow forth,
> Unseen, inquisitive, confounds himself:
> So I, to find a mother and brother,
> In quest of them, unhappy, lose myself.
>
> (1.2.33–40)

Both water-drop images derive ultimately from one of Plautus' favorite similes: "neque aqua aquaeque nec lacte est lactis, crede mi, / usquam similius, / quam hic tui est, tuque huius autem." (*Men*, 1089–90), [No drop of water, no drop of milk, is more like another, believe me, than he's like you, yes, and you like him, sir.] Witness Sosia in *Amphitruo*: "Neque lac lactis magis est simile quam ille ego similest mei" (601), [One drop of milk is no more like another than I is like me.] (Cf. *Bacchides*, frag. 5; *Miles Gloriosus*, 551–2). The simile, a simple, proverbial exercise in visual comparison, might once have supplied the microscopic stylistics of parallel-passage hunting, but its real importance lies in its transformation. For Adriana the image becomes a symbol of incorporate, indivisible wedded love; for Antipholus, a symbol of longing and frustrated desire. Antipholus's metaphor suggests the universal need of people for each other and the threat of self-loss in the ocean of the world. It illuminates Egeon too, again venturing on the high seas, one who "hazarded the loss of whom I lov'd" "of a love to see" the lost son (1.1.130–1). The paradoxes here and above, the complex play on losing and finding, tilt the farce of complication towards a comedy of identity and deliverance.[8]

The significant contrast between the traveling twins also measures the difference between the two plays. Menaechmus of Syracuse says simply that he looks for his lost brother because "ego illum scio quam cordi sit carus meo" (246), [I alone know how dear he is to me.] In Epidamnus he decides to play along for fun and profit, "adsentabor quidquid dicet mulieri, / si possum hospitium nancisci" (417–18), [I'll assent to whatever the wench says, if I can come in for some entertainment here.] "Habeo praedam" (434), [The booty's mine!] he declares later. Thus he, like the other residents, enters the game of false appearances for personal gain. Everyone's on the hustle, even the maid who tries to get gold added to her earrings, and the fun lies in watching the ingenuity of the various players. Trissino deepened the character of the traveling twin in his adaptation of Menaechmi, I Simillimi (Venice, 1548), but even this traveler seeks "qualche guadagnw" [some profit] (sig. Biiii) from the situation. In Ephesus, however, Antipholus of Syracuse wonders in asides about dreaming (2.2.182 ff.), about whether he is "in earth, in heaven, or in hell? / Sleeping or waking? mad or well-advis'd" (212–13). Designated "Errotis" and "Erotes" in the Folio, both terms suggestive of wandering and desire, he follows out the adventure, confused about his experience, uncertain of himself. The romantic melodies of Ovidian metamorphosis sound quietly in his confusion and more forcefully in his lyrically amorous declaration to Luciana.[9] This traveler will not fall upon prey, but into love.

In Menaechmi, the husband comes up against the locked door (661 ff.), but his wife shuts him out intentionally, as does Erotium, leaving him exclusissimus (698), "utterly locked out," or in Warner's translation (1595), "now I am euerie way shut out for a very benchwhistler" (sig. D2). In Amphitruo, probably the direct inspiration for Shakespeare's scene, the wife innocently entertains an imposter while the husband fumes outside (cf. 3.1.1ff and 1081 ff.). He hammers on his door while someone who looks and sounds like his servant taunts him from within. He threatens to break down the door and another dinner guest goes away disappointed. Shakespeare substitutes the self-important business man for the self-important soldier and adds the Dromios, the prefatory discussion on good welcome, and the bouncing rhythm of doggerel fourteeners.

Further, Shakespeare adopts Alcumena, pious matrona, as a

model that elevates and dignifies Adriana, who will rise above the merely dull or shrewish stereotype.[10] The rhetoric of accusation and protest between husband and wife in *Amphitruo* inspires several confrontations in *Errors*.[11] Amphitruo hurls the name of husband in Alcumena's face (813), thus embodying Adriana's fears (2.2.134–35). Both wives protest the perceived impudence of the servants (2.2.168–70; 721–22); both innocently insist that they dined with their husbands at home (4.4.65–99; 804 ff.). The husbands wrongly accuse the wives of infidelity (4.4.101–3; 818–20) and seek outside adjudication. Shakespeare wittily recollects a comic situation and several scattered touches, providing for character complexity and for raucous domestic fun.

Plautus plays the resolution of errors, the *cognitio* [recognition], for laughs: the twins finally meet each other and Messenio unravels the mystery, thereby winning his freedom; the Menaechmi plan to auction off the citizen's goods (and wife) and return to Syracuse together. Shakespeare emphasizes laughter too, but creates a complex closing action with surprising twists and turns. The *summa epitasis* [height of tension] occurs when Adriana stands before the Priory, now locked out herself. This second lockout displays Shakespeare's fondness for mirror episodes that ironically reflect and illuminate each other. Adriana's lock-out initiates a reexamination of her identity and a reevaluation of her moral self. Both occur, remarkably, through the replay of an earlier Plautine reversal. The Wife's father, we recall, turned her complaints about Menaechmus against her:

Sen. Quotiens monstravi tibi, viro ut morem geras,
       quid ille faciat, ne id observes, quo eat, quid rerum gerat.
Mat. At enim ille hinc amat meretricem ex proxumo.
Sen.   Sane sapit.
       atque ob istanc industriam etiam faxo amabit amplius
       (787–91).

[*Father* How many times have I explicitly told you to humor your husband and not to keep watching what he does, where he goes, and what he is about?

   Wife Well, but he makes love to this strumpet, the very next door!

   Father He shows excellent judgment, and he will make love to her all the more, I warrant you, to reward this diligence of yours.]

The Senex humorously upsets expectations: he acknowledges the husband's philandering but scolds the wife for her jealousy.

His sudden turn against the complaining wife inspires the Abbess's sudden turn against Adriana outside the Abbey in "The venom clamours of a jealous woman" speech (5.1.69 ff.). What in Plautus occurs as a humorous surprise reversal becomes in Shakespeare a moment of moral self-revelation about baseless jealousy. Unlike the Plautine husband, Antipholus never plans "Furtum, scortum, prandium" (170), [A raid! a jade! a meal!], but visits the courtesan with a friend and a gift to spite his wife for the lock-out. Adriana's subsequent silence before the Abbess and admission, "She did betray me to my own reproof" (5.1.90), signifies realization of her folly. The Plautine comedy begins and ends as a comedy of doors—doors opening and closing, doors blocking, dividing, concealing, doors locking in and locking out. Shakespearean comedy, as this play suggests, is a comedy of thresholds, of entranceways into new understandings and acceptances.

With *The Taming of the Shrew*, Shakespeare once again reworked the conventions of New Comedy while simultaneously finding in them a deep source of structure, design, and meaning for the play. As Farmer noted, he modeled the Lucentio-Bianca story on Gascoigne's *Supposes*; this play itself is a version of Ariosto's *I'Suppositi*, which frankly acknowledges indebtedness to *Eunuchus* and *Captivi* in its prologue:

> E vi confessa l'autore avere in questo e Plauto e Terenzio seguitato, de li quali l'un fece Cherea per Doro, e l'altro Filocrate per Tindaro, e Tindaro per Filocrate, l'uno ne lo *Eunuco*, l'altro ne li *Captivi*, supponersi: perché non solo ne li costumi, ma ne li argumenti ancora de le fabule vuole essere de li antichi e celebrati poeti, a tutta sua possanza, imitatore.

> [And the author confesses to you that in this matter he has followed both Plautus and Terence, of whom the one had Chaerea substituted for Dorus and the other Philocrates for Tyndarus and Tyndarus for Philocrates, in, respectively, the *Eunuch* of Plautus and the *Captives* of Terence; because the author wishes, as far as he can, to imitate not only the customs but even the arguments of the plots from ancient and celebrated poets.][12]

Behind Shakespeare's Tranio flits the whimsical shade of his classical namesake from *Mostellaria* and also that of another classical *servus* [slave], Parmeno of *Eunuchus*, whose words to the lovelorn Phaedria echo in the play: "Redime te captum quam queas minimo" (1.1.162 cf. *Eun.* 74–75), [Buy yourself out of bondage for as little as you can]. Part of the joke in both Terence and Shakespeare, of course, is that the servant here advises the master, whose infatuation has reduced him to dependence. The other part derives from the mechanical reduction of love to a financial transaction. Lovers in the classics sometimes protest this reduction, even as they yield to harsh economic realities, usually presented by an unsentimental *lena* [bawd]. But the connection between *negotium* [business] and *amor* [love] remains a fact of life in New Comedy, where lovers typically pay to emancipate a slave girl or buy the time of a courtesan. In the subplot of *Shrew* (and in the main one, for that matter) economic considerations still obtain although they have been modernized: here we have the fuss over the daughters' dowries and the bidding for Bianca. In the last scene, Shakespeare takes some pains to reverse the usual dynamics: there Kate's excellence as a wife wins her husband a significant sum of money.

As the above quotation suggests, *Eunuchus* is one of Ariosto's acknowledged sources for the "supposes" plot, a powerful presence in Gasgoigne's translation, and hence a deep source of Shakespeare's play. It sketched an archetypal comic action much imitated by later playwrights, including Chapman in *May-Day*. The play features two complementary wooing actions; in the one most pertinent to *Shrew*, Chaerea, disguised as a eunuch, gains access to Pamphila and has intercourse with her. Her long lost brother appears, reveals that she is Athenian by birth, and arranges a marriage with Chaerea.

Tranio and Lucentio's intrigue is unlike that in Terence's *Eunuchus* or, for that matter, unlike that in any other classical play. By the time of *Shrew*, comedic motifs like Chaerea's disguised entrance had become standard elements in the comic repertory, capable of endless manipulation and refiguration. Lodovico tries the Chaerea trick in Chapman's *May-Day*, for example, only to find the lady a disguised man and to receive a beating, thus literally and literarily confounded by a motif from *Casina*. And later, in Wycherley's *The Country Wife*, of course, Horner feigns impotence to gain access to a number of willing wives. A long tradition of Terentian commentary pointed the way for Shakespeare's adaptation in *Shrew*. The Bembine scholiasts saw in *Eunuchus* love's *furor*, a madness that does not recognize limit or counsel (*modus, consilium*). The humanists likewise glossed the play's double action and particularly the disguise intrigue as illustrations of love's sovereign and irrational power. The opening dialogue, reprised in Lucentio and Tranio's conversation, "exprimitur immoderati amoris insania, & quam difficulter cordatus etiam animus, ex tam impotente malo se eripiat" [expresses the insanity of immoderate love and how difficult it is, even for a reasonable mind, to free itself from this ungovernable evil]. Chaerea's use of disguise likewise shows "Primos adulescentis ardores, & Venereo aestus, posthabita rei domesticae ac publicae cura" [the first ardors of the adolescent and his erotic passions, overruling all concern for private and public responsibilities].[13] Like these commentators, but substituting bemused fascination for censorious disapproval, Shakespeare places love at the center of the action, depicting it as the powerful and irrational raison d'etre for comedic intrigue.

This focus on love, a romanticized version of New Comedic *eros* [desire] generates a number of important changes. First among these is the refiguration of the *virgo* [maiden]. Italian innovators from Ariosto to Oddi had already prepared the way, of course, transforming the slight classical sketches into variously complex women. Bianca too emerges as a character more interesting and important than the mute person of Terence's *Eunuchus*. Pamphila, in fact, has no character at all but is merely a function in the dramatic action. After briefly describing Chaerea's disguise, rape, and escape, one commentator, Muretus, writes, "Hic turbae admirabiles concitantur' [Here wondrous confusions are struck up].[14] He observes wondrous confusions, not guilty or injured persons. Far from being the helpless, voiceless Pamphila, Bianca, capable of willfulness and surprise, actually takes charge of the wooing scene:

> Why, gentlemen, you do me double wrong,
> To strive for that which resteth in my choice:
> I am no breeching scholar in the schools;
> I'll not be tied to hours nor 'pointed times,
> But learn my lessons as I please myself.

> (3.1.16–20)

The student commands the teachers; the lady controls her suitors. From a subordinate position Bianca wields real power and contrasts directly with the insubordinate Kate, who variously asserts her strength and independence only to find herself continually overmastered. By the end of the play, however, Kate will learn what Bianca knows, namely, that acceptance of social role and its limitations need not be demeaning or incapacitating;

played correctly, such acceptance can bring freedom, fulfillment, and power.

Shakespeare's presentation of amatory intrigue plays against classical subtexts in another important way: The disguise creates a two-planed wooing action, one part performed by Lucentio himself, the other by Tranio as Lucentio. Since the disguised Tranio wins Bianca by outbidding Gremio, the odd binary arrangement has seemed to some superfluous and puzzling. Why doesn't Lucentio himself simply bid for and win Bianca, as Tranio does in his name? Marriage is more than simply a matter of social arrangement, and Shakespeare clearly wishes to portray love also as involving personal choice and affection. For this reason he splits the public and private aspects of courtship into parallel actions—one designed to satisfy societal requirements, the other, personal needs; in other words, one for Baptista, the other for Lucentio and Bianca. In classical comedy the emphasis is largely on the first plane only: the marriage action works to reveal or confirm blood lines and citizenship, to establish socio-economic identity. Tranio's performance fulfills the equivalent prerequisites. Lucentio's, however, expands classical comedy in new directions. He seeks to win Bianca's love, which, if not "all in all," is important to them and to the play.

Accordingly, and as he had in *Errors*, Shakespeare changes the blunt sexuality of the subtext to emphasize courtship and romance. Unlike the rapist Chaerea and his descendants in Ariosto and Gascoigne, who enjoy visitation rights for two years and finally impregnate Polynesta, the disguised Lucentio must woo and win the conspicuously chaste Bianca. For the courtship, Shakespeare chooses the unlikely expedient of a Latin lesson. The classical author is Ovid rather than Aristotle and his "checks" (1.1.32), but the wooing is charming and civilized, not passionate or lustful. Sober lines from *Heroides*, rather than a spicy passage from *Ars Amatoria* or the *Metamorphoses*, supply the text which the couple misconstrue purposefully. The Latin exercise is actually an artful linguistic dance that deceives Baptista and the vigilant Hortensio, while giving the lovers a chance to speak.

That Lucentio teaches Latin rather than music (a surprising choice, given Shakespeare's usual portrayals of the two disciplines) illuminates the nature of their courtship. In their own way these two practice rhetoric, the art of civilized communication according to established laws and conventions. Although they forsake the rigors of Latin declensions and conjugations, both work at a complex negotiation through language, one that ends appropriately with this later exchange, whose closing rhyme signals unity and harmony (4.2.6ff). The negotiation in the Latin lesson is replayed in a different form at the end of the play. There Lucentio's belief in his wife's submissiveness is just the first of many foolish misconceptions that marriage will inevitably correct. And Bianca's sharp response, often distorted by critical overreaction, is just the first of many surprises that any real marriage holds. Petruchio's taming school, it may be said, works toward the same ends as the Latin lesson, but with radically different methods and curriculum.

The other deep source of Shrew, Plautus's Captivi, contributes to Ariosto and Gascoigne the main "suppose" of their plays, namely, the exchange of identities between master and servant. Plautus begins Captivi immediately after the exchange; Gascoigne picks up the action several years later; Shakespeare, closer to the classical model, shows the youth falling in love and the switch. In Plautus, the master Philocrates tries to instruct the servant Tyndarus in the device (219 ff.), as does Lucentio Tranio (1.1.198 ff.). Agreeing to the imposture, both servants express their devotion to their master:

Tynd.   Nam tu nunc vides pro tuo caro capite
       carum offerre me meum caput vilitati.

(229–30)

[For that matter, sir, you already see that to save a man I love, I am holding my own life cheap, much as I love it.]

Tra.   I am content to be Lucentio,
       Because so well I love Lucentio.

(1.1.216–17)

In Captivi, the exchange suggests some of the ironies of societal stratification and explores again the dynamics of role-playing. Tyndarus admires Philocrates' performance, especially his smooth adaption of lower-class talk: "ut facete orationem ad servitutem contulit" (276), [How cleverly he's dropped into the servant's jargon], and his ability to philosophize and lie (288). Similarly, Lucentio praises Tranio's assumption of mannered elegance and authority, "Well begun, Tranio" (1.2.224). In both plays, the actors cannot be distinguished from each other "For man or master" (1.1.201) by their faces or manners.

In *Shrew*, however, this change of identity soon becomes charged with a larger meaning and resonates throughout the play, uniting action in "supposes." It echoes in part Sly's promotion from tinker to lord and that of page to Madam wife, providing as well the downside of the process, Lucentio to Tranio. This process, alternating its fields of energy between the poles of dominance and subservience, largely constitutes the main action of taming. In this action, the alternations between service and mastery flash and dazzle. Petruchio asserts his mastery over Kate by serving her with exaggerated solicitousness, by attending to her food and clothes: "'Tis burnt, and so is all the meat" (4.1.161); "It is a paltry cap" (4.3.81); and Kate, in her most imperious, domineering moments, seems most driven, most a slave to her passions, most lacking in freedom as well as in love and happiness. The play works toward redefining mastery and service in a conclusion that transforms rather than articulates the old dichotomy.

The transformation results specifically from Shakespeare's innovative use of New Comedic disguise and deceit. Often in New Comedy, fiction becomes or reveals truth in surprising and unexpected ways. In *Captivi*, for example, Tyndarus, pretending to be Philocrates, says to Hegio, "Tam ego fui ante liber quam gnatus tuos" (310), [Once I was as free as your son], "quam tu filium tuom, tam pater me meus desiderat" (316), [Just as you long for your son, so does my father long for me]. Hegio swallows the lie and arranges the prisoner swap; but since the audience knows that Tyndarus is actually the long-lost son of Hegio, his fiction contains a truth unimagined by the teller. The revelation of this truth, with an emotion more characteristic of Terence than Plautus, constitutes the recognition of the play. Tyndarus' fiction corresponds to a preexistent reality that the audience knows and that the play confirms.

Likewise, Petruchio's fiction about Kate as perfect wife becomes true in ways surprising and unexpected as Kate learns to play the game. The various other fictions in the play, particularly those in the amatory intrigue, provide an illuminating perspective on this one. These fictions require relatively simple masks and performances: people like Tranio, Lucentio, Hortensio, and the Pedant put on costumes, speak set lines, and play well-defined roles. Their performances end and they resume their previous identities. Kate's performance is more complex, less a Plautine imposture than an Ovidian metamorphosis. The role becomes her as she ceremoniously, self-consciously, playfully, becomes the role—the patient, virtuous, obedient wife. Shakespeare's New Comedic action is not revelatory but performative: it concludes not by revealing a preexistent, well-known truth, but by changing fiction into truth. At the end of the play, Kate might well echo Menander's Kichesias, asked to impersonate himself: "gērōn hos eimi gegona" [I am become the old man I am].[15]

The changes in our conception of sources and their relations to texts prompt reevaluation of Shakespeare's plays. Such reevaluation can properly begin with New Comedy. Mixing freely with the bloodlines of other traditions, appearing in various productions, translations, and refigurations, Plautus and Terence bequeathed to posterity the essential genetic makeup of their genre, dramatic comedy. The lines of descent, as is evident from the above demonstration, often run through the Italian intermediaries. Unlike Dennis and Farmer, critics today need not concern themselves with proving direct paternity; instead, four hundred years after the first performances of Shakespeare's plays, we can turn to the more interesting work of establishing ancestry, tracing complicated genealogy, identifying inherited characteristics, and analyzing family resemblance and diversity.

NOTES

1. See Robert S. Miola, *Shakespeare and Classical Tragedy: The Influence of Seneca* (Oxford: Oxford University Press, 1992), 8. See also Thomas M. Greene, *The Light in Troy: Imitation and Discovery in Renaissance Poetry* (New Haven: Yale University Press, 1982); R. J. Schoeck, *Intertextuality and Renaissance Texts* (Bamberg: H. Kaiser-Verlag, 1984); Alan C. Dessen, *Shakespeare and the Late Moral Plays* (Lincoln: University of Nebraska Press, 1986); Patricia Parker and David Quints, eds., *Literary Theory/Renaissance Texts* (Baltimore, Maryland: Johns Hopkins University Press, 1986); Michael Worton and Judith Still, *Intertextuality: Theories and Practice* (Manchester, England: University of Manchester Press, 1990); Heinrick F. Plett, ed., *Intertextuality* (Berlin: W. de Gruyter, 1991); and Jonathan Bate, *Shakespeare and Ovid* (Oxford: Oxford University Press, 1993).

2. For citation I have used *Plautus With an English Translation*, ed. and trans. Paul Nixon, The Loeb Classical Library, 5 vols. (London: Heineman, 1916–38); *Terence With an English Translation*, ed. and trans. John Sargeaunt, The Loeb Classical Library, 2 vols. (London: Heineman, 1912).

3. For this and the following quotations, see Brian Vickers, ed., *Shakespeare: The Critical Heritage*, 6 vols. (London: Routledge and Kegan Paul, 1974–81), 5:77, 2:291–92, 5:275–76.

4. W. H. D. Rouse, ed., *The Menaechmi*, The Shakespeare Library, ed. I. Gollancz (London: Chatto and Windus, 1912), xiv.

5. R. Warwick Bond speculates that *Errors* itself may have suggested both

additions, *The Birth of Hercules,* Malone Society Reprints (London: H. Hart at the Oxford University Press, 1911), x.

6. See William F. Hansen, "An Oral Source for the *Menaechmi,*" *Classical World,* 70 (1977): 385–90.

7. Geoffrey Bullough, ed., *Narrative and Dramatic Sources of Shakespeare,* 8 vols. (London: Routledge and Kegan Paul, 1957–75), 1: 6–7.

8. Treating the play from a similar perspective are Harold Brooks, "Themes and Structure in *The Comedy of Errors,*" *Early Shakespeare,* Stratford-upon-Avon Studies, no. 3 (London: Edward Arnold, 1961), 54–71; R. A. Foakes, ed., *The Comedy of Errors* The Arden Shakespeare (London: Metheun, 1962), xxxix–li; and Vincent F. Petronella, "Structure and Theme through Separation and Union in Shakespeare's *The Comedy of Errors*" in *Modern Language Review,* 69 (1974): 481–88.

9. For an interesting analysis of Ovidian metamorphoses in the play, of the doubling, disguises, and mistaken identities as versions of transformation, see William C. Carroll, *The Metamorphoses of Shakespearean Comedy* (Princeton: Princeton University Press, 1985), 63–80.

10. On Adriana as adapted shrew, see H. B. Charlton, *Shakespearean Comedy* (London: Methuen, 1938), 66–71.

11. This observation is rarely made although Erma Gill has long since provided the evidence in "The Plot-Structure of *The Comedy of Errors* in Relation to Its Sources," *Texas Studies in English,* 10 (1930): 34–37.

12. Farmer, ed. Vickers, 5: 276. For the text and translation of Ariosto, see Brian Morris, "Introduction" in *The Taming of the Shrew* The Arden Shakespeare (London: Methuen, 1981), 79.

13. *The Scholia Bembina,* ed. J. E. Mountford (Liverpool: Liverpool University Press, 1934), 17, 56–57; *Terentius in quem triplex edita est* (Lyons, 1560), 210, 248.

14. *Ibid.,* 202.

15. *Menandri Reliquiae Selectae,* ed. F. H. Sandbach, Oxford Classical Texts (Oxford: Oxford University Press, 1990), 281.

The Tamings of the Shrews

ALAN C. DESSEN

PRINTED in 1594 and reprinted in two subsequent quartos (1596, 1607), *The Taming of a Shrew* (hereafter referred to as *A Shrew* or 1594) is the version of the Katherine story known to readers during the 1590s and early 1600s. Today's reader, however, is familiar with *The Taming of the Shrew* (hereafter referred to as *The Shrew* or 1623), the play as printed in the First Folio, of 1623.[1] Playgoers of the period may have seen either or both versions. Playgoers today often see neither. And thereby hangs my tale.

Scholars have offered a variety of explanations for the existence of two comparable but discrete stage versions of this taming story. For example, the 1594 edition could be an attempt to cash in on the box office success of a production of *The Shrew* by offering readers a play that had been written or staged earlier and had a virtually identical title (albeit set in Athens, not Padua, with only Katherine having the same name). In this formulation, *A Shrew* would therefore be a previous theatrical version of the story and hence a source for Shakespeare (as in the comparable situations of *The Troublesome Reign of King John* being the basis for *King John* and *The Chronicle History of King Leir* leading to *King Lear*). *A Shrew*, however, could equally well be a "bad quarto" (although an unusual, atypical one)—a reconstruction and adaptation of a previously existing *The Shrew*. This latter position has been advanced forcefully by a phalanx of scholars that includes Samuel Hickson, Peter Alexander, G. I. Duthie, Richard Hosley, and most recently, editors Brian Morris, H. J. Oliver, and Ann Thompson.[2]

Proponents of *A Shrew* as the earlier "source" play have been largely silent over the last fifty years, for "bad quartos," memorial reconstruction, and related arguments have dominated the field. Given recent attacks upon this orthodoxy as applied to other plays, however, the 1594-versus-1623 debate warrants reinvestigation. Is, then, the argument in behalf of the "bad quarto" status

of 1594 fully convincing? In particular, does this predominantly
literary argument (grounded upon a chain of descent established
primarily by means of echoes, allusions, and perceived diminu-
tions of superior lines and speeches) fully take into account both
the theatrical evidence and the overall design of both versions?
Perhaps most important for noncombatants, a category that includes most readers of this essay, what difference does the decision about the status of A Shrew (that is, "bad quarto" versus
source versus other options—for example, both 1594 and 1623
drawing upon some common ur-version) make for interpreters
of the Folio script who are not editors or scholars with a large
investment in these competing narratives? To what extent does
one's sense of the 1594 quarto affect how one reads, interprets,
or stages what has survived in the Folio? To invoke those two
immortal words, so what?

Consider but one of the many interpretive implications linked
to the options. If A Shrew is deemed a memorially reconstructed
text that was concocted after The Shrew, it provides a flawed
report that, unlike other supposed "bad quartos," was in turn
tinkered with by an adapter. If this chronology is accepted, the
1594 script could therefore serve as a comment upon, even an
interpretation of, 1623, so as to provide us with The Shrew as
seen through the eyes and ears of X and Y. For example, such an
after-the-fact adaptation could demonstrate how someone (reporter, adapter, compositor) reacted to the taming as revealed in
the Sly coda and other features distinctive to 1594. In contrast,
if in the version that survives in the Folio Shakespeare was building upon an earlier play, the interpreter today can (as with other
situations where the "source" material is fairly certain) gain
some insights into the 1623 version by attending to what was
kept, what was adjusted, what was inserted, and what was further
developed, so as to gain a better sense of the overall design or
strategy.[3]

Admittedly, to tackle this problem yet again is to risk immer-
sion in details and intricate paths of reasoning that can frighten
away everyone except editors and the most intrepid readers.
Nonetheless, to revisit this quagmire might be worthwhile if
questioning again the relationship between 1594 and 1623 leads
to some insights into the moot questions that swirl around this
script (especially in the last scene) so as to arrive at a formulation
of value to a director or a critic not vitally interested in A Shrew
or the competing narratives. My goal therefore is to explore the
differences between 1594 and 1623 with the so what? question

in mind. When are the differences telling or revealing? What difference does or should the precedence of one or another version make to interpretation today on the page or on the stage?

Given such questions, many differences between the two texts are of potential interest. To avoid obfuscation, or sinking into the quagmire, however, I wish to concentrate on three discrete yet related elements: (1) the Sly material; (2) Lucentio and especially Hortensio as opposed to the roughly comparable figures in 1594; and (3) the final sequence.

First consider the Christopher Sly material unique to 1594, the feature of that script that has received the most attention by far and in turn has had the greatest impact upon interpretation today on the page and especially on the stage. The first two scenes of both versions (often referred to as "The Induction" but not cited as such in either script) are different in various details yet roughly analogous, but the Folio Sly is not referred to again after the stage direction at the end of 1.1 ("*They sit and mark*"). In obvious contrast, the 1594 Sly has several scripted interjections after this point, falls asleep, is reclothed offstage, and is finally placed onstage so that his awakening in the presence of the tapster provides a coda that ends the comedy. All three of the recent scholarly editions (New Arden, Oxford, and Cambridge) reprint the Sly material unique to 1594 as an appendix so as to provide a do-it-yourself kit for that reader or director who feels that the Sly story as set forth in the received text (that is, the Folio) is somehow incomplete—a position endorsed as well by various critics.[4]

Such a do-it-yourself-kit approach to the Sly episodes, however, has its pitfalls. For example, the most striking penetration of Sly into the play proper comes in the 1594 equivalent to 5.1, when Sly reacts strenuously to a group of figures being threatened with prison. What is particularly instructive here is the difference between 1594 and 1623 as to who is in trouble and why. Thus, in 1594 Sly intervenes not to save the equivalent to the true Vincentio (the figure threatened with prison in Folio 5.1), but rather to prevent the arrest of the two plotters (Valeria-Tranio and Philotus-pedant), who do not have the success of their analogues in 1623 and are easily cowed by the father of Aurelius-Lucentio. Indeed, the entire sequence is distinctively different, for after the duke (the equivalent to the true Vincentio) rejects Philotus (the substitute father), his son Aurelius (onstage already, not initially offstage as is Lucentio) kneels and begs to be heard, whereupon the duke reacts: "Peace villaine, lay hands on them, / And send them to prison straight" (F2r), at which point "*Phylotus* and *Valeria* runnes away. Then *Slie* speakes."

For a director today to insert the 1594 Sly interruption into a production of *the Shrew*, as in the 1981 Stratford Festival Canada production, the 1991 Oregon Shakespeare Festival production, and the 1992 Royal Shakespeare Company production, is therefore to rescript the scene in more ways than one. Although the threat of prison may motivate Sly's interruption in both scenes, the threat to the true Vincentio (1623) is very different in tone and kind from the threat to the two fleeing tricksters, and the subsequent arrival of Lucentio in 1623 yields a very different payoff. Note too that the 1623 line, "he shall not go to prison" (5.1.95), is spoken not by Sly (who has long been silent or has disappeared), but by Gremio, who quickly backs down and is overruled by Baptista: "Away with the dotard, to the jail with him!" (106). An objection to someone's being sent to prison therefore *is* to be found in 1623 but from a different speaker, directed at different figures, and with a very different impact. What seems to the casual reader simple and straightforward when the "additional" Sly passages from 1594 are printed as an appendix to 1623 in the Arden, Oxford, or Cambridge editions (just plug them in) is, in fact, far more tangled, so that, as with the two versions of *King Lear*, a third conflated version of 5.1 can emerge that corresponds to neither *A Shrew* or *The Shrew*.

Along with the obvious differences in the Sly narrative, another less-noticed but equally telling distinction between 1594 and 1623 emerges when one focuses upon the role of Hortensio.[5] Polidor, the suitor roughly comparable to Hortensio in 1594, is a scholar and a friend of Ferando-Petruchio who courts and wins (without a Gremio or other rivals) Emelia, the youngest daughter of Alfonso; meanwhile, another suitor, Aurelius (Lucentio), son of the duke of Sestos, woos Alfonso's middle daughter, Philema. The most interesting parallel between Hortensio and Polidor, moreover, is that both end up with "untamed" shrews, as revealed by the brief (one scene) but highly charged appearance of the widow in 5.2 of *The Shrew* and by the final beat of *A Shrew* (the last interchange before the Sly coda), where Polidor, "in a dump," tells his new bride "I say thou art a shrew" and Emelia responds: "Thats better then a sheepe" (G2r). The coda that follows immediately after the Polidor-Emelia exchange, moreover, also focuses upon the supposed lesson learned by Sly that, according to him, will lead to a yet-to-be-attempted taming of *his* wife. The 1594 version therefore peaks with its equivalent

to the Petruchio-Kate resolution and *exeunt*, a climax followed
by comments from Aurelius and Alfonso about the departed couple, the Polidor-Emelia exchange (in which a new shrew is revealed), and the Sly coda, with its lesson drawn by one onstage
observer from what the playgoer has just witnessed and a goal
of taming enunciated although not completed or actually staged.

Despite the limits of the verse and overall execution, the 1594
resolution has its own distinctive advantages, but, as I read it, it
offers an unambiguous "taming" of Katherine (without irony or
mutuality) that is played off against a new Kate-like role for Emelia and a linked resolution from Sly. Although anathema to many
sensibilities today, such a package or strategy seems to me of
considerable theatrical interest. This version, moreover, was
Shrew as known to the reading public up through 1623 in three
quartos, whereas such plays as *Love's Labor's Lost*, *2 Henry IV*
and *Much Ado About Nothing* never made it to a second quarto
(whatever that statistic means).

That clearly defined strategy in 1594 should then lead to a
reconsideration of the very different strategy in 1623, and here
is where both "sources' and "bad quartos" can be stimuli in
causing an interpreter to see more clearly the distinctive choices
in the script under investigation. Clearly, the absence of a continuing Sly story denies any obvious closure for that narrative,
but, equally important, that silence in the Folio means that no
moral is drawn, however baldly, by an onstage observer who
plans to put the "lesson" he has learned into practice. Rather,
the rhythm in 1623 takes us to the Kate-Petruchio climax and
then winds down after their *exeunt* in a couplet shared by Hortensio and Lucentio (and no *exeunt* is printed in the Folio for
the ensemble—whatever that omission means, if anything). With
reference to today's productions, moreover, note that neither
1594 or 1623 ends with Petruchio's lines; rather, both call for
the final lines to be delivered by those who constitute the world
left behind. Today's director who lets Petruchio have the last
word (a common theatrical choice—so that "God give you good
night" is directed to the playgoers) is therefore going against *both*
scripts on a strategic choice of some consequence.

To return to Hortensio (and Lucentio), what I had missed, until
encouraged by the 1594 strategy to rethink matters, is the very
different story or rhythm generated by Hortensio in 1623. In the
1623 version of 4.2, Hortensio, unlike Polidor, is soured on his
first love interest, Bianca, the younger sister of Kate, after he sees
her kissing and courting what he thinks is a mere scholar (Poli-

dor is such a scholar in 1594). He therefore refers to Bianca as "this proud disdainful haggard" (39), a clear echo (for the playgoer) of Petruchio's falconry speech at the end of the previous scene, and decides to go to what Tranio describes as "the taming-school" where Petruchio as schoolmaster "teacheth tricks eleven and twenty long, / To tame a shrew and charm her chattering tongue" (57–58). As a failed tutor of Bianca, Hortensio heads off for teacher-training.

Unlike the playgoer, however, Hortensio has not witnessed 4.1, and, despite his use of "haggard," has not heard either of Petruchio's soliloquies on his methods (2.1.169–81 and 4.1.188–211). Somehow in 4.3 he participates in the denial of meat (though the stage business is not clear) and is later asked by Petruchio to pay the tailor, and so ameliorate the situation. Significantly, at the end of this scene, when Hortensio responds to Petruchio's "It shall be what a'clock I say it is," with "Why, so this gallant will command the sun" (4.3.195–96), his reaction is no more informed than Kate's; neither of them has caught on to what underlies Petruchio's method. Rather, during the climactic sun-moon debate, he urges Kate to comply ("Say as he says, or we shall never go"—4.5.11) not out of any understanding of "taming" or insight into Petruchio's procedures, but as a weary traveler who wants to get on with it (enough is enough). Once Kate acquiesces, Hortensio observes, "Petruchio, go thy ways, the field is won" (23). At the end of this scene, he then draws a moral in his own terms: "Well, Petruchio, this has put me in heart. / Have to my widow! and if she [be] froward, / Then thou hast taught Hortensio to be untoward" (77–79). Thus the next time we see him he is married to his (formidable) widow.

What is of particular interest when invoking 1594 then is that it is not Hortensio in that version but Sly who, at the very end, after the finish of the Petruchio-Kate story, draws the moral ("I know now how to tame a shrew / . . . ile to my / Wife presently and tame her too / And if she anger me"—G2v). The verbal links between this passage and Hortensio's speech at the end of 4.5 may not be that close, but the sentiments and the announced purpose are the same, with both the 1594 Sly and the 1623 Hortensio supposedly learning from Ferando-Petruchio "how to do it" ("I know now how to tame a shrew"; "and if she be froward, / Then hast thou taught Hortensio to be untoward") and then going off "to do it" ("ile to my Wife"; "Have to my widow").

The parallels and distinctions, however, can be pursued further. The playgoer must imagine the confrontation between the

1594 Sly and his wife (though that playgoer does witness the final confrontation between Polidor and Emelia). However, Hortensio's declaration of what he has supposedly learned comes at the end of 4.5, so that, in keeping with the emphasis throughout *The Shrew* upon failed education (as in 3.1 with the two rival tutors), the playgoer sees the results of Hortensio's course at The Taming School in 5.2, where he is cowed by his widow, who serves as the Folio's highly entertaining equivalent to Polidor's Emelia and Sly's wife. As a teacher-tamer-educator, Hortensio therefore fails twice with two very different women.

To look closely at the Hortensio story is then to raise some provocative questions about the competing narratives that purport to explain the relationship between 1594 and 1623. Would a putative reporter or adapter move from the strategy of 1623 (Hortensio's decision in 4.5 and his subsequent confrontation with his widow in 5.2) to the strategy of 1594 (the exchange between Polidor and Emelia and Sly's coda)? Such a progression, or perhaps regression, seems to me possible but unlikely. Rather, in this instance I find it more likely that Shakespeare, in building upon some version of 1594, scrapped the Sly coda and the third daughter, set up the rivalry over Bianca (that heightens both the education motif and the mercantile view of this Padua), and developed Hortensio and his widow as a replacement for the *A Shrew* material (along with making Bianca a significant presence in 5.2).

What are the consequences of such weighing of the options? So what? If even some of my argument about the 1623 Hortensio versus the 1594 equivalent has merit, then tacking on the 1594 Sly coda to a production of the Folio script is comparable to conflating the two versions of *King Lear*, indeed is far more suspect, given the substantive differences between 1594 and 1623. Rather, if the Sly coda is included in a rendition of the 1623 script, the playgoer will witness *both* the lesson drawn by Sly *and* the lesson drawn in 4.5 by Hortensio, two components that do not coexist in *either* play.[6] The two versions of *Shrew* do cover much analogous ground on taming, shrews, and lessons, but they do so in a very different fashion and with a decidedly different theatrical rhythm or strategy, as is especially noticeable when one looks closely at what follows the Ferando-Kate *exeunt* in the last scene. Indeed, 1594 ends with a focus upon four marriages, perhaps four different directions to pursue (although little is done with Aurelius-Philema). At stake therefore are two very different trajectories or strategies that cannot be conflated, with the differences having considerable interpretive significance. To conflate them (as in Stratford Festival Canada in 1981 and the Royal Shakespeare Company in 1992) is, even more than with the conflated *King Lear*, to create a third entity that corresponds neither to version one nor to version two.

Such concerns about the Sly material and Hortensio, needless to say, are of less concern to would-be interpreters of *The Shrew* than the many distinctions, small and large, between Kate-Petruchio in 1623 and Kate-Ferando in 1594. For example, the 1594 version of 2.1, their first meeting, is much shorter and less complex, with no initial soliloquy from Ferando and with no clear indication that the father, Alfonso, is to leave the stage during the interview. When offered Ferando's hand, moreover, *A Shrew*'s Kate, unlike her 1623 counterpart, has an angry speech but then says aside: "But yet I will consent and marry him, / For I methinkes haue liude too long a maid, / And match him to, or else his manhoods good" (B3r).

Other 1594 speeches and sequences also differ in suggestive ways, whether in the marriage scene (Folio 3.2) or the taming scenes in 4. For example, in the former, *A Shrew* supplies a specific rationale for Ferando's red cap and outlandish marriage costume ("Shees such a shrew, if we should once fal out, / Sheele pul my costly sutes ouer mine eares, / And therefore am I thus attired a while"—C3v), but has no equivalent to Petruchio's "To me she's married, not unto my clothes" (3.2.117). In the latter, Ferando has a simpler version of the 1623 falconry speech (the comparison between the two versions of this speech is basic to the "bad quarto" argument); the sequence of ordeals for Kate is then basically the same, albeit shorter, simpler, and more violent, with no Hortensio present and no lengthy bit involving Sander-Grumio and the tailor. In 1594, Kate and Ferando are not observers during the equivalent to 5.1 and therefore do not remain onstage after the departure of the ensemble for a kiss "in the midst of the street" and Petruchio's "Is not this well?" (5.1.144, 149). Although rarely cited in the "bad quarto" debate, this last distinction strikes me as significant, for I find it difficult to conceive of a putative reporter who would forget or omit this highly charged and highly memorable theatrical moment.

As already noted in the discussion of both Sly and Hortensio-Polidor, the differences between the two final sequences can be particularly instructive. Overall, the last scene in *A Shrew* has the same general shape as its counterpart in 1623 but, as with other comparable moments, is shorter and simpler. Unlike 1623, the women in 1594 are not onstage at the outset, so that no bantering takes place before the wager. Kate here does provide a major speech on wifely obedience but one composed of different elements (with more emphasis upon Biblical material, especially Eve's sins). Her final lines focus upon women's duty to obey, love, keep, and nourish their husbands, "laying our hands under their feet to tread" to procure their ease; as a precedent she announces: "Ile first begin, / And lay my hand under my husband's feet." The text then supplies a stage direction not spelled out as such in 1623: "She laies her hand vnder her husband's feet," to which Ferando responds: "Inough sweet, the wager thou hast won, / And they I am sure cannot deny the same." At this point Alfonso gives a hundred pounds (not twenty thousand crowns)—"Another dowry for another daughter, / For she is not the same she was before" (G1v)—so that the father's providing of a second dowry comes *after* Kate's big speech, not before as in 1623.

With the *so what?* question in mind, of particular interest is one phrase in another stage direction unique to 1594. In some renditions of the 1623 script (for example, Jonathan Miller's television production for the BBC's "The Shakespeare's Plays"), Kate does not drag in the other two recalcitrant wives but merely precedes them. In 1594, however, the details of this entrance are spelled out. First, Ferando comments: "For see where she brings her sisters forth by force"; then the stage direction reads: "Enter *Kate* thrusting *Phylema* and *Emelia* before her, and makes them come vnto their husband's cal" (G1r). The final phrase—"makes them come vnto their husband's cal"—refers to the wager and the failure of the first two wives (in either version) to respond. No such specific wording, however, is to be found in the Folio.

In itself this 1594 stage direction is unremarkable—apparently merely a "fictional" signal that provides little if any insight into the original staging but merely enhances the narrative for a reader.[7] But when linked to other passages, most notably Ferando-Petruchio's falconry speech, "makes them come vnto their husband's cal" sets up an imagistic and conceptual link otherwise easy to miss, one that can have a fruitful payoff in both versions of the story (and therefore can be operative whether the 1594 adapter "read" *The Shrew* in such terms or whether Shakespeare developed such a motif after he encountered in his "source").

What is at stake here is the relationship between (1) the rationale behind the taming process, as enunciated by both Ferando and Petruchio in their respective falconry speeches, and (2) the

wager and its aftermath. In 1594 (D3v), Ferando announces that
to tame his shrew he plans to use various denials ("curbes of
hunger, ease, and want of sleepe") so as to "mew her vp, as men
do mew their hawkes, / And make hir gently come vnto the lure."
No matter how stubborn Kate proves, "Yet would I pul her downe
and make hir come / As hungry hawkes do fly vnto their lure."
In 1623, Petruchio notes that his falcon, Kate, "now is sharp and
passing empty, / And till she stoop she must not be full-gorg'd, /
For then she never looks upon her lure" (4.1.190–92). He then
describes how he will deny her sleep, with these devices
summed up as "Another way I have to man my haggard, / To
make her come, and know her keeper's call" (193–94). Both Ferando and Petruchio therefore specify that the shrewish wife, like
a falcon or haggard, must be trained to look upon or "gently
come vnto" her lure; Petruchio, moreover, invokes the same
phrase, which turns up in the 1594 stage direction and dialogue
when he states that a major goal of the "taming" process is to
make the wife-haggard "come and know her keeper's call."

To my knowledge, few interpreters have linked these falconry
speeches to the wager and the final sequence, but such links
are potentially there and can be meaningful, particularly if the
interpreter views Petruchio's 1623 reference to "her keeper's
call" in the context of the terms provided in the 1594 final scene.
Consider first the less familiar sequence as scripted in *A Shrew.*
The scene opens with the three husbands and their servants (the
brides' father, Alfonso, joins them a bit later), but does not include either the three women or the equivalents to Vincentio
and the pedant. Aurelius-Lucentio proposes a "trial of our
wiues / Who will come soonest at their husband's cal" (F3v)
and comparable locutions pepper the subsequent discussion (for
example, "For he may cal I thinke til he be weary, / Before his
wife wil come before she list"; "my wife comes as soone as I do
send"; "whose wife soonest comes when he doth cal"). After the
two refusals, Ferando bids his servant, Sander, "command your
mistris to come / To me presently" (F4v). When she complies
("Sweet husband did you send for me?"), he orders her to take
off her cap and tread upon it; the stage direction reads: "She
takes off her cap and treads on it." To "try her further" (G1r),
Ferando asks about Kate's two sisters and then orders: "Fetch
them hither, and if they wil not come, Bring them preforce and
make them come with thee," thereby setting up the stage direction: "Enter *Kate* thrusting *Phylema* and *Emelia* before her, and
makes them come vnto their husbands cal." What then follows is

some bickering among the two couples who have lost the wager, Ferando's order to "tel vnto these headstrong women, / What dewty wiues do owe vnto their husbands," a shorter, highly orthodox version of Kate's speech, her laying of her hand beneath his foot, and the final speeches from Ferando and Alfonso (as described earlier).

The scene as scripted in *The Shrew* is richer and more complex but still has a comparable shape. Initially, a much larger group is onstage (the three couples, the two fathers, the pedant, Gremio, and the three servants). A great deal of banter is provided before the women depart, in part to introduce the widow (and set up a rivalry with Kate), but also to set up Bianca as a bird ("Am I your bird? I mean to shift my bush"—5.2.46), albeit not a falcon, but one that is the object of pursuit. After more hunting talk, again with a focus upon Bianca as "this bird you aim'd at, though you hit her not" (50—and with the emphasis upon dogs, not haggards), the wager is proposed (by Petruchio rather than Aurelius-Lucentio) without any reference to a *husband's call* but in simpler terms: "Let's each one send unto his wife, / And he whose wife is most obedient, / To come at first when he doth send for her, / Shall win the wager. . ." (66–69). What follows is basically the same as in 1594, although (1) Baptista provides the second dowry with Kate offstage; (2) Kate throws her cap "under-foot" (122) in the presence of the other two wives; and (3) the widow provides some strong resistance to Petruchio not found in *A Shrew.* As in 1594, however, Petruchio's initial order conveyed by Grumio is "Say I command her to come to me" (96) as opposed to Lucentio's "bid" (76) and Hortensio's "entreat" (86). Similarly, with regard to the other two wives, he tells Kate "Go fetch them hither. If they deny to come, / Swinge me them soundly forth unto their husbands. / Away, I say, and bring them hither straight" (103–5); when she returns, he notes: "See where she comes, and brings your froward wives / As prisoners to her womanly persuasion" (119–20).

In both versions, then, Kate distinguishes herself from the other two wives by (1) coming at her husband's command; (2) throwing off and treading upon her cap; (3) fetching the wives after they have refused to come at the bidding or entreaty of their husbands; and (4) providing a long speech to "these headstrong women" about "what duty they do owe their lords and husbands" (130–31). Admittedly, Kate is not a falcon-haggard (or a hound-retriever) and therefore possesses language, a mind, autonomy, and many strengths that stretch the analogy beyond the

breaking point. Nonetheless, as an integral part of the final sequence in both scripts, Ferando-Petruchio (1) "commands" her
to come; (2) sends her back to bring-swinge-fetch the other two
women; and (3) orders her to perform two other distinctive actions. Meanwhile, Bianca is set up metaphorically not as a falcon
linked to the will of a master-husband, but as a bird ("Am I your
bird . . . shift my bush") that is a prey or a target for men ("you
hit the white"—186).

To come or not to come at the husband's call is a locution that
is spelled out in 1594 but is less audible in 1623. However, owing
to the far-better-developed "education" motif, the distinctions
among the routes taken by Petruchio, Lucentio, and Hortensio
in *The Shrew* are clearer and more meaningful than the fates of
the comparable figures in *A Shrew.* In both instances, moreover,
the wager and its aftermath constitute the final field-testing of
the approach to taming and education enunciated earlier by both
Ferando and Petruchio in their falconry speeches. In 1623, if not
in 1594, Kate is far more than a trained bird (or hound) being
put through her paces, but there *is* a logic underlying 5.2, in
which the formerly "headstrong" independent shrew now comes
at her husband's call-command, fetches objects to that trainer-
husband, performs a highly visible action, and gives a lengthy
speech as instructed. Such a bald formulation of the links between the falconry speeches and the wager runs the risk of flat-
tening out many significant qualifications that critics and
theatrical professionals have found in the Kate-Petruchio relationship. Nonetheless, the wording of the 1594 stage direction
and speeches does bring into sharp focus a strategy or relationship that has significant implications for any interpretation of
this final sequence.

Such interpretations will continue to vary widely. As a final
response to my *so what?* question, note that in 1594 Sly is not
present during the wager and its aftermath; nonetheless, the lesson he, for one, learns from the rest of the Kate-Ferando story is
simple and blunt ("I know now how to tame a shrew"). The
absence in the Folio, however, of (1) this after-the-fact drawing
of a "lesson" and (2) any specific signal that Kate "laies her hand
vnder her husbands feet" leaves open a space that is closed down
in 1594. In today's productions, after entreating the wives to "vail
your stomachs . . . / And place your hands below your husband's
foot," Kate often starts to do so, but her actual lines read: "In
token of which duty, if he please, / My hand is ready, may it do
him ease" (5.2.176–79). Given the specific stage direction, the

1594 Kate and Ferando have few options at this point, but the 1623 Petruchio ("Why, there's a wench! Come on and kiss me, Kate!"—180) can prevent Kate from completing or even starting this action: "my hand is ready" can be played with no more than a small gesture with that hand. Indeed, I have seen one production (directed by Homer Swander at the University of California, Santa Barbara, in 1991) in which Petruchio, after lifting Kate's hand from the floor, placed *his* hand in the same spot.

That space left open for interpretation in 1623 but not in 1594 should be factored into the "bad quarto" versus "source" controversy. If *A Shrew* is indeed the later version, then those responsible for the adaptation remembered, read, or interpreted the final sequence of *The Shrew* in a manner consistent with the Sly coda and Kate's placing her hand beneath Ferando's foot. In this formulation, at least one set of interpreters of the Folio version of this comedy understood the taming story in such straightforward, hierarchical, patriarchal terms. On the other hand, if *The Shrew* is the later version, Shakespeare adapted the raw materials found in *A Shrew* so as to complicate a simpler narrative, eliminate any unambiguous lesson from Sly, and leave open the disposition of Kate's hand and Petruchio's reaction. If *A Shrew* is deemed a memorially reconstructed "bad quarto," the reader today with a patriarchal bent can argue that the reporters responsible for the 1594 text are remembering accurately the original stage business: in the terms of this narrative, when Shakespeare's *The Shrew* was staged in the 1590s, Kate put her hand beneath her husband's foot. However, if *A Shrew* is deemed a "source," the reader today with a penchant for mutuality or irony can argue that such a disposition of the wife's hand was acted out in an earlier, cruder version of the taming story, but was softened or eliminated completely in Shakespeare's adaptation. In this formulation, either the 1623 Kate did not complete such a submission or the 1623 Petruchio did not allow it. In short, the various elements that constitute the basis for the "bad quarto" versus "source" debate need not provide fodder only for editors and bibliographers, but can have major consequences for the ideological wars that arise out of this controversial scene.

To return to my beginning, my fresh look at some of the facets of the competing narratives that "explain" the relationship between *A Shrew* and *The Shrew* has yielded no definitive answers. Admittedly, in a few instances I find the prevailing account (which would place the 1623 version earlier) unsatisfactory, for I cannot imagine a theatrical adapter forgetting or finessing the Kate-Petruchio kiss at the end of 5.1 (a high point in many productions today) or turning Hortensio-Bianca-widow into Polidor-Emelia. Such doubts, however, may complicate rather than disprove the prevailing narrative and certainly do not provide a telling blow in this combat.

What does emerge, however, is the value of attending closely to the evidence provided by 1594 as a window into a better understanding of 1623. The "completed" Sly story in the former may appeal to many readers of the latter frustrated by an apparent lack of closure, but, upon investigation, the carefully wrought closure in 1594 calls attention to a distinctively different and in its own terms compelling strategy in 1623. Both plays, in fact, present multiple "shrew" stories, so that the 1594 title, with its emphasis upon "a" shrew, may signal a deliberate ambiguity that can encompass Kate, Emelia, and even Sly's wife. Admittedly, while many of the differences between the two versions (I have omitted numerous examples) result not from conceptual or strategic choices but from differing levels of execution, other differences (some features of the Ferando-Kate material unique to 1594, the very different trajectories for the non-Kate material, and the variations in the placing of Kate's hand beneath her husband's foot) are significant and worthy of our attention. Not to take such evidence into account is then to indulge in yet another taming—this time a diminution of the Folio's *The Shrew* into one or another rigid category that cannot do justice to its richness and complexity.

NOTES

1. Citations from 1594 are from *The Taming of a Shrew*, ed. John Farmer, Tudor Facsimile Texts (Amersham, 1913). I know of no evidence that anyone in the 1590s or early 1600s distinguished between *A Shrew* and *The Shrew.*

2. For lucid summaries of the debate (along with arguments in favor of the "bad quarto" thesis), see Brian Morris's introduction to his New Arden edition (London and New York: Methuen, 1981), 12–50; H. J. Oliver's introduction to his Oxford edition (Oxford: Oxford University Press, 1982), 13–34; and Ann Thompson's "textual analysis" appendix to her New Cambridge edition (Cambridge University Press, 1984), 164–74.

3. Admittedly, some changes could also be attributed to theatrical exigencies. For example, a playing area "above" is not needed in 1594 (where, in the second scene, "Enter two with a table and a banquet on it, and two other, with *Slie* asleepe in a chaire, richlie apparelled, & the musick plaieng"—A3v) but is needed at least twice in 1623. Several of the explanations for the two versions, moreover, are linked to the number of actors available, so that, in one formulation, the disappearance of Sly and his entourage after 1.2 in 1623 is necessary

so that those actors could take on other parts, an exigency not faced, it is argued, in 1594. See, in particular, Karl P. Wentersdorf, "The Original Ending of *The Taming of the Shrew*: A Reconsideration," *Studies in English Literature* 18 (1978), 201–15.

4. For a useful summary and critique of such arguments, see Margie Burns, "The Ending of *The Shrew*," *Shakespeare Studies* 18 (1986), 41–64. Burns argues that "Sly's loss can be discussed as the play's gain, because the discontinuation of Sly's story actually helps develop the Kate-Petruchio story" (41). She concludes that "in the absence of textual or historical evidence, the idea of a missing ending must be regarded as myth with the usual function of myth, to explain puzzling sensations or puzzling phenomena, such as the impression created at the end of *The Taming of the Shrew* that much does indeed hang in the balance" (61).

5. In some scholarly debates, Hortensio does play a significant role. For example, those who argue in behalf of a Shakespeare version of *The Shrew* that precedes what survives in the Folio point to supposed anomalies in Hortensio, for he is not included in the 2.1 negotiations over Bianca (or he is forgotten), and Tranio-Lucentio in 3.2 seems to be taking over his role (as one who is intimate with Petruchio). Like most recent editors (for example, see Morris, New Arden, 37–39), I find such arguments unconvincing.

6. A comparable argument can be made against the copresence in a modern conflated text of both Hamlet's last soliloquy, "How all occasions do inform against me" (4.4.32–66), that is omitted in the Folio and the Folio-only material that follows Hamlet's allusion to "perfect conscience" (5.2.68–80) and includes "the interim is mine." The two passages cover comparable ground on *conscience* but do not coexist in either Q2 or F.

7. I am building here upon Richard Hosley's distinction between *theatrical* and *fictional* stage directions. See "The Gallery Over the Stage in the Public Playhouse of Shakespeare's Time," *Shakespeare Quarterly* 8 (1957): 16–17. In Hosley's formulation, "theatrical" directions refer to "theatrical structure or equipment" (for example, *within, at another door, a scaffold thrust out*) as opposed to "fictional" signals that refer "to dramatic fiction" (for example, *on shipboard, enter the town*). Compare *enter above* and *enter on the walls* [of a city] as signals for the same action. Editors sometimes link "fictional" stage directions to authorial drafts as opposed to playhouse manuscripts or memorially reconstructed "bad quartos," but such distinctions are not supported by the extant evidence. The presence of "makes them come vnto their husbands cal" is therefore not inconsistent with the putative "bad quarto" status of *A Shrew*.

Love's Labor's Lost:
Burn the Parasols, Play the Quarto!

HOMER SWANDER

IN performance, *Love's Labor's Lost*, a very great play, is unusually easy to loathe. Or if the experience is pleasant, there is too often an unpleasant aftertaste, an uneasy feeling that one has yielded to—even colluded with—a concoction of unrelentingly adolescent and manufactured charm created by designers in love with parasols and by actors who seem light-years past adolescence. The revoltingly aristocratic, fake-eighteenth-century, Victorian, or flapper-era charm comes to seem a bland and patronizing substitute for the real energy of the young and the real energy of the original script. For that, too—the script itself—has also been diluted in the Editorial House of Charm. It should thus, I suppose, be no surprise that dilution—the "Harrod's Window Approach"—is what we get in the theater.[1]

Staring in the morning-after mirror, even dyed-in-the-wool bardolaters may sense an ugly question fighting to get out: "If I hadn't known that play to be Shakespeare's, would I have thought it so delightful?" But ah—what if the play we saw last night wasn't Shakespeare's? What if it was based on a blurred and distorted version of his script? Would that matter? Would it make a difference? Is there, somewhere, perhaps under several centuries of debris, a lost *Love's Labor's Lost* that could provide the deeper theatrical experience one has a right to expect from an evening labeled "Shakespeare"? Is there a Berowne, a Rosaline, a Costard out there in the wings somewhere—in the Quarto, say—whom we have never seen? These are the questions I wish to place before the house.

Such questions may, of course, seem to be leading to something like the kind of inflated claims that have always littered the Shakespearean landscape: "I alone, among all the peoples of the earth, can interpret this line or speech or play accurately for you, and can, moreover, tell you what is and what is not the real

Shakespeare." God help us. Let me see if I can distinguish my efforts here from all such claims. I do not wish to argue with, or to supplant, anyone's interpretation of the received text of *Love's Labor's Lost*. I have, in fact, no interpretation of that text to offer, and no wish to seek one. My argument is, instead, with the received text itself: it is, I believe, an editorially diminished version of what the editors themselves believe to be the closest thing we have to Shakespeare's original. What I shall therefore try to do in the following pages is to report and support the claims of that original—as represented in the Quarto of 1598—against unauthorized and damaging revisions that now help to shape all popular and scholarly editions of the play, and that therefore also shape even the best professional productions. I intend only to call attention to points at which Shakespeare's script has disappeared behind the screen of the standard literary text, and to suggest some of the consequences. I shall be, in other words, radically conservative and with a single motivation: when I do turn to "interpretation"—in my study or, more appropriately, in the theatre—I want to be exploring, as near as daylight, Shakespeare's own *scripted* words. What follows is for those who share that desire.

Even if literary interpretation is your game, there is a long-hidden text of *Love's Labor's Lost* to explore. And, more importantly, if you inhabit the theatre—as actor, director, designer, or audience—there is an exciting "new" script pointing to an exciting new play that, in widely contrasting productions from a thousand theater companies, could free us forever from the forest of parasols and straw hats, and from the bland acting that takes place under them.

The editors are, of course, merely performing their important scholarly duty as they see it. Yet their activity, which seems so quiet—often, in their own technical term, actually "silent"—and innocent on the page, can, in the theater, result in definitive transformations of character and event. Smoothly, insidiously—the differences from Shakespeare unnoticed after centuries of residence in print—the editorial text becomes "Shakespeare's Text"—and, thus, the actor's script. On stage, then, actors speak or remain silent as directed not by Shakespeare but by the editors. Without realizing it, the actors become the puppets of editors, who empower them or silence them at will.

In comments from critics, scholars, and editors, the two words most frequently generated by the received text of *Love's Labor's Lost* are—quite understandably—"artificial" and "symmetrical."

In its turn, the received theatrical tradition, guided by such a text and influenced by such comments, generates productions that are also—of course—artificial and symmetrical. The women, especially, tend to be formal, statuesque, given to static posing, and distanced by what the director must suppose to be elegant performing. The men—each matched sartorially with the "right" parasolled lady—are, in the tradition, mind-chillingly silly and boyishly charming.

In spite of the frequently bawdy language that Shakespeare constrains both men and women to speak, the acting in the usual production (whether amateur or professional) utterly stifles any possibility that these young people are capable of, or even know about, coition: they clearly neither think nor feel the bawdry that they speak. The decorum of Harrod's window defines the territory. How shocking it would be were we to sense there the presence of living flesh actually capable of opening or rising to desire. And thus how impossible for any serious sexual or marital value to surface in the theatrical event. Anything like real life is a long way away.

But there is, thank God, a world elsewhere. It begins with what may at first seem to be small textual differences, with only a local impact in performance, but that have in fact the power to alter our basic perception of the entire script, releasing hitherto ignored elements for scrutiny and theatrical exploration. What is most amazing about this kind of textual research is the revelation (and even revolution) that even the tiniest discovery—a single altered mark of punctuation, for example—is capable of generating.[2] The rehearsal room and the stage are where the practical side of the research, the testing of textual possibilities, takes place. We find there a rule that must, for Shakespeare's plays, alter the fundamental procedure of editorial work. If the original text—in a phrase, a stage direction, a mark of punctuation, a speech heading, whatever—works for the actor in rehearsal and performance, a powerful signal is created for editors. DANGER! PROCEED AT YOUR OWN RISK.[3]

Over and over again, editors perceive (conceive?) difficulties where none exist. For example, Costard says, "Come Jaquenetta, away" (1.2.145), and yet he clearly does not leave (for he continues to speak) though she certainly seems to go, and the Quarto's stage direction—Exeunt—suggests that she is not alone. In the editor's study, this is A Difficulty, and the only solution over the centuries has been to alter the script by giving the line to Dull: he and Jaquenetta then make an exeunt unremarkable except for the possibility that Dull violates his character by speaking when speech is unnecessary. But let us move to the rehearsal room: Costard speaks the line, starts to sweep Jaquenetta off (perhaps headed for the bushes again), is stopped short by the jealous Armado—"Villaine, thou shalt fast for thy offences ere thou be pardoned" (146)—and Dull makes off, silently and triumphantly, with the "Wench." Actors will invent the comic business. It is a lovely, scripted moment, with a wide range of freedom in which to invent the precise details of staging. Armado and Costard are, in an odd sense, rivals for Jaquenetta's favors. Armado, openly panting for her—"I do betray myselfe with blushing" (133)—thinks he has rescued her from Costard's lecherous arms, Costard (as always, without taking a breath) goes right on jesting—and there is at least a brief moment in the play when sexual opportunities seem, perhaps, to open up for, of all people, Dull.

All right: the play can survive without it. But is there any reason to deprive Dull, the actor playing him, and the audience of such an unexpected sexual triumph over the two more obvious rivals? Or the actors playing Armado and Costard of a lovely bit of fun? For in its small but solid way, the moment also beautifully develops the Armado-Costard relationship. But the real point is this: beginning with Lewis Theobald over 250 years ago, editors have seen a difficulty where none exists. Among the ten most popular and influential modern editions, all have (with no authority whatsoever) made a change in the original text, and have thus *unscripted* the Quarto. Or: with a flick of the pen, they have given us their play instead of Shakespeare's.[4] Do we really want that kind of gift?

The perception that something needs fixing in this brief episode actually started very early in the history of the text, long before Theobald. Constable Dull, performing official duties, brings Costard and Jaquenetta on, gives Costard over to Armado, and says, "I must keepe her at the Parke ... Fare you well" (130–32). Normally, that scripting would be clear: Dull leaves, taking Jaquenetta with him. But no: she stays, to reply to Armado's foolish wooing. However, the mystery person (or persons) whose interventions in or around 1623 prepared the Quarto text for the Folio printing took Dull's farewell at face value and sent him off with an "Exit" in the Folio text that leads the Constable to desert both Jaquenetta and his duty. Our ten modern editors quite properly ignore this stage direction but keep Dull on only so that he can, twelve lines later, speak Costard's line.

The two interventions—one from 1623 and no longer active, the other born in the eighteenth century and still defining a moment of *Love's Labor's Lost* in the 1990s—illustrate simply and quickly the extreme vulnerability of a script under the care of those who, while clearly trying as editors to "stage" the lines for a reader, are not themselves reading the text in its own scripted terms. The field is full of mines. To read and negotiate it, one must know what kind of map one is holding and how to respond to the very specialized signs that it employs.

This little example from the Folio not only demonstrates that unfortunate responses have a long, long history, but also suggests that whoever was responsible for the revisions that gave us the Folio text, though he gets some things right, could violate the script as radically as any subsequent editor.

None of the interventions that I shall be examining is new. Some started with the Folio, others with eighteenth century editions, one in the nineteenth century. And the modern editorial community has failed to purge these and other errors that thus still separate readers and actors alike from Shakespeare's theatrical scripts.

Though in *Love's Labor's Lost* dozens of questionable interventions demand to be discussed, I shall limit myself to a single category: speech headings. Giving Costard's speech to Dull is but one of several times in the play when all or nearly all modern editors, following their predecessors, take words from the mouth of one character and put them in the mouth of another. To deprive one character of speech and to force that speech upon another is a particularly audacious editorial act, a kind of surgical violation perhaps of both characters. In *Love's Labor's Lost*, this particular editorial activity is especially significant, for to explore specific examples therein will lead us straight to the most damaging textual intervention in the play, the famous (among editors) Rosaline-Katherine "tangle" of the third scene (2.1). The editorial activity in that scene is what has most deprived the play of the complex theatrical life signaled by the Quarto Text, and it is the alteration that we shall be moving toward as we explore others that are less famous.

In rehearsal, however, the textual rule is simple: if the script works, don't fix it. In Act Five, for example, hearing the Princess who is now a Queen promise (albeit conditionally) to marry the King, "The young Dumaine" presses Katherine with the urgent energy of repetition and a premature possessiveness: "But what to me my Love? but what to me?" (5.2.823). In the context, the direction of his question is perfectly clear, and when Katherine answers, "A wife?," do the words burst out of her as she shakes her head, amazed at his immature audacity? After all, her first six words about him early in the play twice emphasize his youthfulness (2.1.56), and here now, in some of her last words, she does so twice again: she wishes him a "beard," he is a "smooth-fast wooer." Or is her question spoken quietly, mostly to herself— "A wife?"—startled and perhaps frightened to find herself suddenly confronted with the serious possibility of marriage? She is, after all, the woman whose sister died of love and the woman who in a moment will amaze and puzzle us all by saying to Dumaine, "Then *if* I have much love, Ile give you *some*" (my italics). Among the women, hers is the strangest response of all to the hurried, probing proposals of the men. Those two simple words—"A wife?"—can be a defensive irritation with Dumaine's impulsiveness, a sudden bursting forth of her unique anguish in which love and death are too closely linked, a startled expression of some passionate though reluctant longing, a quick cry of fear at any man really laboring for her love, or the brief moment of a hushed seeking to know herself. She might even breathe the words softly or fiercely to Maria or Rosaline, sharing the emotional moment with such a friend. However the actress takes and plays the scripted question, it can, in an infinite number of ways, be one of those quick, deep, defining revelations through which Shakespeare brings very specific beauties into our lives.

But this particular moment is a beauty that few readers or viewers have experienced. You will find it in none of our ten modern texts, in none of the mainline scholarly or teaching editions, and therefore we would be foolish to expect to encounter it the next time we visit *Love's Labor's Lost* in the theater. If you were working with the Quarto, would it seem to you that, to make sense of this passage, the two words must be shifted from Katherine to Dumaine, presumably so that he can exercise his conventional male right to pop the question?

> But what to me my Love? but what to me?
> A wife?

This alteration of the Quarto text, which first surfaced in the nineteenth century, seems now to the editors *obviously* required. They perform the surgery in the belief that they have "restored" the words to Dumaine and thus returned us to Shakespeare's play. But by fixing something that is not broken, they have, in

that moment, trimmed both Dumaine and Katherine down
to a size that allows us conventional folk to see them effortlessly
with our conventional eyes. A more challenging Shakespeare
has, for the moment, disappeared under the rubble of editorial
playwriting.

Is the same true of the editorial decision that earlier in the
script takes lines from Longaville and gives them to Berowne? In
the first scene, Berowne—reading from the recently formulated
decrees that will govern life in Navarre—finds that any woman
who comes within a mile of the Court will have her tongue cut
out, and he wants to know "Who devis'd this penaltie?" (124)
The Quarto reads:

Long.   Marrie that did I.
Bero.   Sweete Lord and why?
Long.   To fright them hence with that dread penaltie.
        A dangerous law against gentletie.
Item.   Yf any man be seene to talke with a woman within the tearme
        of three years, he shall indure such publique shame as the
        rest of the Court can possible devise.
Ber.   This Article my liedge your selfe must breake.

                                        (1.1.125–133)

No modern editor would script the play this way, so it is unlikely
that any of us will ever in the theater hear Longaville speak
more than the first line of the five-line speech. The editors—and
theater companies working from modern texts—give the other
four lines to Berowne (beginning, that is, with, "A dangerous law
against gentletie."). Which, on the face of it, does seem to make
more sense.

I confess that my every conventional impulse—and which of
us is without them?—agrees with the editors. In all three of my
productions, we allowed Berowne to chastise Longaville ("A dangerous law") and then to continue reading the next "Item" of the
decrees. It of course works that way, works easily that way. It is,
after all, Berowne's strategy to create and dominate a confrontation about the "Proclamation," and it is clearly the logic of the
scene to let him, at least for the most part, do so. Then each of
the first two lines of Longaville's speech is punctuated as an
independent statement, and the second may therefore seem more
appropriate in the mouth of another speaker. Moreover, the obvious way to play "A dangerous law against gentility" is as a criticism of Longaville, not as a comment by him.

But my most recent Longaville developed a strong impulse to defend more vigorously his authorship of the horrendous decree—he didn't want so easily to be a patsy for Berowne—and we should at once have realized why. He was, I believe, sensing the scripted energy and direction of the Quarto. In a postproduction workshop, we have now explored that energy, taken the action in that direction, and found the Quarto not only playable but fascinatingly so. Suddenly, we have a Longaville who, in his self-defensive rage, is wonderfully comic, stealing the play for just a moment from Berowne, thus enabling the latter to take it back with a great leap of triumphant fun in "This Article my liedge yourself must breake."

The fun of the moment—at least as we have now found it to be—is far more competitive, and grows as follows. *One:* Longaville, proud of his contribution to the King's new laws and angry at having his work questioned, shouts, "Marry that did I." *Two:* Berowne, fast as a whip, interrupting, not allowing Longaville to complete the pentameter, strikes with a strong rhyme—his "why" noisily subduing Longaville's "I." *Three:* Longaville drives across the stage as he speaks, using the surprising, strong stress on "that" to grab the proclamation away from Berowne, waving it emphatically as he actually and wildly brags that the penalty and law are savage—"dread," "dangerous," *and* "against gentility." *Four:* having taken the initiative and the strategy away from Berowne, he uses the next *"Item"* as a threat: "Berowne, if we see you once talking with a woman, we'll inflict on you the most terrifying public punishment that the three of us can devise." *Five:* but Berowne, bursting (jumping? dancing?) with delight, snatches the decrees back from Longaville, and turns the tables on his buddies. The Princess is coming, and the King himself will be the first to break the law.

I am now convinced that any two good actors for Berowne and Longaville can make the Quarto work, that the Quarto version is more fun in the theater (is more truly theatrical), and that the Quarto gives us a more interesting Longaville and a more complex scene. All we need for editing purposes, of course, is to know that the Quarto works: if so, don't change it. But the consequences also matter. It is wonderful, in these passages, to see characters like Dull, Katherine, and Longaville becoming, in small but revealing ways, more complex—less stereotypical, more surprising—as we turn back to the Quarto. And a pattern is already beginning to appear: as we move away from the editors, toward what is more likely to be Shakespeare, the play takes on a new, less conventionally predictable thrust.

But in what sense is the Quarto in this Berowne-Longaville exchange "more likely" to be Shakespeare? The question rises directly out of another that I confess I'd love to stifle: "Could the editors, after all, be right?" Oh, yes. Yes. Yes! "Certainty" is not the name of this game. But that doesn't mean that we are reduced to flipping coins. It means, instead, that we are required to make a rational choice. In their studies, at their desks, the editors don't like or don't understand the Quarto at this point, and they act, therefore, on the basis of speculation: "A printer must have dropped the speech prefix for Berowne, so we'll just put it back." Well, actually, Theobald put it back over two-and-a-half centuries ago. That is part of the problem. Theobald's way, carrying all the seductive force of conventional logic and an obvious pattern of action for Berowne, has come so thoroughly to seem Shakespeare's way that none of us can easily think otherwise.

In the rehearsal room, however, we at long last came round to thinking that perhaps Theobald and his modern followers have been putting back something that was never there. Of course, we can't prove it was never there. But it is fair, I think, to insist that the burden of proof is on those who are altering the text. And finally it seems reasonable to believe in an unaltered script that stands the test of rehearsal instead of accepting an alteration based on no more than an arguable interpretation of the text and pure speculation about the compositor—especially when the theatrical consequences of the Quarto seem to be more interestingly unexpected than the play the editors give us.

When the twentieth-century editors of any of the Shakespeare plays place words in the wrong mouth, they are normally succumbing to an editorial tradition born in the eighteenth century: in Love's Labor's Lost they are—usually in a distressing lockstep—following Theobald, whose editions appeared in 1733 and 1740. He it was who, in the above examples, first deprived Costard and Longaville of their lines, and he it was, again, who first gave one of Berowne's lines to Boyet (5.2.159) and one of Rosaline's to the King (5.2.216). The script that Theobald thus refashioned continues to be the text that our editors present as Shakespeare: eight of the ten, following Theobald, move Berowne's line to Boyet's mouth, and all ten of them force the King to speak words that before 1733 Rosaline spoke to the King.

In this scene, when the lords enter disguised as Russians, they are confronted with women also disguised. Moth's prepared

speech—"All haile, the richest Beauties on the earth" (5.2.158)—
must, ludicrously, be delivered to four masks. Berowne sees at
once what this does to the entertainment he and his fellow
wooers have created and says, "Beauties no richer than rich Taffata." Does he mutter, whisper, grumble, hiss, whine? Is he
stunned, angry, despairing, already fighting back? Does he speak
to Moth, the other lords, himself, the audience? These are the
questions that must be answered in rehearsal, and the answers
will, of course, vary from production to production. But they are
also the questions that most Berownes never face. In all productions guided by the ghost of Theobald, the line belongs to Boyet.

Of all the editors, Hibbard explains most fully why he follows
Theobald: "because the King says explicitly and angrily that it
was Boyet who 'put Armado's page out of his part'" (5.2.336).
And Wilson provides the kind of bibliographical fiction by
which editors typically justify their interventions: "'Boy.' or 'Bo.'
in the MS. might easily be misread [by the compositor] 'Ber.' or
'Be.'." First, you invent the manuscript you need; then, you invent the compositor you need. But, as is too often true, the jus-
tifying fiction arrives to support an unsupportable explanation.
When the King later blames Boyet, he does so because the latter
has, in two other speeches (165 and 171), taunted the flustered
Moth. For his anger and his target, the King has no need to be
fueled by a speech that—if we trust the Quarto, the Folio, rehearsal, and performance, all of which agree—Shakespeare
wrote for Berowne. Moreover, one has only to think for a moment
to discover that the speech is wittier, funnier, richer, more revealing of character when it comes from an astonished, dismayed,
quick-thinking Berowne instead of a tauntingly superior Boyet.

What makes the editorial explanation fail, however, is that even
the King gets it wrong. Boyet—no matter whether he has two or
three speeches—is not the villain. The ladies are. And the script
requires a play in which that is clear. There is no evidence in
the script that Moth even hears the line under debate, whoever
speaks it: he goes right on with his speech, gets one more line
out, "A holy parcell of the fayrest dames" (160), and suddenly
doesn't even have masks to address: "*The Laydes turne their
backes to him.*" It is then, because of their move, that he first
stumbles—understandably, says "backes" for "eyes." Under Berowne's angry guidance, Moth quickly corrects himself: "That
even turnde their *eyes* to mortall viewes." As Moth begins another line—"Out" (in both early texts, the only word printed on
that line)—Boyet speaks: "True, out in deede" (165). This can be

played as an interruption, or, after a pause, as a comment on
Moth's inability to continue: rehearsal will tell. In any case, the
script suggests that Boyet's remark has not the least effect on
Moth, who simply repeats "Out" and finishes the line. It is the
women who continue to force him out of his speech. Still mes-
merized by their backs, he says, "Not to beholde" (167) when he
is (as Berowne reminds him) supposed to say, "Once to beholde
with your Sunne beamed eyes" (169). When he then repeats himself—"With your Sunne beamed eyes"—he seems at a loss, un-
able to continue; or, perhaps, as rehearsal may reveal, he is
deliberately repeating, shouting at the women to get them to turn
their eyes toward him so that his speech will make sense.

The script places Boyet on the periphery of all of this. He has
himself predicted what will happen when the women mask and
then turn away:

> Why that contempt will kill the speakers hart,
> And quite divorce his memorie from his part.
>
> (5.2.149–50)

Boyet seems no more than a happily unfriendly commentator as
the women carry out their plan. As scripted, Moth ignores him.
Even when Boyet speaks again,

> They will not answere to that Epythat,
> You were best call it Daughter beamed eyes,
>
> (5.2.171–72)

Moth, again as scripted, ignores him. Instead of responding in
any way to what seems a direct address from Boyet (though it
could be an aside), Moth verifies the accuracy of Boyet's predic-
tion, explaining as clearly as possible that his memory has been
undermined by the ladies: "They do not marke me, and that
brings me out" (173). In rehearsal it would of course be necessary
to discover how to play Boyet's two speeches, but nothing in
those speeches—and nothing in the speeches of Moth or Berowne—suggests that the King and Hibbard are right to claim
that it was Boyet who "put Armado's page out of his part."

I do not argue that when Theobald took Berowne's words from
him, he thereby gave us an unworkable script. But he did fix an
original that did not need fixing, and the result is a play that
is, for one more moment, less interesting in the theater than is
Shakespeare's. The version most editors prefer—thus the version

that most of us know and think genuine—skews the action toward a Boyet-Moth skirmish, marginalizing the impact and theatrical centrality of the women as we watch Boyet amusing himself at the expense of Moth. In Shakespeare's version, we do not lose even for a second the central fun—the women's masks and the force of four female backs. The authoritative script of the Quarto-Folio texts gives us a play in which the women, with little or no help from Boyet, baffle two of the cleverest characters in the play and throw the carefully rehearsed wooing entertainment into complete disarray.

Theobald's blinding influence harms the play again a few moments later when the King, mistaking Rosaline for the Princess and foolishly borrowing her moon imagery, begs her and her "stars" to dance. She seems at first to agree, then quickly to decline:

> King. Wil you not daunce? How come you thus estranged?
>
> Ros. You tooke the moon at ful, but now shee's changed?
>
> King. Yet still she is the Moone, and I the Man.
>
> Ros. *The musique playes, vouchsafe some motion to it,*
> Our eares vouchsafe it.
>
> King. But your legges should do it.
>
> (5.2.213–17)

Not one of our ten editors can resist the seductive Theobald. They are unanimous in their belief that the passage makes sense only after they have intervened to steal from Rosaline the line I have italicized. They give it to the King, apparently so that he can beg the women even more emphatically to dance. Ah, yes, once again: their script works. Of course it works. But—once again—in the theater (and surely even in the study) so does the Quarto. Which is more likely to be Shakespeare's?

And to whom, other than the editors, can it be surprising that the Quarto version—Shakespeare's script (let us call it that)—is more interesting than Theobald's? And that Shakespeare's speech heading is truer to the event of which it is a part? The event is composed of men with a blatantly sexual goal and of women with a witty counterattack. Throughout the dialogue, then, runs an undercurrent of possible sexual suggestion.[5] And in the relentless battle of wits, the women always win. Here, their winning goes like this: apparently agreeing to dance, Rosaline (as the Princess) orders the musicians to play, but before the men can take a breath, she says, "no daunce: thus change I like the

Moone" (212). The baffled King asks, "How come. . .?" And from
Rosaline, suggestively and theatrically: "You tooke the moone at
ful, but now shee's changed?" Just how the King speaks and acts
his next line must be found in rehearsal, but he must surely
think himself very clever: "Yet still she is the Moone, and I the
Man—in the moon, he hopes. In rehearsal it is not our task to
join the editors in speculating, as they do, about a missing line
(to rhyme with "Man") but to discover why that blunt sexual
innuendo draws to it no rhyme to make the expected couplet. It
is even possible that he means "Moone" and "Man" to be a slant
rhyme, and it could be played that way. If not, we must take the
absence of a full-length rhyming line as a scripted signal: there
is a discoverable action to turn the script into a play. Perhaps
appreciative male laughter from Navarre's friends will convince
him, prematurely, that he has triumphed. And Rosaline's reply—
this is the line the editors take away from her—may then catch
him as he and they bask in that illusion. In any case, coming
from her the line taunts him again for not responding to the
dance music, but also now taunts him for not "dancing" in the
sexual sense: if you are going to talk so big, let's see "some motion to it" (with the "it" deliberately ambiguous).

These women of France are a far more bawdy lot than are the
men of Navarre; elsewhere (especially in Act Four, Scene One)
they have some of the bawdiest lines in all of Shakespeare. However, I need not (and would not wish to) argue that my suggestion
here is *the* meaning. I only claim that it (or something like it) is
an actable sense of the passage, and that played in such a way,
the line would function usefully and be satisfyingly compre-
hensible to an audience. Theobald's editorial tinkering is unnecessary and destructive. Modern editors—and actors—should
reject it.

I have now pointed to five moments in *Love's Labor's Lost* in
which editorial action has hidden the play from modern readers,
actors, and audiences. But I hear some impatient voices. So, yes,
I confess, none of the violated speeches is long; one is but two
words; only one is longer than a line and that is but four lines.
And I grant the voices: it may even be true that no one of the
altered speech prefixes profoundly violates the character of the
new speaker, deprives the former speaker of a defining speech,
or substantially alters any major event. The five moments are,
that is, *relatively* minor. In performance, no one in the audience
notices, and even in rehearsal an acting company using the editorial version, as most do, normally senses nothing at odds with

the defining drive of the play. And yet, in each case, as I have argued, the loss is real. How many such losses must we suffer before we see that something typical in current editorial procedure is methodically reducing the theatrical vitality of the play? And how many such losses must we suffer before we notice that the typical editorial procedure creates just as methodically losses of a much larger kind? This last question brings us directly to the famous "Rosaline-Katherine Tangle."

In the first moments of the first meeting between the women of France and the men of Navarre (2.1, the third scene of the play), the words and actions of five of the major characters— Katherine, Rosaline, Berowne, Boyet, and Dumaine—have been, from at least as early as 1623, a central editorial and theatrical challenge. Who says and does what, and with whom? As different scripts yield different plays, the Quarto offers one play, the Folio another, and no modern editor that I know of has fully accepted either. For the seeker of *Love's Labor's Lost*, there are now available—out there in the market—at least seven different scripts offering, in a major sense, seven different plays. Exploring this territory in rehearsal and performance, one discovers—not surprisingly, after all—that what happens in that first meeting of the men and women very intimately shapes and colors what happens thereafter. It is not enough to say "shapes." One must add "colors" because the impact of those first few moments on all the rest is so enormous, complex, and detailed. As an acting company, we are at this early point learning what kind of a play Shakespeare was scripting. Is it as sunny, light, charming, symmetrical, and parasolled as our twentieth-century theater has been led by the editors to believe?

The flight from the 1598 Quarto started early, but the story in it and all subsequent versions begins like this: four young men, having taken an oath to study for three years and to see no women, are confronted by four young ladies, three of whom bring with them a strong interest in three of the men, thus creating three couples before the men have anything to say about it. The couples are Rosaline and Berowne, Katherine and Dumaine, and Maria and Longaville. It is at this point, upon the entrance of the men, that in 1623 the story divides, becoming two (one in the Folio), and then, much later (in modern editions), splintering into several different stories. Though different, the post-Quarto stories have much in common. They are all trying to "correct" or "untangle" a very "muddled" Quarto, and their shared motivation is founded in a desire for the artificial charms of symmetry.

The editors inhabit a world in which the young men must enter and each take his place with absolute precision within the couples that the women have arranged for them.

But let us face the challenge as an editor must. Here, from the Quarto, is the first of two sparring matches in which Berowne participates. It occurs while the King is examining a governmental document presented to him by the Princess.

Ber.	Did not I dance with you in *Brabant* once?
Kath.	Did not I dance with you in *Brabant* once?
Ber.	I know you did.
Kath.	How needles was it then to ask the question?
Ber.	You must not be so quicke.
Kath.	Tis long of you that spur me with such questions.
Ber.	Your wit's too hot; it speedes too fast, twill tire.
Kath.	Not till it leave the rider in the mire.
Ber.	What time a day?
Kath.	The houre that fooles should aske.
Ber.	Now faire befall your maske.
Kath.	Faire fall the face it covers.
Ber.	And send you manie lovers.
Kath.	Amen, so you be none.
Ber.	Nay then will I be gon.

This is of course the passage that causes most of the trouble. Berowne, unschooled in the virtues of symmetry, talks to the *wrong* woman. From the editorial point of view, he fails to redeem himself when, some fifty lines later, he at last tries his luck with the "right" lady:

Ber.	Ladie I will commend you to my none hart.
Ros.	Pray you, do my commendations, I would be glad to see it.
Ber.	I would you heard it grone.
Ros.	Is the foole sick.
Ber.	Sicke at the hart.
Ros.	Alacke, let it blood.
Ber.	Would that do it good?
Ros.	My Phisicke saies I.
Ber.	Will you prickt with your eye.
Ros.	*No poynt*, with my knife.

Ber. Now God save thy life.
Ros. And yours from long living.
Ber. I cannot stay thankes-giving.

Immediately thereafter, each of the young lords, one after the other, asks Boyet to identify one of the ladies. Longaville points at Maria, which is as it should be. But Dumaine stuns all lovers of symmetry by asking about Rosaline, and Berowne—now entirely out of control—swings wildly back to Katherine. Clearly, something must be done about these two: their asymmetrical sexual prowling here completes what all editors perceive to be the incomprehensible "tangle." That in their next scene the two lords have, without explanation, recovered their senses—pursuing for the rest of the play the "right" ladies—only makes their early wavering the more incomprehensible to the editors. Editorial policing has become obligatory.

The first to accept the obligation was that mysterious person whose on-again, off-again "editing" (it isn't quite fair to call him an editor) produced the changes that distinguish the Folio from the Quarto. Whoever he was, whatever his connection with the acting company or the printing house, both his dissatisfaction and his solution are important. The Quarto apparently made no more sense to him than it does to modern editors, and he was pulled, as they are, toward symmetry. But the most interesting part of his revision modern editors unanimously reject or seem, in fact, to ignore. In this Folio version of the story, Berowne goes at once to the "right" lady—Rosaline—the one, that is, who has earlier, before he enters, announced her interest in him and to whom therefore all of Katherine's speeches are transferred. In the second duet, however, it is, surprisingly, Boyet who "commends" himself to her heart. He speaks throughout exactly the same words that Berowne speaks in the Quarto, but the last speech—"I cannot stay thankes-giving"—is still Berowne's. In our rehearsal room and on our stage what the Folio version prompted us to present was a Rosaline who is offended by Berowne's state-of-the-art masculine line in the first duet and who then deliberately flirts with Boyet in front of Berowne, thus offending him so that he stalks off with no "thanksgiving" and, a moment later, takes a brief, perhaps retaliatory, interest in Katherine, asking Boyet for her name just as he does in the Quarto.

One of the oddities of modern editorial argument, I think, is that dissatisfaction with the Quarto has apparently never convinced anyone—not even those for whom the Folio is "potentially authoritative"—to adopt, argue for, or even mildly admire the Folio solution to the "tangle." It is clear, however, that the often careless reviser here had his mind on his job. His alteration of speech headings, without changing a word of dialogue, creates a good story that is great fun in the theater: our audiences loved watching Rosaline unsettle Berowne in the first duet and conspire with Boyet to taunt him without mercy in the second. Once again, however, the reviser's poor theatrical judgment ultimately undermines his revisions. He saw clearly that one duet between Berowne and Rosaline is enough, and having inserted Rosaline into the first, he could simply have cut the then-superfluous second. But he was more adventurous than that, and must, I think, have been quite pleased when he thought of bringing in Boyet. However, words scripted for a Berowne-Rosaline sparring match simply will not work as a Rosaline-Boyet maneuver against Berowne. The idea is so good—Berowne's frustration is so deserved, comic, and theatrical—that it seems worthy of Shakespeare. In the audience, one is tempted to ignore the words and love the fun. Many members of our audience, perhaps unknowingly, did just that. But at last the words triumph. They arise convincingly from a Berowne-Rosaline relationship, but they are at last not convincing in the quite different relationship of Boyet and Rosaline. After a thorough testing in rehearsal and performance, we felt we had learned the hard—and proper—way that the series of speeches belonging to Berowne cannot simply be shifted to Boyet. Shakespeare would surely have rewritten them had he desired the new story line. However good the new story, the editorial changes in the Folio fail as a scripted signal.

Other ideas, most of them not nearly so good, have prevailed. Here are some of them (with the editions that present them):

1. Cut both duets (New Cambridge and Arden).
2. Cut the first duet and substitute, in its place, the second (Penguin).
3. Keep the two duets just as they are in the Quarto but alter Boyet's subsequent replies to the would-be wooers so that each man is showing an interest in the "right" lady (Riverside).
4. Replace Katherine with Rosaline in the first duet (as the Folio does), keep the second unchanged, thus presenting two Rosaline-Berowne duets, and alter Boyet's speeches so that each man asks about the "right" lady (Pelican, Signet, Festival, Oxford/Hibbard, Oxford/Wells, and Bevington).
5. Follow the version just described but cut the second duet (BBC TV and many theatrical productions).

For *Love's Labor's Lost*, then, we have (counting the Quarto and the Folio) at least seven scripts: six competing revisions of the Quarto. However different from one another they may be, the revisions are alike in one important way. In their shared belief that the Quarto is confused (a "tangle," a "muddle"), they all try to lead us out of the confusion by creating a dramatic world in which the simplicities of symmetry are the clarifying force. This is especially true of the version that has come to dominate the market (bookstores, libraries, schools of all kinds, theaters for performance purposes, even scholarly studies) and is thus, for most people, in every practical sense, *The Play*—the version that is number four above and is presented by eight of our ten editors, even by the two who believe that both duets should be cut.

Being as brainwashed as the rest of the world, I have twice directed that Mainline Version and have spent most of my professional life (some forty years) teaching it. But having now directed both the Folio and the Quarto, I know how profoundly we have all been cheated. Some time ago—while pursuing the editors beyond their editions and into the scholarly journals where, in pages remote from any theater, they debate among themselves— I encountered an attack upon the Quarto, and thus a defense of editorial revision, from the justly famous director John Barton of the Royal Shakespeare Company. His remarks, quoted in a scholarly context by John Kerrigan, the editor of the Penguin edition of *Love's Labor's Lost*, reveal that even Barton has been cheated:

"There certainly is a tangle—no audience could cope with the complications in the wooing as early as II.I, the first scene where the lovers are together. . . . An audience can only take in so much at once. Shakespeare knew that better than anyone."[6]

I must, however, ask myself: what kind of evidence do I bring into this arena when, against a world of editors and the voice of such an experienced theatrical authority, I testify to the simple truth that our audiences—from high school students to research scholars and the general public—did "cope" with the "complications" of the Quarto and enjoyed doing so? Unlike the editors, we took the "tangle" into the rehearsal hall and onto the stage; and unlike Barton, we allowed the audience to speak for itself. As a script, the Quarto works; as a play, it is amazing—especially, perhaps, for those who, like the scholars in our audience, thought they thoroughly knew *Love's Labor's Lost*. The power of the editors to hide Shakespeare from us registers both in that and in the fact that even the Royal Shakespeare Company has never freed itself to bring its actors and audiences into the very great pleasures of the Quarto.

Having, as an acting company, fought our way through the Editorial Version to the Folio—for a time believing in each—and only then, with a struggle, moving on to the Quarto, we are sure of our ground. For us, there is no longer a "tangle." The story the Quarto tells in the theater is not only simple and clear but more theatrical and more believable, offering a more complex view of sexual maneuverings, than any other version. Its "new" story drew us into a world we recognized: our world, the world of students and young would-be lovers at any contemporary American university.[7]

What a lovely irony: Shakespeare's script from the 1590s seemed, as soon as we started *doing* it, closer to the 1990s than any of the versions offered by "modern" editors. The young actors could finally stop merely pretending to believe what was going on. To be sure: at first, the same four men, the same four women, but Berowne—who has, even while signing the oath, been dreaming of "some mistress fine"—is here at once on the prowl, making (in the first duet) a fast, macho play for Katherine, then (in the second) for Rosaline, back briefly to Katherine (checking on her name), and at last settling (apparently, but not until we see him in the next scene) on Rosaline. "The young Dumaine," as Katherine significantly characterizes him in her first words about him, is also making his move: Rosaline looks good to him, and the editors haven't told him about symmetry.

So in this new-old play we found Berowne trying his line— and it is so clearly a "line"—on Katherine: "Did not I dance with you in *Brabant* once?" Ah, Katherine: she whose beloved sister— "melancholie, sad, and heavie" (5.2.14)—died of love, she who late in Act Five will say even to Dumaine, "Then *if* I have much love, Ile give you *some*" (830), and she who knows that her dear friend Rosaline (standing right over there, listening and watching) has a very special interest in this man. Berowne couldn't have found a less promising way to break his oath, and for his pains he gets the verbal equivalent of a knee to the groin. Retreating in haste—"Nay then will I be gon"—he almost at once brazenly puts an even more outrageous move on Rosaline: "Ladie, I will commend you to my none hart."[8] Ah, right: he for whom this is the second lady in the last three minutes. Her replies—if taken simply as they come—are stunning: she has a knife for his heart and wishes him soon dead. When Boyet later says that the "tongues of mocking Wenches" are like arrows and bullets (5.2.256–61), we will know what he means. They hurt, can even kill.

No wonder that after this defeat, Berowne decides at once to switch back to his first choice: even Katherine seems a more likely pick-up than this brunette fury. And in the playing, as we soon realized, the actor (speaking to Boyet) needs only to hesitate at the right second: "What's her name"—pause, eyes roaming over the field, finger pointing at last to her—"in the capp?" Katherine!—"by good *happ*"?—yes, indeed, as Boyet says. Apparently the Elizabethan audience recognized this brash young man; certainly our modern audience did. Laugh at him or loathe him, he is as familiar—especially to women—as a street corner, a college party, or a day at the beach. And he is infinitely more interesting for the actors and the audience than the bland editorial Berowne—funnier and yet a more serious threat to comic form, more problematic for the female characters, and with a more complex sexual and intellectual impact on the rest of the play. As we thought about it, he seemed a far more likely candidate for a play in which the *"Labor"* of *"Love"* is *"Lost."*

Our reward came in many forms. It is a critical commonplace that Armado is some kind of parody of the oath-breaking, romantic young men of the court, especially, perhaps, of Berowne. Discovering how to convert the scripted signals of the parody into amusing and revealing stage action is, however, not as easy as one might wish. It was, therefore, always a moment of pure joy when, with the insight provided by the Quarto, we saw signals that had been hidden from us by the other scripts. In the fourth scene (3.1), the major elements of the parody are, in all versions, clear enough: Armado, melancholy in love, asks Costard to deliver a letter to Jaquenetta and tips him a "remuneration"; Berowne, melancholy in love, asks Costard to deliver a letter to Rosaline and tips him a "guerdon." There is no missing the parallel. But why, for example, does Armado forget Jaquenetta's name—"But o but o"—and Moth drive home so emphatically in some eighteen lines (3.1.26–43) the forgetting: "Negligent student, learne her by hart"? The moment, just in itself, is funny enough, but could there be another payoff?

In all versions of this scene, Berowne enters with the letter, but the Quarto is by far the most interesting, for there the audience cannot know at once which lady (Katherine, Rosaline, or

even Maria) he is now pursuing. Groaning for love and begging
Costard to deliver the letter to a "gentle Lady," he says:

> When tongues speake sweetely, then they name her name,
> And *Rosaline* they call her . . .

(3.1.166–67)

Suddenly, in rehearsal, we knew that the Berowne of the Quarto
would (of course) forget her name, that—even in the midst of his
moony talk about naming her name—he would have to glance
quickly at the letter to name "Rosaline." An action of one or two
seconds only, but it is true to character, is based (we believe)
firmly on the script, enriches the function of Armado, and employs the parody wonderfully to ridicule Berowne's ability to
"love" (to dress lust, that is, in the conventional language and
actions of love). Our audiences loved it. And we, once more, were
grateful to the Quarto.

Another consequence of playing the Quarto script is that the
women, too, become more interesting. Startled and challenged
by the disorderly surprises of life instead of simpering into the
prearranged simplicities of neatly symmetrical patterns, they
blossom into real women, women with more passions than parasols. In the first duet, Katherine is suddenly on the front line,
deeply offended, even wounded (she may have known just such
a man as the lover of her sister), and deeply embarrassed, suffering for Rosaline. But what Katherine (and the audience) won't
know until much later is that Rosaline has lied about Berowne,
lied outrageously, and this in a play that is prominently about
the value of honesty. Only minutes earlier, in the same scene
(2.1.64–76), she has said to her friends that Berowne's wit—
unlike that of the men the two of them fancy—remains always
"Within the limit of becomming mirth," that his tongue is
"fayre," his words so "apt and gracious" that older folk are delighted and the young "quite ravished" by his "sweete . . . discourse." What a lovely man! He has, in Rosaline's description,
no faults. What a contrast to Longaville—of whom the painfully
honest Maria has just confessed (2.1.40–51) that his "sharpe
Wit" and "blunt Will" spare "none . . . that come within his
power"—and to Dumaine, of whom Katherine, in a bonding with
Maria, says that he has "Most power to do most harme" and "wit
to make an ill shape good" (2.1.59–60). But Rosaline is hiding
the truth, trying perhaps to hide it even from herself. Berowne
is, as she has known from the beginning but does not admit until

her next-to-last speech in the play, at least as dangerous as the other men:

> Oft have I heard of you, my Lord *Berowne*,
> Before I saw you: and the worldes large tongue
> Proclayms you for a man repleat with mockes,
> Full of comparisons and wounding floutes:
> Which you on all estetes will execute,
> That lie within the mercie of your wit.

(5.2.841–46)

The actress playing the Quarto will know that, as Rosaline watches Berowne in that first scene trying to manipulate first Katherine and then herself, she is already beginning to pay for her lie. The passion of her response to him has its source in guilt as well as anger. No such complication troubles the life of the editorial Rosaline.

Maria has watched it all, heard it all: heard Rosaline's unqualified praise for Berowne, felt the force of the comparison against Longaville and Dumaine, and watched as Berowne puts his arrogant, oath-breaking, sexual moves on her two friends. With all that, we suddenly discovered that it isn't easy to find Maria's tone of voice when, upon Berowne's exit, she says, "That last is Berowne, the merrie madcap L[ord] / Not a word with him but a jest" (2.1.215–16). In his exchange with Boyet just before leaving, he has in no sense justified such a comment—nothing "merry," nothing of the madcap, no jesting. She must, then, be commenting on Berowne's behavior with Katherine and Rosaline—with an ironic look back at Rosaline's glowing characterization of him. As Maria may not know that Rosaline has been lying, there need be no resentment toward her in the irony. What Maria certainly does know is the great contrast between Berowne's "apt and gracious" ways in Rosaline's report and his ungracious ways in the last few minutes. Our actresses came to believe that the women are united in their feelings about this man who seems to think that, even as he breaks his oath, he is God's gift to any lady, and we all agreed that Maria, with her scornful and amazed irony, is speaking for them all.

"So why do I continue to put up with the guy?"—an anguished question from the actress playing Rosaline, and a very good question it is, revealing a level of difficulty, of complexity, a depth of characterization that challenged us only when we had switched to the Quarto. In each succeeding rehearsal and performance, we discovered that, under the impact of the Quarto script, this kind

of deepening continues right through the play. But for my purposes here I shall carry the story no further. Though there is
more to say about the superiority of the Quarto over both the
Folio and all modern edited versions of the play, I hope I have
sufficiently answered the questions with which, in my second
paragraph, I started. Is there a new/old *Love's Labor's Lost* waiting
to be discovered for the stage? If so, as I believe, then we must
find a way to break through the mask that editors, largely because
of their literary bias, place between us and Shakespeare's scripts.
The ultimate purpose of my examination here of *Love's Labor's
Lost* is, in other words, to call for a fundamental reexamination
of editorial policy. Most immediately, the editorial interventions
in this script have limited and distorted our understanding of
Shakespeare's early work in comedy, but they are unfortunately
typical. Much, throughout the entire canon, remains to be recovered so that theater companies will be able to bring us closer to
the plays that the original texts imply.

To edit Shakespeare's sonnets and narrative poems is to undertake a literary task. To edit his scripts is to undertake a theatrical
task (in which, of course, literary skills and knowledge are extremely important). When the text is a script, what in the editor's
study appears to be a severe textual difficulty—a dreadful "tangle"—may actually be a richly scripted opportunity for staging.
Imposing a literary process on theatrical material, editors arrive
at solutions that not only violate the scripts but more often than
not are presented so quietly that only a textual expert is likely
to see that the work is not Shakespeare's. A new kind of theatrical
evidence must begin to make its proper contribution to editorial procedure. It will usefully guide bibliographical and historical evidence and radically demote editorial speculation and
interpretation.

"*Must*"? Well, yes, so says the optimist. I can, in my dreams,
see an Edenic time, with a new breed of editors: editors who,
when they encounter a word, a passage, a stage direction, a
speech prefix in the "authoritative" text that "fails to make
sense," hold the difficulty open as a challenge to be explored in
depth and at length in the theater. That is, editors who work in
the belief that the original text—being of the theater, being a set
of scripted words—contains a world of possibilities that can
never be fully revealed in any literary arena. Until such an Eden,
however, with such editors, one of those worlds—*Love's Labor's
Lost* in all its wonderful complexity—will for most people remain hidden behind a simpler, more conventional, less interest-

ing play devised by literary scholars and perpetuated on the stage by directors, designers, and actors with parasols who think they are doing Shakespeare.

Ah, well, you may think I've gone and done it—joined that chorus of inflated claims that tells us "what is and what is not the real Shakespeare." All right, I admit to this much: I claim that there is a more trustworthy way than that employed by professional editors to find what is most likely to be the "real" Shakespearean text. This "way" comes down to two simple rules: (1) trust the original texts far longer and more deeply than do the editors, and (2) explore and test theatrical texts with theatrical methods in theatrical arenas. Even as individuals in our own studies—in our work as scholars, teachers, actors, and directors—we need not continue to depend so unquestioningly upon the literary, and thus masked, versions of Shakespeare's scripts produced by the Editorial Establishment. We live, after all, in a time when the Folio and the Quartos are easily available to us all. And in the case of *Love's Labor's Lost*—a typical example— the Quarto Version, even with its many serious blemishes, proves to be the most exciting and complex script from which to teach, study, and perform. Does this mean it is reasonable to believe (even though we have no final proof) that the Quarto brings us closer to Shakespeare's working script than does any of the "corrected" versions? But, well: isn't that a rhetorical question?

NOTES

1. I owe this characterization of a Royal Shakespeare Company production to one of the actors in it.

2. I have previously explored this territory in the following: "Menas and the Editors: a Folio Script Unscripted," *Shakespeare Quarterly* 36 (Summer 1985), 164–87); "Editors vs. a Text: the Scripted Geography of *A Midsummer Night's Dream*," *Studies in Philology* 87 (Winter 1990), 83–108; "No Exit for a Dead Body: What to Do with a Scripted Corpse?" *Journal of Dramatic Theory and Criticism* 5 (Spring 1991), 139–52.

3. My own research was conducted through the process of directing *Love's Labor's Lost* for the American Shakespeare Company (the University of California, 1992). It was the third time I had directed the play.

4. The ten modern texts include both popular and scholarly versions, ranging over time from 1951 to 1992: Pelican, Penguin, Signet, New Cambridge, Arden, Riverside, Harper Collins, both Oxford editions (in the Complete Works and the independently edited version), and the New York Shakespeare Festival edition. For quotations from the Quarto text, I use *Shakespeare's Plays in Quarto*, eds. Michael J. B. Allen and Kenneth Muir (Berkeley: University of California Press, 1981), 292–330. I have not known quite what to do about the

relatively new Guild Edition edited by John Andrews. It has had no wide public distribution and is not yet significantly consulted by scholars, teachers, or directors. As I write, however, Mr. Andrews is revising it for publication and some of the plays have already been published individually as part of the Everyman Shakespeare, under which label it may have greater impact. Textually, his *Love's Labor's Lost* is already far closer to the Quarto than any other modern edition, and he has said that he is even more conservative in his revisions. As his edition has yet to become an influence, I have not included it in this essay with those that continue to define our idea of the play. But I wish it an influential future.

5. In, for example, the King's speech (repeated by Boyet and played on by Rosaline): "Say to her we have measured many miles, / To treade a Measure with her on this grasse." See Eric Partridge, *Shakespeare's Bawdy*, rev. ed. (New York: E. P. Dutton, 1969), 204.

6. "The 'Rosaline-Katherine Tangle': A Correspondence," *The Library*, 6th Series, 5 (December 1983): 401.

7. This paragraph and the seven-and-a-half that follow are borrowed from "Love's Labor's Lost: Finding a Text, Finding a Play," an essay that forms my contribution to *Acts of the Imagination*, a projected volume of essays in honor of O. B. Hardison (edited by Arthur Kinney and Marifrancis Hardison).

8. A strange reading from the Quarto. Among modern editors, only Andrews keeps and defends it. We did not keep it in performance because we thought our actor could communicate Berowne's deliberately faked passion (in "my own heart") better than he could get the audience to savor an awkward pun that Berowne himself is not aware of. How can Berowne, of all people, be less aware of a pun than the audience is? We couldn't find a way to act it. But we know that doesn't mean it can't be done.

Convents, Conventions, and Contraventions:
Love's Labor's Lost and *The Convent of Pleasure*

JEANNE ADDISON ROBERTS

THE temptation is strong to argue for *Love's Labor's Lost* as Shakespeare's most feminist play. Such an argument would be supported most obviously by the fact that the Princess of France and her three noble ladies control the action from their first appearance to their last. In spite of their exclusion from the inner sanctum of the court of Navarre because the King and his three noble followers have resolved on a cloistered life and have forsworn the company of women, the ladies arrive as visitors and soon become love objects for the four men. However, the women continue to defer capitulation to marriage even beyond the end of the play, assigning to the men a year of penance for their oath-breaking, to be followed by possible reconsideration. Such an ending has no parallel in Shakespearean comedy, and it looks like not only a violation of the conventions of New Comedy, but also a clear example of women on top.

From their first appearance, the women show unaccustomed signs of power. At the beginning of Act 2, after the men have established their resolution to renounce such indulgences as sleep, food, and the company of women, the Princess and her ladies arrive at the court in the ambiguous guise of "suitors," a role normally commanded by men in a potentially matrimonial climate and only assumed by women when, like the three widowed queens of *The Two Noble Kinsmen* or Volumnia at the end of *Coriolanus*, they are helplessly suing for assistance or concession from powerful males. Although the Princess orders Boyet, her attendant Lord, to say that she and her ladies have come "Like humble-visag'd suitors" seeking the King of Navarre's "high will" (2.1.34), her behavior is anything but humble. Boyet describes her as a royal emissary negotiating between equals—the King of France and the King of Navarre. She instructs Boyet to say to Navarre that she has arrived on "serious business craving quick dispatch" and that she "[Importunes] personal conference with his Grace" (2.1.29–32). When the princess meets Navarre, she commands him preemptorily to conduct her to the forbidden court and charges him that it is a deadly sin either to keep his oath or to break it (2.1.96–106). She concludes with an injunction that he

> Vouchsafe to read the purpose of my coming,
> And suddenly resolve me in my suit.
>
> (2.1.109–10)

And she finally rebukes him for initially rejecting her claim:

> You do the King my father too much wrong,
> And wrong the reputation of your name,
> In so unseeming to confess receipt
> Of that which hath so faithfully been paid.
>
> (2.1.153–56)

As the women actively demonstrate their power, the men seem curiously passive. Because the King of Navarre has forbidden the Princess to "come within [his] gates" (2.1.171), he takes on the aura of the female virgin immured in a secluded garden. The aura of aggressive female power, on the other hand, is enhanced by Boyet, who notes that the women are being treated more as invaders come to besiege the court than as humble suitors. The word "suitor" slips from a female to a male connotation. The ladies are not begging, but attacking. And, indeed, the word "suitor" is later conflated with the word "shooter," apparently a homophone in Elizabethan English. Rosaline, one of the Princess's ladies, is identified as the "shooter" in the deer hunt. An elaborate quibble on deers and horns evokes both the traditional affinity of the hunt for deer and the hunt for love, and the ubiquitous specter of cuckoldry. The Princess herself becomes a shooter who actually kills a deer, which may or may not have been a suspiciously male-sounding "pricket" (4.2.56).

The women's physical presence is, of course, accented by their beauty, which is repeatedly attested to. Boyet, as chorus, celebrates Nature's prodigality, after starving the general world, in bestowing all graces on the Princess (2.1.9–12). Beauty, traditionally the passive female lure for attracting the opposite sex, here, like skill with the bow, becomes a signal of dominant power.

While the women may be "in love," as the Princess suggests after hearing how every one of them "her own [prospective mate] hath garnished with . . . bedecking ornaments of praise" (2.1.78–79), they show few signs of melting emotion. They are suitors not for spouses, but for money and land—a hundred thousand crowns and Aquitaine are at stake. The Princess urges that the suit should be settled quickly because, she tells the King prophetically, "you'll prove perjur'd if you make me stay" (2.1.113). After the first meeting, Boyet describes the King's reaction in curiously passive terms: "Methought all his senses were lock'd in his eye, / As jewels in crystal for some prince to buy (2.1.242–43). Again the usual gender roles are reversed—the male is waiting to be bought rather than negotiating a sale. And Boyet correctly assures the Princess that Aquitaine is now hers for the taking.

There is no fainting, no protestation among these women that their love, like Rosalind's in As You Like It, is as deep as the bay of Portugal, little anxiety about whether they are loved. They accept diamonds, gloves, and pearls with aplomb, but Rosaline's response is to resolve to torture her love. She wants to make him fawn, beg, seek, and spend, fancying that "he should be my fool and I his fate" (5.2.62–68). There is a nice disruption of Shakespeare's usual sun/son pun when Moth fails to get the women's attention to "sun-beamed eyes" and is advised by Boyet to shift to "daughter-beamed eyes" (5.2.170–72). And Berowne complains, "The tongues of mocking wenches are as keen / As is the razor's edge invisible" (5.2.256–57). Finally, each woman declines the offer of marriage and imposes a year's penance on her admirer. Compared with the instantaneous matrimonial imaginings of a Juliet, a Rosalind, or a Miranda, the behavior of these ladies seems strikingly cool. Is this a feminist's dream? a conventional comedy? or perhaps an idiosyncratic Shakespearean vision?

Love's Labor's Lost is one of the very few Shakespeare plays with no known source—the others are A Midsummer Night's Dream, The Merry Wives of Windsor, and The Tempest—and I should like to imagine that Shakespeare, with mind unfettered by sources, reveals himself to be a closet feminist. The first three of these plays have in common the depiction of powerful women. There may be some echo of the viragoes of Love's Labor's Lost in Hippolyta, the Amazon of A Midsummer Night's Dream, and in the formidable Titania, who is a dominant presence until Oberon succeeds in tricking her into relinquishing her changeling boy and renouncing her animalistic erotic adventure with Bottom as ass. The merry wives are repeatedly victorious in shaming Falstaff. And all three of these plays exhibit the deception of men by women. The Tempest, of course, is a serious impediment to a theory of a Shakespeare with feminist leanings when unencumbered by an inherited plot, but three out of four is not bad.

And yet the case for a feminist Love's Labor's Lost remains unconvincing. The sense persists that the play is actually not about women at all. The noble ladies appear in only three scenes (the last admittedly a long one): one scene in Act 2, one scene in Act 4, and one scene in Act 5 and not at all in Acts 1 and 3. The peasant Jaquenetta appears also in only three scenes, and she has a total of thirteen lines. Her main function in the two latter scenes is as an instrument of plot—to deliver letters to the wrong people. Her only distinguishing qualities are stupidity, physical appeal, and fertility, all of which amusingly attract both the aristocratic Don Armado and the lowly Costard. Although the court ladies, especially the Princess and Rosaline, are slightly individualized, they lack the marked distinctions between Helena and Hermia in A Midsummer Night's Dream, Portia and Nerissa in The Merchant of Venice, Rosalind and Celia in As You Like It, or Beatrice and Hero in Much Ado About Nothing. The focus is almost entirely on the men. We are diverted with the pleasures of male bonding, male frailty, male pedantry, male posturing, male dullness, and male wit, but the women remain fixed points to be reacted to.

But if Love's Labor's Lost is not about women, it is certainly about male reactions to women, and it raises the question of what is behind the portraits of the men? The question has puzzled generations of critics. The play seems to have a specifically topical agenda, now lost. The King of Navarre, de Mayenne, the Duc de Biron, and the Duc de Longueville were actual historical French characters, and many identifications with real Englishmen have been suggested for Don Armado, Holofernes, Nathaniel, and Moth.[1] In 1936, Frances Yates advanced the theory that the play was written as a tribute to the brilliant sisters of the Earl of Essex, Penelope and Dorothy Devereaux, in refutation of a tract by the Earl of Northumberland, a friend of Sir Walter Raleigh, which argued that "the entertainment of a Mistress was inconsistent with the pursuit of learning."[2] And most persistently, following Muriel Bradbrook's 1936 book, the play has been explained as a satire of Raleigh and his followers and friends—

supposedly united in a School of Atheism, obliquely referred to in the play as "the school of night" (4.3.251).[3] Connections have also been made with George Chapman, another Raleigh ally, whose two poetical hymns, "To Night" and "To Cynthia," were published together, probably about the time of Shakespeare's play, in 1594 as *The Shadow of Night.*

The evidence for all of these identifications is murky and ambiguous. The reference to the school of night may be a textual error or an explainable image, and there is no solid evidence that such a "school" existed. If Shakespeare means to attack Chapman, why do so many passages echo Chapman rather than reject him?

Chapman laments the corruption of the present "day" where men's faces glitter while their hearts are black.[4] But, like Shakespeare, he celebrates the power of women and their association with night, especially Cynthia/Diana, the goddess of night, saying,

> But thou (great Mistresse of heavens gloomie racke)
> Art blacke in face, and glitterst in thy heart.
>
> (Biiv)

He conjures great Hercules to "shoote, shoote" and stop the pride of the sun, suffering

> . . . no more his lustfull rayes to get
> The earth with issue . . .
>
> (Biii)

Night shall then live forever as "the Planets Queene" (Eiiv). He prophesies that maids will subdue the might of Jove "with well-steeld lances of [night's] watchful sight" (Eiiv). He praises the pureness of Cynthia/Diana's "never-tainted life, / Scorning the subject title of a wife" (Civ) and urges her to seek hounds and archery and "shun faithlesse men's society" (Ciii). And he concludes "Musicke, and moode, she loves, but love she hates" (Ci).

Much of this rhetoric and the determined rejection of marriage is obviously relevant to Queen Elizabeth as well as to divine philosophy. But it is not foreign to the mood of *Love's Labor's Lost.* Rosaline is repeatedly associated with black—black eyes, ebony, pitch, Ethiopes, colliers, and chimney sweepers. Berowne insists that "No face is fair that is not full so black" (4.3.249), and she repeatedly refers to herself as a moon. Both she and the

Princess are archers, and both end by shunning faithless men's society. True, in the play there is also attack on blackness—the King declares black "the badge of hell," while Berowne argues that Rosaline is "born to make black fair" (4.3.250–57). But this is the matter of witty debate. It seems to me unthinkable that satire is meant to be directed against the women. The audience stands with Berowne in admiring and enjoying Rosaline as well as the other ladies. If satire of women is intended, at least for modern audiences, it misses its mark. And if there is local satire of London dramatists or courtiers, we no longer get the point. The eccentrics seem rather incarnations of recurring types from traditional comedy and the *commedia del'arte*.[5]

If the play cannot be read by us as either a precociously feminist or a specifically satirical drama, how can we view it? The 1598 Quarto confidently advertises it as "A Pleasant Conceited Comedie," and it is generally accepted as such. But not within the play, where Berowne declares with apparent regret that the comic structure is unfinished and self-consciously distinguishes it from the comedic tradition:

> Our wooing doth not end like an old play:
> Jack hath not Gill. These ladies' courtesy
> Might well have made our sport a comedy.
>
> (5.2.874–76)

The implication is clearly that, although comic, the play does not fit the traditional pattern of New Comedy.

Like Berowne, most modern scholars, under the powerful influence of Northrop Frye, have taken as the very essence of New Comedy a movement toward erotic consummation and the establishment of a new society.[6] But I suggest that this definition, while useful, is not fixed in stone. Students tend to define comedy as drama that is funny and ends happily. But the arbitrarily predetermined marriages that terminate Roman comedy may not be "happy endings," especially for women.

I think one might argue that Shakespearean comedy, while not clearly feminist in the modern sense of promoting equality of fully developed genders, may be read as evolving toward such an end. As *Love's Labor's Lost* experiments with the rejection of comedic convention, other early Shakespearean comedies modify comedic expectations. In *The Comedy of Errors*, the Abbess, relic of the older generation, remains firmly in charge, and the reunion of her son with his wife is shadowed by the memory of the courtesan who earlier entertained the husband. But a new generation is established, and lovers are united. In *The Taming of the Shrew*, two out of three of the new marriages seem headed for trouble, but there can be no doubt that the inexorable movement toward coupling and presumably toward fertility has been reenacted. This process recapitulates what audiences are assumed to want and what society needs and is therefore provided ritualistically as the "happy ending" of comedy. Hollywood colludes in such unlikely unions as that of a prostitute and a millionaire at the end of the film *Pretty Woman*, apparently because preview audiences would not accept the original "unhappy ending" in which the two were separated.

But comedy is not ritual, and the inherited generic traditions are strongly patriarchal. While the marriages of classical New Comedy are arranged by and for men, Shakespeare's comedies seem to be evolving toward a newer and more female-oriented form. The wishes of audiences and societies are neither simple nor univocal; and as women grow in power, comedic patterns change. Shakespeare's early comedies modify tradition; his later ones show further evolution. As female characters are more fully developed in the later comedies, it might be argued that the real pleasure is not in their rather perfunctory promise of consummation at the end, but in their exquisite prolonging of the slow movement toward it, their achievement of what Milton describes as Eve's mastery of "sweet reluctant amorous delay" (3.311).[7]

Male resistance to commitment is axiomatic in modern self-help literature as well as in Elizabethan drama. Benedick in *Much Ado About Nothing* displays this quality at some length, and Bertram in *All's Well that Ends Well* is the quintessential personification of it. Don Armado in *Love's Labor's Lost* says, "there is no evil angel but love" (1.2.173), and Cyrus Hoy sees in him the blend of aversion and desire "to be noted whenever passion long withstood is yielded to."[8] Women, however, are often thought of as the great romantics. For this very reason, they too may relish delay, as Rosalind obviously does in *As You Like It*, in order to enjoy the process rather than its outcome.

Most of Shakespeare's heroines are eager for love—the notable exceptions are Kate in *The Taming of the Shrew*, who seems (to put it mildly) resistant at first; Luciana in *The Comedy of Errors*, who fears what seems to be adultery; Hippolyta in *A Midsummer Night's Dream*, who has been wooed with the sword; and Emilia in *The Two Noble Kinsmen*, who prefers not to marry at all, cherishing rather the memory of her dead female companion and arguing

> That the true love 'tween maid and maid may be
> More than in sex [dividual].
>
> (1.3.81–82)

The more typical eagerness for love and marriage in Shakespeare's young women may reflect social and economic necessity or, indeed, may be constructed by male projection of a vision of what woman want. But surely some of Shakespeare's female audience could relate to the country's Virgin Queen and to Chapman's Diana in wishing to scorn "the subject title of a wife" and to "shun faithlesse men's society." In opening up this possibility, Love's Labor's Lost might be thought of as a pioneer work. The deviant comic structure encourages a realization of revolutionary possibilities. And indeed, men in the audience as well as women may take pleasure in the violation of convention at the end of this play.

For ambivalent audiences, male and female, the ending of Love's Labor's Lost may well be a happy one—endlessly postponing the perils as well as the pleasures of consummation. Like the lovers of Keats's Ode on a Grecian Urn, the "lovers" of this play are frozen eternally in time. The year will never end; and, indeed, if it did, all the couples might well have changed their minds. The faint promise of fertility in Jaquenetta's pregnancy is demoted to the cursory subplot. The "message" of nonconsummation is encapsulated in the song of spring followed by the song of winter at the play's end. Spring brings flowers and fertility, but also the fear of cuckoldry. The regression to winter provides a temporary safe haven where "blood is nipp'd" and where unthreatening domesticity can offer the childish comforts of food and warmth without the hazards of sex (5.2.894–929). Resistance has its victories no less renowned than capitulation. Modern comedies, especially those written by women, increasingly celebrate this fact. Love's Labor's Lost may not be a protofeminist play or a specifically satiric one, but in its violation of convention it has come to seem like an amazingly modern one. We might claim it as at least a forerunner of feminism.

The absence from the Renaissance stage of female playwrights has made it almost impossible to determine how dramatic visions by women might compare with those by men.[9] In the case of Love's Labor's Lost, however, we have the good fortune to possess a play by a woman, published in 1668, which seems extremely likely to have been inspired by Shakespeare's play. Margaret Cavendish, Duchess of Newcastle, wrote the first known prose assessment of Shakespeare's plays in an undated letter to a friend published in 1664. She defends Shakespeare from carping criticism, displaying a wide knowledge of his plays, mentioning comedies, tragedies, and histories, and speaking of his works in a way that implies a familiarity with one of the early Folios. Describing Shakespeare's versatility, she praises his female characters as so accurate that "one would think that he had been Metamorphosed from a Man to a Woman." She may have been especially fond of *The Merry Wives of Windsor*, since four of the eight women she mentions specifically are from that play. All eight are notably independent. Her knowledge is so specific and so wide-ranging that it is hard to imagine that she did not know *Love's Labor's Lost*. She declares Shakespeare so superior that "those, who writ after him, were Forced to Borrow of him, or rather to steal from him."[10]

She herself was probably of this number, for in 1668 she published *The Convent of Pleasure*, a closet drama that seems in part a witty reversal of Shakespeare's plot.[11] Lady Happy, young, beautiful, and very rich because of the recent death of her father, resolves to retire with her female friends to a convent, to live "incloister'd from the world" (6). But her convent will be like Rabelais's Abbey de Théleme, where the motto is "Do as you list." Not for her is Navarre's ascetic devotion to study at the expense of food and sleep. She says she intends "to enjoy pleasure, and not bury [herself] from it" (6). Only poor women, she adds, need men; "those Women, where Fortune, Nature, and the gods are joined to make them happy, were mad to live with Men, who make the Female sex their slaves. . ." Accordingly, although her Cloister is to be "a place for freedom, not to vex the Senses but to please them" (7), men are duly excluded.

Cavendish's play seems to have a stronger claim to feminism than Shakespeare's since it focuses on women and celebrates their freedom and independence. And yet by the end, her play is as puzzling and ambiguous as Shakespeare's. The beginning seems a joyous vision of a world of women, celebrating their competence and independence. Like the Princess of France at the end of *Love's Labor's Lost*, Lady Happy has achieved absolute power and wealth through the death of her father—the disappearance of the patriarch. The convent is described much more extensively than Navarre's court. It has women physicians, surgeons, and apothecaries, and is provided with "Gardens, Orchards, Walks, Groves, Bowers, Arbours, Ponds, Fountains, Springs, and the like" (11–12). The decor changes with the seasons, and the general delight is such that Madam Mediator declares that she had rather be in "the *Convent of Pleasure*, than Emperess of the whole world" (14–17). Unlike Shakespeare, who satirizes the folly of the men, Cavendish seems to applaud the liberated feminist vision. The only overt satire is directed against the male would-be suitors to the encloistered women. Excluded from the convent, they consider such drastic measures as knocking down the walls, setting the place on fire, and even disguising themselves as women, but reject each plan as impractical.

Also unlike Shakespeare's, Cavendish's play has an unconventional beginning and, in the middle, an unprecedented recital of the woes of women in marriage. For the first half of the play, her main purpose has seemed to be to imagine an idyllic reversal of the male-centered cloister at the start of *Love's Labor's Lost*. But the ending of her play reverts in a rather cursory fashion to the standard New Comedy closure based on marriage and the creation of a new society. If satire of the women is intended, it becomes apparent only retrospectively.

As in the case of Navarre's court, into the cloistered world arrives a "great Foreign Princess," "a Princely brave Woman truly, of a Masculine Presence" (16). A warm friendship develops between the Princess and Lady Happy—so warm indeed that Lady Happy seems called upon to insist on its purity, avowing

> More innocent Lovers never can there be,
> Than my most Princely Lover, that's a She.

(23)

The two "imbrace and kiss, and hold each other in their Arms." And the Princess now declares that

> These my Imbraces though of Femal kind,
> May be as fervent as a Masculine mind.

(33)

As the relationship intensifies, Lady Happy does wonder

> . . . why may not I love a Woman with
> the same affection I could a man?

But answers

> No, no, Nature is Nature, and still will be
> The same she was from all Eternity.
>
> (32)

Like *Love's Labor's Lost*, *The Convent of Pleasure* has a play within a play and both playwrights people these plays with lower-class characters. But where Shakespeare's actors absurdly assume the personas of the Nine Worthies, great men of history, Cavendish's play provides nine scenes of the miserable lives of average wives. There is nothing satiric about their treatment, and the effect is to stunningly testify to the evils of marriage. Her internal play is a grim and extended catalog of the woes of married women. It features in rapid succession (1) women who pull their drunken husbands out of the ale house, expecting to be beaten when they get them home; (2) a sick pregnant woman; (3) male gamblers who waste their estates and entertain whores; (4) a mother of a dead child; (5) women drinking to cure their melancholy over unfaithful husbands; (6) a woman painfully giving birth; (7) ancient ladies discussing the trials of motherhood; (8) a dead child born to a dead mother; and (9) a married man pursuing a virgin (24–30). The Epilogue to this internal play declares, quite understandably after what we have seen, that

> Marriage is a Curse we find,
> Especially to Women kind.
>
> (30)

So far the "message" seems clear. Only in retrospect does the reader begin to wonder whether the juxtaposition of the miseries of the poor with the pleasures of the rich may reveal some satiric social commentary on the frivolity and excess of the rich. Could Cavendish intend to criticize the detailed devotion to decor and physical pleasures that characterize the Convent? Or is she merely demonstrating that it is better to be a rich woman than a poor one? The answer is simply unclear.

Both plays also contain masques, but where the men in *Love's Labor's Lost* make fools of themselves in pretending to be Russians, the two masques of *The Convent of Pleasure* are much more traditional, at least on the surface. The Princess expresses the desire to affect male dress, which she does through the rest of the play. In the first masque, she is a shepherd come to woo

Happy, who appears as a shepherdess and who agrees to marry "him." In the second masque, the Princess appears as the sea-god Neptune and Lady Happy as a sea goddess. They seem a well-matched couple.

As in *Love's Labor's Lost*, the festivities are interrupted by the arrival of an ambassador to the Princess, who now reveals that "she" is actually a prince, and the Prince now claims Lady Happy as his "Soveraigness." Lady Happy is silent, and she says almost nothing through the rest of the play, but the two are quickly married. She loses her name and seems to dwindle complacently into a conventional New Comedy wife. The extended vision of female independence and self-sufficiency fades, and the sustained flirtation with the celebration of a lesbian relationship is disavowed, although in the mildest and most ambivalent terms. Madame Mediator (in a scene apparently written by the Duke of Newcastle, Cavendish's husband) merely suggests that the couple's earlier kissing has been too enthusiastic to have been the "unnatural" and presumably tepid amorousness of two women. She says,

> . . . you know Women's kisses are unnatural, and me-thought they kissed with more alacrity then Women use, a kind of Titillation, and more Vigorous.
>
> (24)

Except for the brief contention after the play-within-a-play by the "Princess" that

> . . . though some few be unhappy in Marriage, yet there are many more that are so happy that they would not change their condition.
>
> (31)

the impetus of the first part of Cavendish's play is to preach against marriage for women, and she is clearly enjoying the titillation of a conceivable lesbian alternative. But her two masques lay the groundwork for a marriage to follow by presenting the two protagonists in each masque as a male and female couple. The pull of social and artistic conventions seems to be so strong that Cavendish cannot resist the "happy ending" of matrimony, thus satisfying the expectations of New Comedy.[12] Shakespeare's play, on the other hand, begins like a conventional New Comedy, and only with the failure of the masque does the movement toward consummation seem to grind to a halt. There is no reconciliation after the women's trick, no concession to commitment on the women's part. The tongues of mocking wenches continue as keen as a razor's edge, and we are not wholly unprepared for their rejection of the men's proposals.

Both plays, then, change course in mid-stream. Both move from artificially imposed systems of regulating society to a re-organization based on unforeseen experience—thus creating, in some sense, a new society. But unlike the usual New Comedy, neither play includes the older generation—usually the blocking force working against the consummation of the young. Lady Happy's father is dead as the play begins, and Shakespeare's Princess of France's father is inoperative during the play and dead at the end. The forces that block consummation are inter-nal, and in both plays they are in the women themselves. Both playwrights contravene conventional expectations as well as re-versing the directions established within their own plays. Both draw out the pleasures of amorous delay, but Shakespeare ends by denying them closure and Cavendish ends by redefining the terms.

After permitting his audience the delights of witty courtship and laughter at the rapid capitulation of the men, Shakespeare reveals that the women have never taken the men seriously. The Princess says,

> We have receiv'd your letters full of love;
> Your favors, embassadors of love;
> And in our maiden council rated them
> At courtship, pleasant jest, and courtesy,
> As bombast and as lining to the time;
> But more devout than this [in] our respects
> Have we not been, and therefore met your loves
> In their own fashion, like a merriment.
>
> (5.2.777–84)

The "new society" is more like a revision of the cloister than a celebration of fertility. The King must go "To some forlorn and naked hermitage, / Remote from all the pleasures of the world" (5.2.795–96). The Princess will shut her woeful self in "a mourn-ing house" to grieve for her father. (5.2.807–8), while Berowne must "jest a twelvemonth in an hospital" (5.2.871).

Margaret Cavendish, on the other hand, paints a happy and prosperous world of women, contrasts it with an extended depic-tion of the woes of wives in marriage, and then, in collaboration with her husband, imposes on her unconventional play a conventional ending. Mimick, in the Epilogue, separates himself from his author in order to declare,

> I dare not beg Applause, our Poetess then
> Will be enrag'd, and kill me with her Pen;
> For she is careless, and is void of fear;
> If you dislike her Play, she does not care.

(53)

But it is hard to avoid the conclusion that she has not escaped completely the pressures of society and of the traditional dramatic form that supports that society. The surprise is that she ventures as far as she does. If her play had been put on in a public theater, it probably would have been seen "to show virtue her feature" and to satisfy "the age and body of the time" (*Hamlet* 3.2.22–24). Only those who took pleasure in the end of *Love's Labor's Lost* might have grieved for the loss of the Convent of Pleasure.

Both Shakespeare and Cavendish show some signs of incipient feminism. Both enjoy satirizing men—the one at length and the other in passing—and both demonstrate considerable originality in shaping their dramatic forms. Cavendish in the preface to the readers of her volume calls into question whether her works should be called plays at all because

> . . . it would be too great a fondness to my Works to think such Plays as these suitable to ancient Rules, in which I pretend no skill; or agreeable to the modern Humour, to which I dare acknowledge my aversion . . . (n.p.)

and she insists

> I regard not so much the present as future Ages,
>   for which I intend all my books. (n.p.)

It is a great strength of both these plays that their authors were able to imagine dramatic form not "suitable to ancient rules." In this regard, both were indeed writing for future ages and providing clues as to how ancient rules might be changed with the passage of time and the impact of social revolutions.

NOTES

1. For a sustained discussion of possible topical relevance, see G. R. Hibbard's "Introduction" to *Love's Labor's Lost* in the Oxford Shakespeare (Oxford: Clarendon Press, 1990), 49–57.

2. *A Study of "Love's Labour's Lost"* (Cambridge: Cambridge University Press, 1936), 25–26. The text of the tract, discovered by Yates in manuscript in the Public Records Office, is reprinted in her book, 206–11.

3. Bradbrook, *The School of Night: A Study in the Literary Relationships of Sir Walter Raleigh* (Cambridge: Cambridge University Press, 1936). Hibbard traces and finally dismisses these theories, but the idea of a School of Night persists, reinforced most recently by a play by Peter Whelan called *The School of Night*, which deals with Raleigh and his circle in connection with the death of Christopher Marlowe. The play was produced by the Royal Shakespeare Company at The Other Place in Stratford-upon-Avon in 1992.

4. G[eorge] C[hapman], *The Shadow of Night* (London, 1594).

5. See Yates, 177–82.

6. *Anatomy of Criticism* (Princeton: Princeton University Press, 1957; repr., 1973), 44.

7. See, for example, my article, "Strategies of Delay in Shakespeare's Comedies: What the Much Ado is Really About," in *Renaissance Papers 1987* (Durham, North Carolina: The Southeastern Renaissance Conference, 1987), 95–102.

8. *The Hyacinth Room* (New York: Knopf, 1964), 25.

9. A small ray of light has been cast on the question in recent years by the new attention given to Elizabeth Cary's closet drama, *Mariam*, a play about a jealous husband who kills his wife, written probably about the same time as Shakespeare's *Othello*. Elizabeth Cary, The Lady Falkland, *The Tragedy of Mariam, the Fair Queen of Jewry*, eds. Barry Weller and Margaret W. Ferguson (Berkeley: University of California Press, 1993).

10. Letter CCXI, *Sociable Letters* (London, 1664), 246–47. I am extremely grateful to Professors Elizabeth Hageman and Susan Green for generously sharing with me their knowledge of Cavendish and her work.

11. Duchess of Newcastle, *Plays Never Before Printed* (London, 1668). Pages of each play are numbered separately: Numbers in the text refer to pages.

12. Cavendish herself seems to have been happily married to a much older husband. He was an appreciative spouse. Writing in his wife's book, *Nature's Pictures* (London, 1656), Biiv, the Duke of Newcastle compares her to Homer, Aristotle, Hippocrates, Cicero, Virgil, Horace, Lucian, Lucan, Plutarch, Esop, Terence, Plautus, Tully, Seneca, Tibullus, Orpheus, and the Apocrypha.

"Errors" and "Labors":
Feminism and Early Shakespearean Comedy

Ann Thompson

Most feminist critics have simply ignored *The Comedy of Errors* and *Love's Labor's Lost*: the bibliographies on these plays in the pioneering anthology, *The Woman's Part* (1980), are minimal,[1] and the number of items specifically devoted to them in the Garland Annotated Bibliography of *Shakespeare and Feminist Criticism* (1991) is still very low.[2] On one level, feminist critics are simply perpetuating the general critical neglect of the earliest works in the canon, whatever the genre, which is disappointing in itself if one had entertained hopes that something genuinely new was happening in Shakespeare criticism. It is indeed quite baffling that plays like *Titus Andronicus* and the *Henry VI/ Richard III* tetralogy have not attracted more attention, with their strong but demonized women (Tamora, Joan of Arc, Margaret). The only exception amongst the early comedies has been, predictably enough, *The Taming of the Shrew*, which has been rediscovered and reread with, as it were, a vengeance.

I do not propose to attempt to appropriate *The Comedy of Errors* and *Love's Labor's Lost* for feminism, nor to attack them for not making themselves available for this kind of appropriation. Rather, my emphasis is on how these texts raise issues that are of real interest to feminist critics. One part of my project is to collect and survey such work as has been done so far. The other part is to consider lines of investigation that might be undertaken in the future.

A particular reason for critical neglect in the case of *Errors* and *Labor's* may be that these two plays do not contain instances of the transsexual disguise that has been such an immensely fashionable topic among feminist and other gender-conscious critics recently. But a substitute or counter-attraction might have been the relatively strong presence of women at the end of each play: *The Comedy of Errors* is unusual in the pre-*Pericles* comedies in restoring the mother in the last scene, while in *Love's Labor's Lost* the four women remain unmarried, holding out, albeit provisionally, against the power of patriarchal control.

If as feminists we are looking for strong female characters—and it can hardly be denied that we enjoy them when we find them—both plays show the women as distinctly superior to the men in terms of their behavior in the courtship plots. As often in Shakespearean comedy, they are constant in the objects of their affection, judicious in their responses to the men's advances, and supportive of each other. By contrast, the men in *The Comedy of Errors* are made to seem confused and inconstant throughout the play by the mistaken-identity plot, while the men in *Love's Labor's Lost* are ridiculed in the same way in the scene (5.2.79–483) where they make love to the wrong (masked) ladies. In both plays (again, as in the other comedies and in *Romeo and Juliet*), the men make extravagant vows or declarations of affection that are treated skeptically by the women. In 3.2 of *The Comedy of Errors*, Luciana rejects the advances of Antipholus of Syracuse, reminding him of his marriage vows to her sister (which were of course made by Antipholus of Ephesus). In *Love's Labor's Lost*, all four young men begin by vowing not to see women at all, but they quickly break their vows and resort to sophistry for "some salve for perjury" (4.3.285). Not surprisingly, they have difficulty at the end in convincing the women that they are serious.

There are some specific feminist discussions that are relevant here. Deborah T. Curren Aquino has argued that the women in the early plays, though not yet dominant forces like Rosalind in *As You Like It*, possess highly developed survival skills that make them more adaptable and resourceful than the men.[3] She concentrates especially on their verbal skills, demonstrating how the women in *Love's Labor's Lost* outsmart and outmaneuver the men, while Adriana at the end of *The Comedy of Errors* reasons logically with the Duke, in contrast to her emotional, irrational husband. Aquino also argues that the female characters are more practical and more efficient.

Irene G. Dash, in a chapter on *Love's Labor's Lost* in her book *Wooing, Wedding and Power: Women in Shakespeare's Plays*, specifically champions the Princess as a strong, self-assertive woman: "original in her thinking, she is unafraid and undominated".[4] She points out that this character has been the victim of editorial and stage tradition: Pope cut many of her lines in his 1723 edition, and Johnson in 1765 voiced a general disapproval:

> In this play, which all editors have concurred to censure, and some have rejected as unworthy of our poet, it must be confessed that there are many passages mean, childish, and vulgar; and some which ought not to have been exhibited, as we are told they were, to a *maiden queen*.[5]

It was this 'vulgarity' (of which I shall have more to say below) that led to the part of the Princess being much abbreviated on stage; as elsewhere in her book, Dash proves the stage tradition to have been more sexist than the text. Dash is also refreshing in her analysis of the critical tradition, demonstrating how the Princess has been consistently ignored or underestimated by writers who take it for granted that Rosaline, who is Berowne's amorous partner, must also be his intellectual foil. Such critics then prove, to their own satisfaction, that Rosaline does not seriously rival Berowne in this area, conveniently ignoring the princess, who arguably does.

There is a slight problem of essentialist naivety in these discussions, as when Dash writes that "the exchange between [the Princess] and Boyet illustrates the dramatist's remarkable insight into the mind of a woman and his ability to create, as Pope observed, characters as 'Individual as those in Life itself'."[6] Nevertheless it is true that even at the end of the play these women remain independent, at least temporarily, refusing the men the closure of immediate marriage.

A male feminist critic, Peter Erickson, has explicitly contrasted the ending of *Love's Labor's Lost* with that of *As You Like It*, where the men's control is reaffirmed and the women are rendered nonthreatening. In that play, Rosalind explicitly submits to male power, saying to both her father and her husband "To you I give myself, for I am yours" (5.4.116–17). Moreover, the Epilogue reminds the audience that the performer of the heroine's role is not really a woman at all: as Erickson puts it, "Not only are women to be subordinate; they can, if necessary, be imagined as nonexistent."[7] The formal awkwardness of the ending of *Love's Labor's Lost* perhaps renders it aesthetically inferior to *As You Like It*, but from the viewpoint of sexual politics the later play does not represent an unqualified advance.

The ending of *The Comedy of Errors* is significant among the early or middle comedies due to the prominence of the mother.

Feminist and other critics have recently explored some of the missing mothers in Shakespeare in essays such as Coppélia Kahn's "The Absent Mother in *King Lear*"[8] and Stephen Orgel's "Prospero's Wife."[9] Kahn has also written on *The Comedy of Errors* in her book *Man's Estate: Masculine Identity in Shakespeare*, where she focuses on the identity crisis in the play and its relation to the sea:

> In [*The Comedy of Errors* and *Twelfth Night*], the fear animating the identity crisis is the fear of losing hold of the self; in psychoanalytic terms, the fear of ego loss. Often it is expressed as the fear of being engulfed, extinguished, or devoured in the sea or in some oceanic entity.[10]

Another psychoanalytic critic, Ruth Nevo, explores the same idea, finding the sea an:

> archetypal symbol of vicissitude in human life—yes; but "oceanic," it will be recalled, was Freud's term for those fantasies of merging, union and dissolution which are rooted in yearnings for the primal symbiosis of infant and mother.[11]

Both critics quote the words of Antipholus of Syracuse:

> I to the world am like a drop of water,
> That in the ocean seeks another drop,
> Who, falling there to find his fellow forth
> (Unseen, inquisitive), confounds himself.
> So I, to find a mother and a brother,
> In quest of them (unhappy), ah, lose myself.
>
> (1.2.35–40)

Antipholus' search for his mother represents a nostalgia for a lost state of bliss—the undifferentiated union of mother and child. The fantasy of merging with another human being is also a nightmare of losing one's own identity. The ultimate reunion with the identical twin (as also in *Twelfth Night*) both satisfies the longing for a return to some kind of original union and re-establishes individual identity by resolving the confusions that have built up.

There is a curiously strong emphasis on the act of giving birth both at the beginning and at the end of *The Comedy of Errors*. In the opening scene, Egeon describes how he had been obliged to leave his wife when she was "almost at fainting under / The

pleasing punishment that women bear" (1.1.45–46) and how she
subsequently became "A joyful mother of two goodly sons"
(50), adding

> That very hour, and in the self-same inn.
> A mean woman was delivered
> Of such a burthen male, twins both alike.
>
> (1.1.53–55)

In the final scene, the Abbess, revealing herself to be the long-
lost mother, celebrates:

> Thirty-three years have I but gone in travail
> Of you, my sons, and till this present hour
> My heavy burthen [ne'er] delivered.
>
> (5.1.401–3)[12]

However, the actual dramatic role of the mother here is to criticize her daughter-in-law, Adriana, and especially to tell her that
her husband's blatant infidelity is her own fault—indeed that her
jealousy may have driven him mad. She interrogates Adriana at
some length, leading her on to incriminate herself by admitting
to a more extreme form of jealous behavior than she has in fact
practiced. This is perhaps the most remarkable example of the
double standard in the entire canon: is it possible to imagine
someone scolding Othello in this way and telling him that he
should have put up with his wife's infidelity quietly?

Moreover, although the mother is present in this scene, the
main emphasis is on the reunions of the male twins. Janet Adelman has even argued that both *The Comedy of Errors* and *Love's
Labor's Lost* are not primarily concerned with marriage at all
but with male identities, male bonding, and male friendship, all
of which are potentially threatened by women and marriage.[13]

This threat to male relationships perhaps underlies the wildly
shifting attitudes to women displayed by the men in both plays.
They veer from worshipping them as quasi-divine beings to de-
spising them as mere sensual animals. Their language about
women ranges from romantic lyricism to bawdy innuendo and
downright obscenity. This is most obvious in *Love's Labor's Lost*
when, in 4.3, the men produce extravagant sonnets in praise of
their mistresses. Longaville, for example, speaks of the "heavenly
rhetoric of [Maria's] eye" (58) and claims,

> A woman I forswore, but I will prove,
> Thou being a goddess, I forswore not thee.
> My vow was earthly, thou a heavenly love;
>
> (4.3.62–64)

On which Berowne comments,

> This is the liver-vein, which makes flesh a deity,
> A green goose a goddess; pure, pure [idolatry].
>
> (4.3.72–73)

Nevertheless, Berowne's own subsequent "salve for perjury" is much in the same style, arguing that it is the women who are the true inspiration of all learning:

> For when would you, my lord, or you, or you,
> Have found the ground of study's excellence
> Without the beauty of a woman's face?
> From women's eyes this doctrine I derive:
> They are the ground, the books, the academes,
> From whence doth spring the true Promethean fire.
> . . . .
> For where is any author in the world
> Teaches such beauty as a woman's eye?
> . . . .
> For when would you, my liege, or you, or you,
> In leaden contemplation have found out
> Such fiery numbers as the prompting eyes
> Of beauty's tutors have enrich'd you with?
> . . . .
> From women's eyes this doctrine I derive:
> They sparkle still the right Promethean fire;
> They are the books, the arts, the academes,
> That show, contain, and nourish all the world,
> Else none at all in aught proves excellent.
>
> (4.3.295–351)

Yet Berowne has begun the scene with a very negative description of his own experience of being in love, "I am toiling in a pitch—pitch that defiles" (2–3), and has spoken harshly of his choice:

> And among three to love the worst of all,
> A whitely wanton with a velvet brow,
> With two pitch-balls stuck in her face for eyes;
> Ay, and, by heaven, one that will do the deed
> Though Argus were her eunuch and her guard.
>
> (3.1.195–99)

The play provides no justification for this attack on Rosaline's morals: it is just assumed (as in *The Taming of the Shrew* at 2.1.294–96) that a spirited or outspoken woman must be unchaste.

The "war against the affections" undertaken by the men in the opening scene of Love's Labor's Lost, although supposedly a general one against "the world's desires" and involving devotion to study as well as abstinence from food and sleep, quickly turns out to focus exclusively on the vows about women and the threat they pose to the all-male utopia. The first item Berowne reads from the paper he is about to sign is "That no woman shall come within a mile of [the] court. . . . On pain of losing her tongue" (1.1.119–24). While women are, as usual, stereotyped as talkative, it is the men's language in this play that is actually out of con-trol—explicitly so at 4.3.270 when, during the competitive prais-ing of mistresses, Berowne says of Rosaline (apparently forgetting her pitch-ball eyes) "I'll prove her fair, or talk till doomsday here."

Of course the utopia is doomed. From the beginning, Costard the "clown" has pointed out "it is the manner of a man to speak to a woman. . . . Such is the simplicity of man to hearken after the flesh" (1.1.209–18). The country wench Jacquenetta finishes the play two months pregnant with Don Armado's child. There seems to be a class differentiation here, with the lower-class char-acters accepting the basic facts of life in a way the higher-class characters find difficult, but the play does not simply endorse the lower classes. Berowne's own put-down of Rosaline quoted above ends with a class-insult: "Some men must love my lady, and some Joan" (3.1.205). Don Armado is anxious to justify his love by the precedents of "great men" such as Hercules and Samson (1.2.65–76), and Berowne also cites Solomon, Nestor, and Timon (4.3.165–68). Both class and gender hierarchies are evoked by the patronizing analogies of the king and the beg-garmaid (1.2.109–17 and 4.1.64–66) and that of Jove turning mortal for love of a woman (4.3.115–18). There is a comparable class differentiation in The Comedy of Errors, where the greasy kitchen wench is a joke and her pursuit of Dromio of Syracuse a parody of courtship. She is "a very beastly creature" (3.2.88), "a mountain of mad flesh" (4.4.154).

Women of all classes are identified with "flesh," the body, sex-uality—what Lear is later to call "the sulphurous pit" (4.6.128). In The Comedy of Errors, they are also seen as witches and dev-ils: the Courtesan is addressed as "Satan" by Antipholus of Syra-cuse, who tells his servant she is worse than the devil—"she is the devil's dam" (4.3.48–51). They subsequently call her "fiend" and "sorceress" (64–66)—this is again reminiscent of the way Kate is demonized in *The Taming of the Shrew* (for example, at 1.1.66, 105, 121–25). The supposed threats to male identity of enchantment and physical transformation are also specifically associated with women at the end of *The Comedy of Errors,* when the Duke says "I think you all have drunk of Circe's cup" (5.1.271).

The other way that women turn men into beasts is of course through infidelity: they give them cuckolds' horns. This is an obsessive theme in both tragedy and comedy in this period. Coppélia Kahn points out that it depends on three things:

> First, misogyny, in particular the belief that all women are lustful and fickle; second, the double standard, by which man's infidelity is tolerated, while woman's is an inexcusable fault; and third, patriarchal marriage, which makes a husband's honor depend on his wife's chastity.[14]

The Comedy of Errors contains Shakespeare's longest and most explicit discussion of the double standard. In 2.1, Adriana, whose husband is being unfaithful to her, asks, "Why should their [that is, men's] liberty than ours be more?" (10), to which her sister Luciana replies with a general chain-of-being argument:

> The beasts, the fishes, and the winged fowls
> Are their males' subjects and at their controls:
> Man, more divine, the master of all these,
> Lord of the wide world and wild wat'ry seas,
> Indu'd with intellectual sense and souls,
> Of more pre-eminence than fish and fowls,
> Are masters to their females, and their lords:
> Then let your will attend on their accords.
>
> (2.1.18–25)

This is the same appeal to cosmic/civic order (as opposed to theological decree) used by Kate at the end of *The Taming of the Shrew.* Later in the scene, Luciana, like the Abbess in 5.1, scolds Adriana for her "self-harming jealousy" (102) and advises patience. When Luciana is courted by Antipholus of Syracuse, whom she takes for Adriana's husband, Antipholus of Ephesus, she accepts the double standard while rejecting his advances:

> If you did wed my sister for her wealth,
> Then for her wealth's sake use her with more kindness:

Or if you like elsewhere, do it by stealth,
Muffle your false love with some show of blindness:

. . . .

Tis double wrong, to truant with your bed,
And let her read it in your looks at board:

(3.2.5–18)

Feminist critics have differed in their use of this material. Juliet
Dusinberre cites the debate as evidence that in real life women
were arguing for their rights within marriage,[15] while Lisa Jardine
sees Adriana's articulateness in defense of women as ironically
underlining the actual helplessness of a wife: when the wronged
wife does (albeit unwittingly) finally shut her husband out of
the house, he sends for a "rope's end" to beat her with (4.1.16).[16]

Another relevant aspect of women-as-flesh is the whole issue
of verbal obscenity in these plays. People who encounter Shakespeare as readers of edited texts are to some extent protected
from the high level of obscenity in his work by squeamish editors
who have traditionally passed over certain phrases or simply
labeled them "*double entendres*" or "*sexual equivoques*" without further explanation. Similarly, in the theater, audiences have
been protected by cuts justified in the past by propriety and in
the present by obscurity. As Irene Dash says of the chief heroine
in *Love's Labor's Lost*, "the remarkably outspoken Princess [is]
infrequently heard."[17] Unlike their editors and producers, Shakespeare's female characters are frank and direct about sex: the
Princess and her women in *Love's Labor's Lost*, twice described
as "mad wenches" (2.1.257 and 5.2.264), give as good as they get
in terms of bawdy repartee, despite occasional criticisms, as
when Berowne says to Rosaline "Your wit's too hot" (2.1.119), or
when Margaret comments to Boyet and Costard "Come, come,
you talk greasily; your lips grow foul" (4.1.137).

Nevertheless, verbal obscenity is most likely to be directed
against women in these plays, given the association between the
female and sexuality in general. Without quite descending to the
reductionism of Launce in *The Two Gentlemen of Verona* ("This
shoe with the hole in it is my mother" [2.3.17–18]), both plays
seem obsessed with the physical aspects of sex and with female
genital parts: women constitute a "lack," both in the Freudian
sense and as a literal absence from the Elizabethan stage. The
itemized or fragmented *blazon*, or catalog of a woman's physical
beauties, is parodied in the description of the kitchen maid in

The Comedy of Errors (3.2), where both the master (supposedly in a state of romantic infatuation with Luciana) and the man relish the comedy of listing the woman's "parts" in increasingly grotesque physical detail, much as the qualities of Launce's mistress are cataloged in 3.1 of The Two Gentlemen of Verona. The extravagant eulogy of women's eyes in 4.3 of Love's Labor's Lost (quoted above) follows on from the fantasy elaborated by Longaville, Dumaine and Berowne:

> Long. Look, here's thy love, my foot and her face see.
> Ber. O, if the streets were paved with thine eyes,
> Her feet were much too dainty for such tread!
> Dum. O vile! Then as she goes what upward lies
> The street should see as she walk'd overhead.
>
> (273–77)

Women's eyes are impossibly idealized as part of the display of erotic attraction, while men's eyes are devoted to "vile" voyeurism.

Despite the dangers of falling back into the more naive forms of character-criticism, I think there is still a case for feminist critics to explore further the roles allocated to women in The Comedy of Errors and Love's Labor's Lost. We don't need to "identify" with them, or argue that they are "just like real women," in order to analyze the ideology of femininity that is represented within the text by such things as women's function within courtship, the double standard regarding infidelity, and so forth. Similarly, we don't need to treat the plays as documentary dramas about Elizabethan England to allow them to spark off investigations of such relevant social and historical issues as witchcraft, royal marriages, class relations between men and women, and illegitimate births.

We should continue to build on work already done on the reproduction of these texts, both in the theater and in the classroom or study. The editorial tradition might also be investigated, since it too has arguably been more antifeminist than the texts it presents and interprets. It has neglected many of the issues that feminists might be interested in and has at times displayed a casual misogyny in its commentary, especially on obscene passages. Gary Taylor has even argued that sexism has determined male editors' responses to a textual crux in The Comedy of Errors.[18] We do, happily, have some feminist criticism of these plays: can we have a feminist production or a feminist edition?

Notes

1. Carolyn Ruth Swift Lenz, Gayle Greene, and Carol Thomas Neely, eds., *The Woman's Part: Feminist Criticism of Shakespeare* (Urbana: University of Illinois Press, 1980). The bibliography lists just one item on *The Comedy of Errors*, an essay by C. L. Barber published in 1964. It manages three items on *Love's Labor's Lost*, though one of them dates from 1953.

2. Philip C. Kolin, *Shakespeare and Feminist Criticism: An Annotated Bibliography and Commentary* (New York: Garland Publishing Company, 1991). In the Play/Poem index, *The Comedy of Errors* and *Love's Labor's Lost* have the lowest numbers of references among the comedies, significantly fewer than those to *The Taming of the Shrew* and (even) *Two Gentlemen of Verona*.

3. Deborah T. Curren Aquino, "'Toward a Star that Danced'" Woman as Survivor in Shakespeare's Early Comedies," *Selected Papers from the West Virginia Shakespeare and Renaissance Association* 11 (1986): 50–61. See also Louis A. Montrose, "'Sport by Sport O'erthrown': *Love's Labor's Lost* and the Politics of Play," *Texas Studies in Language and Literature* 18 (1977): 528–52.

4. Irene G. Dash, *Wooing, Wedding, and Power: Women in Shakespeare's Plays* (New York: Columbia University Press, 1981), 15.

5. Ibid., 15

6. Ibid., 23

7. Peter Erickson, *Patriarchal Structures in Shakespeare's Drama* (Berkeley: University of California Press, 1985), 35.

8. Coppélia Kahn, "The Absent Mother in *King Lear*," in *Rewriting the Renaissance*, ed. Margaret W. Ferguson, Maureen Quilligan, and Nancy J. Vickers (Chicago: University of Chicago Press, 1986), 33–49.

9. Stephen Orgel, "Prospero's Wife," *Representations* 8 (1984); 1–13. See also my own essay "'Miranda, Where's Your Sister?': Reading Shakespeare's *The Tempest*," in *Feminist Criticism: Theory and Practice*, ed. Susan Sellers (Harvester Wheatsheaf: Hemel Hempstead, 1991), 45–55.

10. Coppélia Kahn, *Man's Estate: Masculine Identity in Shakespeare* (Berkeley: University of California Press, 1981), 197.

11. Ruth Nevo, *Shakespeare's Other Language* (London: Routledge, 1987), 46–47.

12. There is a discrepancy about dates here. In 1.1, Egeon says that his son left home to look for his brother when he was eighteen years old (1.1.125) and that he himself took up the search after "five summers" (132). In 5.1., he claims he last saw his son "but seven years since" (321). Theobald emended the Abbess's figure to "twenty-five," but modern editors assume these inconsistencies will not be noticed by audiences or even readers, and they therefore leave them alone.

13. Janet Adelman, "Male Bonding in Shakespeare's Comedies," in *Shakespeare's Rough Magic*, ed. Peter Erickson and Coppélia Kahn (Newark: University of Delaware Press, 1985), 73–103.

14. Coppélia Kahn, *Man's Estate*, 121.

15. Juliet Dusinberre, *Shakespeare and the Nature of Women* (London: Macmillan, 1975), 77–82.

16. Lisa Jardine, *Still Harping on Daughters* (Brighton: Harvester Press, 1983), 44–47.

17. Irene Dash, 14.

18. Gary Taylor, "Textual and Sexual Criticism: A Crux in *The Comedy of Errors*," *Renaissance Drama* 19 (1989): 195–225.

A Night of Errors and the Dawn of Empire: Male Enterprise in *The Comedy of Errors*

BRUCE R. SMITH

THE first recorded performance of *The Comedy of Errors*, on 28 December 1594, almost didn't happen. It was preceded by a near-riot when too many spectators tried to find places for themselves on stage. Some of them, an eyewitness noted, were "worshipful Personages . . . that might not be displaced"; others were "Gentlewomen, whose Sex did privilege them from Violence." Only when some of the most conspicuous members of the audience walked out in discontent and displeasure did the "Throngs and Tumults . . . somewhat cease," permitting the players, after a spell of dancing, to get on with "a Comedy of Errors (like to *Plautus* his *Menechmus*)."

Such throngs and such tumults are just what contemporary detractors of London's commercial theaters would lead us to expect, but the venue for this particular episode was not The Theater in Shoreditch, the usual playing place of Shakespeare's company in 1594, but the great hall of Gray's Inn. The occasion was not a few hours stolen from other pursuits, but the dedicated business of celebrating Christmas; the time was not afternoon, but night; the audience, though it included "many disordered Persons" whom the porters had failed to keep out, was made up not of anybody who could afford a penny, but a household of *gentlemen* and their invited guests—including "divers Ladies and Gentle*women*" with whom the law students of Gray's Inn intended to dance and to flirt, and a delegation from a rival household whom they intended to impress. It was, in fact, the gentlemen from the Inner Temple who walked out in disgust. In the written record of the whole affair, Shakespeare and his fellows are set down as "a Company of base and common Fellows" hired "to make up our Disorderes with a Play of Errors and Confusions."[1] The Lord Chamberlain's Men, on this occasion, played what amounts to a single scene in a much larger plot—a plot that extended from 20 December to Shrove Tuesday, more than two months later.

Printed in 1688, nearly a century after the event, as an already venerable piece of antiquity, *Gesta Grayorum: Or, The History of the Prince of Purpoole, Anno Domini, 1594* sets in place a social context for the first recorded performance of *The Comedy of Errors* that is far more specific than the context new historicists have built up for performances of Shakespeare's other early scripts on the public stage.[2] Part of that specificity of context is its gender. Diverse ladies and gentlewomen may have been present in Gray's Inn hall on that December night in 1594, but the entire evening, and all the revels that preceded it and followed it, are cast by *"The Deeds of the Grays"* as a ceremonial affirmation of the all-male household's self-identity. The very fact that the chronicler takes such pronounced notice whenever ladies are present serves to mark the gender of the whole affair with an even heavier hand than if he had neglected to do so. Reinserted into the social context in which it was given its first recorded performance, *The Comedy of Errors* offers itself as a particularly revealing document about what it meant to be male—for one privileged group of men, at least—in early modern England.[3]

MEN'S STUDIES: 1994 AND 1594

The very term *Men's* studies implies its progenitor, *women's* studies, and suggests the complicated relationship between the two. In more ways than one, maleness as a subject of academic inquiry is a *sequitur* to feminism. If for men's *studies* we substitute the men's *movement*, it is tempting to read that *sequitur* as primarily political. Politics alone, however, can't quite explain why ritualized group therapy sessions like Robert Bly's "New Father" conferences have attracted such numbers of participants and such notice from the media, or why a book like Bly's *Iron John: A Book About Men* could enjoy best-seller status in the United States through the whole of 1991 and well into 1992. An attention to maleness—what it is, what it has been, how it can be lived—seems at this particular juncture in western civilization to satisfy needs that are as much psychological as political.[4] (Indeed, neo-Freudian theorists like Eric Erikson and Margaret Mahler might ask us to see in the self-declared identity of men's studies no more than an unusually sophisticated instance of the basic necessity that all males face in finding and asserting an identity that separates them from the femaleness that has given them birth and nurture.[5] After the radical redefinitions of femaleness that have been going on during the past twenty years, males must necessarily now readjust their own identity.) Beyond politics, beyond psychology, men's studies can, if we prefer, be understood as a logical next step beyond women's studies. That is to say, men's studies takes the epistemological lessons of women's studies and applies them to a new subject—the male.

Much of the recent writing on masculinity has been as radically essentialist as any misogynist treatise of the sixteenth century. Maleness has been taken as a universal given, present in the subconscious if not in the very bones and blood of the male members of *homo sapiens*. Sociobiology practiced by the likes of E. O. Wilson and Lionel Tiger may be suspect to many people, but Jungian assumptions by the likes of Robert Bly about male master-plots that transcend time and culture have by and large gone unquestioned. Feminist theory would caution us to scrutinize such essentializing assumptions very carefully. Exceptions like Luce Irigary to the contrary, the important lesson of feminist theory is that "feminine" is a not a universal given but a cultural construct that is different in different times, in different places, in different cultures. If that is so with "feminine," why not also with "masculine"?[6]

There is one important epistemological reason why that might not be the case. Under the ineluctable laws of bipolar thinking, the process of marking a difference always privileges one thing over another. Implicitly if not explicitly, one thinking is taken to be the radical that defines the "otherness" of the other, and usually that radical is the particular thing of the two with which the person making the distinction identifies himself or herself more closely. In the distinction between "male" and "female," it has been "male" that traditionally has stood as the radical of difference. Females are imperfect versions of males: that commonplace in early modern medical thinking is no more than a blatant example of the bipolar privileging of "male" that continues to structure the subject of gender in more subtle and insidious ways. The fundamental challenge in men's studies is simple to state but hard to do: we must unthink "male" as a radical. Instead of assuming that maleness is an essential universal something, we must learn to read "male" in culturally relative terms.

In a survey of cultures ranging in time from antiquity to the twentieth century and in place from Andalusia to Tahiti to Japan to the rainforests of Brazil, David D. Gilmore has discovered only the barest minimum that can be said to constitute universal ideas of manhood. Three basic things seem to be expected of males all over the world: impregnating females, provisioning one's dependents, and protecting one's family or tribe. Beyond those three imperatives, maleness is constructed by different cultures in startlingly different terms, but always in terms that functions within the material environment, that reinforce the controlling ideology and that help prevent regression to the passive, mother-dependent state in which all males start their lives. However differently maleness may be constructed, the one thing that all cultures seem to share is an implicit sense that maleness is not a natural given but something that has to be earned through time with difficulty and that can be lost in a moment with ease.[7]

If we apply this anthropological method to the subject of masculinity in early modern England, *The Comedy of Errors* in its original social content emerges as an important piece of evidence. *Gesta Grayorum* is just the kind of all-male rite looked for by Gilmore and the anthropologist whose work he has summarized in *The Making of Masculinity*. To read *The Comedy of Errors* as part and parcel of the *Gesta Grayorum* is to extend the critical method of the, by now not-so-new, new historicism to a genuinely new subject area—male identity. Instead of privileging the play as an independent work of art, we study it as part of a social process. In doing so, we give up our position as objective observers of the play as a work of art (as if we could ever be truly objective observers) and try to assume instead the perspective of the men who actually saw the play on 28 December 1594. Or rather, we entertain two perspectives at once, theirs in 1594 and ours in 1994, as anthropological critics with a particular interest in how masculinity is socially constructed.[8] Our task in this case is made easier than it might be by the fact that "men's studies" is exactly what Gray's Inn was set up to foster.

ERRING IN PASSAGE

Between 20 December, at the beginning of winter, and Shrove Tuesday, on the verge of spring, the gentlemen of Gray's Inn did anything but trace a straight line. Instead, as the *Gesta Grayorum* recounts, they formed the nonce princedom of "Purpoole," centered on Gray's Inn, and they demanded homage and tribute from all the localities round about—Holborn, St. Giles's, Totten-

ham, Bloomsbury, Islington, Kentish Town, Paddington, and
Knightsbride (16–20); they twice went in procession around the
streets of London (57, 73–74); they followed the Thames' winding course from London to Greenwich (72); they circled the floor
of Gray's Inn hall in "Old Measures" (28), galliards (28), courants
(86), and "new measures" (59, 86); they evolved an elaborate
fiction, sustained through the whole ten weeks, that some of their
members went out to Russia, helped the emperor win a campaign
against the "Tartars," and came home to London in triumph
(59–63, 73). In a word, the gentlemen of Gray's Inn erred. Literally speaking, they wandered, they roamed, they strayed from the
straight and narrow path that ordinarily constrained legal study.[9]

In two senses *Gesta Grayorum* and *The Comedy of Errors* enacted a rite of passage. For the entire household of men it cele-
brated the transition from winter to spring. For the younger
members it also epitomized the rite of passage from adolescence
into adulthood that each of them, in his own time, according to
his own age, was pursuing as a young man who had left home
and taken up residence at one of the inns of court. Most newly
admitted members to the inns were between sixteen and twenty
years old; by the late sixteenth century, nearly half of them had
spent some time at one of the universities before they arrived.
Although membership was for life, 70 percent of the men actually in residence were between seventeen and thirty years old.[10]
The elder "benchers" of the inn sat, figuratively at least, as
authority figures and role models for the younger "outer-
barristers," who stood waiting on the far side of the bar that
separated students from attorneys, adolescents from adults. The
Princedom of Purpoole, presided over by young Henry Helmes,
"a very proper Man of Personage, and very active in Dancing
and Revelling" (6), may seem just the sort of topsy-turvy mock-
kingdom that C. L. Barber, Victor Turner, Robert Weimann, and
others have taught us to expect in the seasonal celebrations of
early modern England, but the elder benchers never really abdi-
cated their control over *Gesta Grayorum*, as the chronicler makes
clear when he registers the outer-barristers' disappointment that
"the Readers and Ancients of the House" forbade, "by reason of
the Term," two of the "grand Nights" planned to celebrate the
heroes' supposed return from Russia (70). The all-male hierarchy
of Gray's Inn shapes up as just the sort of apparatus for passing
along codes of manhood that the anthropologists in Gilmore's
survey have found in cultures all over the world. As a ceremonial
rite of passage that likewise resembles the formal rites noted by

Gilmore's anthropologists, *Gesta Grayorum* exposes early modern codes of manhood in a much more obvious way than they would have been in everyday life or even in literary texts not tied specifically to a ceremonial occasion.

For finding out what manhood meant in the past, four distinct approaches suggest themselves. The most obvious, perhaps, is ethical discourse—conduct books like Castigilione's *The Courtier* or Sir Francis Bacon's essay "Of Friendship" or the six counselors' speeches that Bacon is reputed to have contributed to *Gesta Grayorum*. Against these ethical ideals we can measure the lived realities recorded in biographies and autobiographies— or, rather, the interplay between ethical ideals and the untidy facts of life that these narratives typically inscribe. (In the context of the inns of court, one thinks of Izaac Walton's "Life and Death of Dr Donne." Donne was admitted to Lincoln's Inn at about age seventeen, remained in residence for at least two years, and returned to take up a readership in divinity at the age of forty-four.[11] Psychoanalytic theory, particularly the neo-Freudian notion of a series of "life crises" that all individuals must negotiate, offers a way of reading the record of past experience that transcends the particularities of early modern culture. Those particularities are, by contrast, the very subject of cultural anthropology, which asks us to read documents like *Gesta Grayorum* and *The Comedy of Errors* not as aesthetic products but as social processes. Ethical discourse and biography are, of course, well established ways of reading the past—*The Courtier* once ruled as a kind of master-text for interpreting Renaissance literature—but psychoanalytic theory and cultural anthropology are able to bring to light things that ethical discourse and biography may neglect or attempt to reconcile or consciously cover up: the incongruities between one ethical ideal of manhood and another, conflicts between the neatness of ideals and the intransigence of political and economic realities, the power struggles among peers that male maturity seems to entail, the unarticulated subconscious underside of achieved manhood, and above all the differences among men as individuals. As an instance of ideas put into social actions, *The Comedy of Errors* positively invites all four critical approaches to the subject of masculinity. Any pattern of behavior that remains central to a culture's self-identity, Gilmore points out, must satisfy two sets of needs: the social needs of the group and the psychic needs of individuals.[12] *The Comedy of Errors* in its first recorded performance seems calculated to have done just that.

The "Throngs and Tumults" that played prologue to *The Comedy of Errors* on 28 December 1594 were clearly not part of the plan. Once the disturbance had happened, however, it did become part of the plan. "So that Night was begun," the chronicler concludes, "and continued to the end, in nothing but Confusion and Errors; whereupon, it was ever afterwards called, *The Night of Errors*" (32). Given a proper name, *The Night of Errors* was written into the script. The very next day the Prince of Purpoole and his courtiers set up a judicial investigation into the whole affair (32–34); picking up perhaps on Ephesus's reputation for sorcery in Shakespeare's play, they lay blame for the whole misadventure on "a Sorcerer or Conjurer" who sounds very much like the play's Dr. Pinch (32–33); they recouped their honor before the Templarians with a mask-like "Shew" of Amity five days later (35–37); the episode was still on their minds in March.[13] Whether or not *The Comedy of Errors* was written specifically for performance at Gray's Inn has been the subject of philological inquiry for some time.[14] From the standpoint of cultural anthropology, however, it doesn't really matter which is the chicken and which the egg. More important is the fact that *The Comedy of Errors* and the *Gesta Grayorum* that occasioned its first recorded performance constitute a single datum, a single piece of social process.

ADOLESCENT ANXIETIES

Separation, transition, incorporation—the three phases that Arnold Van Gennep has distinguished in rites of passage all over the world articulate a program of Renaissance self-fashioning (no reflexive implied) wherein an individual (1) is divested of his old identity, (2) is assigned a new identity, and (3) affirms that identity before the whole society to which he belongs. The second of these phases, because it is neither one thing or the other but stands instead as the threshold (Latin *limen*) between the two, opens up a "liminal" space within which we can observe the new identity in the process of being formed.[15] *The Comedy of Errors* belongs to this second phase of *Gesta Grayorum*. The play was staged just after the outer-barristers had given up their real identities as law students and had taken on the grandiose titles of retainers to "Henry, Prince of Purpoole, *Arch-Duke of* Stapulia *and* Bernardia, *Duke of* High and Nether Holborn, *Marquis of* St. Giles's *and* Tottenham, *Count Palatine of* Bloomsbury and Clerkenwell, *Great Lord of the Canton of* Islington, Kentish-Town, Paddington *and* Knights-Bridge, *Knight of the most Hero-ical Order of the* Helmet, *and Sovereign of the same"* (21), some-time Henry Helmes.

One obvious way of acquiring a new identity is to take on a new name; another way, less obvious but more fundamental psychologically, is to distinguish who one is from who one is *not*. Eric Erikson sees "identity versus identity confusion" as the particular life crisis that must negotiated in the period between childhood and adulthood, regardless of how a particular culture may define that period or arrange that negotiation. One mark of this adolescent identity crisis, Erikson observes, is an especially strong sense of *group* identity, which typically is affirmed by a brutal exclusion of those who are "different."[16] As participants in *Gesta Grayorum* and as spectators of *The Comedy of Errors,* the outer-barristers of Gray's Inn identified themselves as knights errant. Against whom, once they had claimed that identity, did they distance themselves? Some of those "others" are named explicitly, some are implied, some nervously keep getting named only to be repressed.

One thing the gentlemen most certainly are not is Puritan. They demonstrate that fact in the very act of staging the revels and engaging the Lord Chamberlain's Men to put on a play. But they explicitly state the fact, too, in the requirements they lay down for the so-called "Knights of the Helmet," who take their name from Henry Helmes:

> Every Knight of this Order shall endeavour to add Conference and Experience by Reading; and therefore shall not only read and peruse *Guizo,* the *French* Academy, *Galiatto*[,] the Courtier, *Plutarch,* and *Arcadia,* and the Neoterical Writers, from time to time; but also fre-quent the Theatre, and such like places of Experience; and resort to the better sort of Ord'naries for Conference. (41)

Reading Stefano Guazzo's *Il Civile Conversazione,* Pierre de la Primaudaye's *The French Academy,* Giovanni della Casa's *Gala-teo,* Castiglione's *The Courtier,* Plutarch's *Moralia* (or perhaps his *Lives of the Noble Grecians and Romans*), and Sidney's *Arca-dia* are interestingly allied here with two other activities with which reading conduct books and romances (or is the *Arcadia* being classed as a conduct book?) might seemingly have little to do—going to public playhouses and conversing in taverns. The common demoninator among these pursuits of "experience" is the disapproval these activities earned from Puritan polemicists like Philip Stubbes.[17] One problem with this anti-Puritan stance is the compromising social position in which it puts the Gray's Inn gentlemen as frequenters of theaters and denizens of taverns. The chronicler's reference to Shakespeare and his troupe as "a Company of base and common Fellows" is not easy to read. On the one hand, it can be taken ironically, as a parody of Puritan anti-theatrical prejudice. On the other, it can be taken straight, as a genuine index of social superiority over men who legally were some noble person's "servants" and earned their living by acting plays.

More obvious among the threatening "others" that environ the Princedom of Purpoole are foreigners of various stripes, colors, and genders. The journey of the brave barristers to Russia and to the lands of the Tartars in the frameplot of *Gesta Grayorum* finds a counterpart in the various journeys that converge on Ephesus in *The Comedy of Errors*. The life story of wanderings and separations that Egeon tells the Duke of Ephesus in 1.1, sets up Ephesus as a kind of hyper-liminal space within the already liminal space of play and revels. A town of deceiving appearances, "full of cozenage" and "liberties of sin" (1.2.97, 102), Ephesus may supply the scene for all the play's action, but Syracuse remains, for Egeon, his wife, and his sons, the home base against which the strange and threatening otherness of Ephesus is measured. It is in the same Middle Eastern venue that the five Knights of the Helmet who go out from the Prince of Purpoole's court prove their valor. The "Tartars" they defeat there are not limited to the ruthless infidels we might expect from medieval romances but include specifically "an Army of *Ne-gro-Tartars*; whose wretched Devices ceased not to work the Confusion and Combustion" of the Russian emperor's domains (61). These "*Negarian Tartars*" maintain their separate identity from the "*Barbarian Tartars*" (69) to the very end of *Gesta Grayorum*, two months after the performance of Shakespeare's play. In the masque before Queen Elizabeth that concluded the season of revels, the Prince of Purpoole's "glorious Conquests of the *Negarian Tartars*" (71) are marked in the person of a "*Tartarian Page*," who silently attends the Squire representing the Princedom of Purpoole, as well as in a troupe of "Pigmies" who lead out the dancers at the end (76, 86). Not only Islam but blackness haunt the borders of the Princedom of Purpoole and, within those borders, Shakespeare's city of Ephesus.

The Phoenix, The Porpentine, The Abbey—the three sequential places of action specified in *The Comedy of Errors*—may have been realized on the stage in Gray's Inn hall as three stage houses of the sort familiar from medieval drama or as three openings in the hall screen, each with a label to identify it.[18] Home, the brothel, the shrine of the lost Mother—these three sequential places also define a certain psychological space in which the flesh is given just as much room as the spirit, though flesh yields to the spirit in the end. "Unlawful love," as "the Lady Abbess" (so she is styled in the stage directions) observes in the end, is "A sin prevailing much in youthful men,/Who give their eyes the liberty of gazing" (5.1.51–53). Of unlawful love, the spectators of *The Comedy of Errors* have, by this point in the play, been able to see and hear plenty. Some of the play's most hilarious business has been Antipholus of Ephesus's solace-seeking with the Courtesan—"a wench of excellent discourse,/Pretty and witty; wild and yet, too, gentle" (3.1.109–10)—and the spectacle of her own rapacious tricks. Though she doesn't enjoy the play-long prominence of Plautus's Erotium, Shakespeare's unnamed Courtesan nonetheless enters just in time to tie the knot of confusion to its tightest. Her soliloquy at the end of 4.3 (81–96) establishes an easy familiarity with the audience that none of the other female figures, most especially the Lady Abbess, can claim. In the end, Adriana gets back her husband; the Abbess gets back her sons; and the Courtesan gets back her diamond ring, all forty ducats' worth.

Such dealings with the prickly porcupine are endlessly joked about in *Gesta Grayorum*. So frequent and so detailed are the references to brothels that *Gesta Grayorum* might almost serve as a guidebook to the stews of Clerkenwell, Stoke Newington, and the South Bank. A "Letter from the Sea" arrives with news of "an huge *Armado* of *French Amazons*," commanded by an "Admiral" called "the *Rowse-flower*," who prey on men and rob them of their goods: "They exact so unreasonably of those that trade into *Netherland*, that they leave them neither Lands, Goods, nor good Wares." The Admiral of the Amazons herself—she who has "been known to have borne nine hundred fighting Men in her Poup"—has proved the undoing of one, particularly unfortunate fellow who "came up with her in such close manner, that he brake his Boltsprite in her hinder Quarter." The report is signed "John Puttanemico" (that is "John Whore-hater"), "*From the Harbour of* Bride-well" (65–67). While it is not surprising that adolescent young men, at the very height of their sexual desires and

yet ten years away from the average age of marriage, should find
it so funny to joke about prostitutes, it is remarkable that they
should repeatedly cast their jokes in terms of battles and conquests. Among the tributes the prince of Purpoole exacts from
his retainers is Amarillo de Paddington's promise "that when
the Prince maketh a Voyage Royal against Amazons, to subdue
and bring them under, he do find, at his own Charges, a thousand
Men, well furnished with long and strong Morris-pikes, black
Bills, or Halberts, with Morians on their Heads" (18). Knowing
that "Morris" is a corruption of "Moorish" seems no less important, in this particular context, than knowing that Morris-
pikes are phallic clubs. In the case of "Lucy Negro, Abbess de
Clerkenwell," whose "nuns" owe the Prince of Purpoole "Night-
Service in Cauda" (that is, "in the tail," with a pun on the legal
obligation of "entail"), the image of adversarial Amazon is fused
with that of Negro Tartar (17). No less than pagan infidels,
women in Gesta Grayorum are cast as a threatening "other."

Knowing the narrative context gives added significance to the
sweaty and predatory mountain of female flesh that threatens to
engulf Dromio of Syracuse in the person of Nell, the kitchen
wench in The Comedy of Errors. The images of trade and geography in which Dromio casts his blazon of Nell's all too ample
beauties anticipate the "Letter from the Sea" that the Gray's Inn
gentlemen enjoyed two weeks later. After hearing about the bogs
of Ireland in Nell's buttocks, the barren hardness of Scotland in
the palms of her hands, the warring hairs/heirs of France on her
forehead, the salty rheum of the English Channel down her chin,
the hot air of Spain in her nostrils, and the carbuncles of
America on her nose, Antipholus of Syracuse asks Dromio about
the Nether-lands. "O, sir, I did not look so low" (3.2.139). John
Puttanemico's jokes, two weeks later, about how the ravenous
French Amazons "burn all those Vessels that transport any dry
Wares into the Low-Countries" (66) make one wonder if The
Comedy of Errors was not in fact the specific inspiration for this
"Letter from the Sea."

If "Amazons" stand for prostitutes in particular, there is nonetheless in both Gesta Grayorum and The Comedy of Errors a
highly charged ambivalence about women in general. On the one
hand, the ladies invited to the revels are objects of solicitude—
and solicitation. Between the tumults that sent the Templarians
home in discontent and the performance of "a Comedy of Errors
(like to Plautus his Menechmus)" there was a period of "Dancing
and Revelling with Gentlewomen" (32). Women figure so promi-

nently in the catalog of "Pass-times and Sports" that the sixth counselor advises the Prince of Purpoole to adopt revelry in preference to war, philosophy, building projects, fiscal control, and gracious government: *What! Nothing but Tasks, nothing but Working-days? No Feasting, no Musick, no Dancing, no Triumphs, no Comedies, no Love, no Ladies?* (55). The linkage among dancing, comedies, love, and ladies is most suggestive for understanding *The Comedy of Errors* in its original social context. Henry Helmes, so proper a personage and such a dancer and reveler, takes up the sixth counselor's advice forthwith, leading his courtiers in making choices among the ladies and spending the rest of the evening in dancing. "The Mask of Proteus and the Adamantine Rock" that brought the whole season of revels to a close on Shrove Tuesday is, in effect, an elaborate invitation to the dance in which the gentlemen masquers step out of the fiction to lay claim to ladies in the audience. For all the deference they are shown on occasions like these, women figure more frequently in *Gesta Grayorum* as faceless objects of sexual conquest. One of the Prince of Purpoole's first official acts is to extend a general pardon to all his subjects for their offenses—with certain exceptions that, once itemized, end up excepting everybody. Side by side in this itemized catalog of unpardonable offenses are two that catch exactly the ambivalence that the gentlemen bring to women. All the Prince's subjects shall be pardoned except, first of all, those who neglect "the Profession, Practice and Perfection of a compleat and consummate Gentleman or Courtier" by failing "to entertain, serve, recreate, delight, or discourse with any vertuous or honourable Lady of Gentlewoman, Matron or Maid" (23–24). But in the very next item, pardon is withheld from anyone who fails to take full advantage of any such "Lady or Gentlewoman, Woman or Maid, Sole or Covert" whom he manages to lure "into his Possession or Convoy" (24). In particular, pardon is to be withheld in the case of "All Intrusions and Forcible Entries, had, made, or done into or upon any of the Prince's Widows, or Wards Female, without special Licence" (24)—which implies that the only license that is needed in such cases is licentiousness. The topography of *The Comedy of Errors* turns this ambivalence about women into a visible fact. Standing between the house of the Courtesan and the house of the Lady Abbess, the Duke of Ephesus hears all the confusions that have made the male characters doubt their own identities and offers this exclamation in sum: "Why, what an intricate impeach is this,/I think you all have drunk of Circe's cup" (5.1.270–71).

One situation in which the Prince of Purpoole's Knights of the Helmet may forfeit the privileges of their order is the unlikely event of "every Maid of His Highness's Province of *Islington*, continuing a Virgin after the Age of fourteen years, contrary to the Use and Custom in that place always had and observed" (40). The fact that the *Gesta Grayorum* chronicler should specify the maids of *Islington* as particularly fair game for the gentlemen's gambols suggests a subtler but no less important "other" against which those gentlemen find their identity, merchants and trades-men. Difference in the deference that Gray's Inn gentlemen were prepared to show to women seems to have turned, in part at least, on the social station those women happened to occupy. The *gentlewomen* "whose Sex did privilege them from Violence" during "the night of errors" were objects of respect; the virgins of Islington were quarry for love sports. Gentlewomen belonged to the world of chivalric romance; widows and wards female to the altogether different world of city comedy.

The border between the two was policed by armed guards. To avoid a repetition of the night of errors "there was provided a Watch of Armed Men, to ward at the four Ports . . . that none but those that were of good Condition might be suffered to be let into the Court" (34–35). Whether the likes of Antipholus of Syracuse would have been admitted to the Prince of Purpoole's court on a subsequent night is questionable. Merchants and their sons are, of course, stock protagonists in Roman comedy, but in chivalric romance they figure as intruders of a sort. "Merchant of Syracusa, plead no more" (1.1.3): "merchant" is the first word out of the Duke's mouth in 1.1, and "merchant" remains his epithet for Egeon through all his talk of "our well-dealing countrymen" (1.1.7), of "traffic" (1.1.15), of "marts and fairs" (1.1.17), of "goods" and "substance" as they are "valued" in marks (1.1.20–25). Ephesus may be a place of sorcery and seduction, but the most prominent physical props we see there are a thousand marks in coin that Antipholus of Syracuse sends ahead to his inn (1.2.81), a purse of five hundred ducats (4.1.103–5, 4.4.13), a gold chain worth two hundred three ducats (4.1.27–31, 4.4.134), and a diamond ring worth forty (4.3.96). The audience not only sees these objects, it is told the objects' exact value. Egeon's freedom carries an equally precise price: a thousand marks, the very sum that Antipholus of Syracuse has brought with him to Ephesus.

Such concern with objects, prices, and values would not be surprising in a city comedy, but it sorts oddly in a romance world where the worth of a man is measured in honor, not in coin. The distinction between the two value systems is drawn as sharply as possible in Sir William Segar's *Honor Military, and Civill*:

> There are but two arenas of action for men, business and honor: The principall markes whereat every mans endevour in this life aimeth, are either Profit, or Honor, Th'one proper to vulgar people, and men of inferior Fortune; The other due to persons of better birth, and generous disposition. For as the former by paines, and parsimony do onely labour to become rich; so th'other by Military skil, or knowledge in Civill government, aspire to Honor, and humane glory.[19]

What we find described in this piece of ethical discourse are, in effect, two distinct and competing codes of manhood in early modern England. It is tempting to associate these two ethical codes with the two economic systems that likewise existed side by side in England of the 1590s; the older feudal system based on land and the newer capitalist system based on money. The difficulty we have now of imagining a code of manhood in which power is measured by honor, not my money, shows just how completely capitalism has supplanted chivalry.

To understand the social and economic situation of the gentlemen barristers gathered in Gray's Inn hall in December 1594 however, we must make that imaginative leap backwards. Just where the outer-barristers were positioned vis à vis Segar's social dichotomy was not so fixed as the fiction might make it seem. *Gesta Grayorum* may speak the language of chivalry, but not every participant in the revels was wealthy enough or wellborn enough to afford the "generous disposition" that Segar specifies as the mark of an honorable man. In the usual hierarchical census of the estates of the realm—(1) gentry, (2) the burgesses of cities and towns, (3) yeomen, and (4) artisans, servants, and laborers—the place of professional men remained ambiguous. Were they gentlemen or were they burgesses? In general, gentility derived from *landed* wealth. Whether that land had been inherited through the centuries or had recently been bought with money amassed somewhere else was another question entirely. Within this ambiguous situation, the inns of court offered a solid foothold toward upward mobility, particularly for younger sons of gentry who did not stand to inherit the land on which their father's wealth and gentility were based. Among the practicing attorneys of early modern England, estimates of younger sons of gentry range from three-quarters of the common lawyers to half or three-quarters of the civil lawyers.[20] Many of the young men gathered at Gray's Inn had come there not just to learn the social graces that, by the sixteenth century, were more than an adjunct to the study of the law; many of them were there actually to learn the law as a means of making a living and of maintaining, if not attaining for the first time, a claim to gentility.

For these particular members of the audience, the merchants of The Comedy of Errors would have been less easy to mark as "other" than Puritans, foreigners, and women. Implicitly at least, the processions that the Prince of Purpoole and his consorts made through the streets of London were designed to put citizens in their place as passive on-lookers before the spectacle of "Honor Military, and Civill." When the Prince and his party rode to and from a banquet at the Lord Mayor's house, the streets were "thronged and filled with People, to see the Gentlemen as they passed by; who thought there had been some great Prince, in very deed, passing through the City" (57). When the Lord Chamberlain's Men put on The Comedy of Errors, the roles, symbolically and literally, were reversed. It was the gentlemen who were the spectators; the enterprising capitalists, the performers. The chronicler may be parodying certain gentlemen of his own social station, as well as Puritan polemicists, by writing off Shakespeare and his troupe as "a Company of base and common Fellows," but the merchandizing fiction of the play engaged economic and social uncertainties that, for this particular audience, were not so easy to dismiss.

ADULT ASSURANCES

Incorporation, the third and final phase in a rite of passage, calls for some gesture of public action to affirm the new identity the subject has just accepted—some outward sign that can be read by others of the new inward reality he has embraced. In an act of incorporation, the subject is, literally, "embodied" in the society of which he has now become a member. In The Comedy of Errors as a self-contained play, that act of incorporation is marked by the events of the play's last scene—the revelations of true identities, the reunions among lost siblings and their parents, and the reconciliations between masters and servants, husbands and wives, prostitute and customers, Ephesus and Syracuse, law and mercy, illusion and reality. In Gesta Grayorum as a whole, it is marked by "The Mask of Proteus and the Adamantine Rock" that the gentlemen of Gray's Inn took to court and danced before Elizabeth on Shrove Tuesday. Both endings to this particular adolescent rite of passage lay to rest the "others" who have been singled out as objects of anxiety—Puritans, foreigners, women, merchants. The identity of "Gentleman" is achieved, in large part, through negotiation of these differences.

The Puritan prejudice that would see the play itself as a form of sorcery is exorcised in *The Comedy of Errors* not only by the farcical send-up of Dr. Pinch, whose knowledge of devils and demons is exposed as a fraud, but by the image of Nativity-with-a-capital-N that closes the Lady Abbess's last speech and marks the whole play as a celebration of Christmas. Ephesus may seem to be a place full of cozenage and liberties of sin, but the ending lays bear a Providential design that transcends such appearances. "This *sympathised* one day's error" is how the Lady Abbess describes the accidents of the play in the serenity of retrospect (5.1.398, italics added). Artifice and illusion have been deployed in service to a higher truth. That effect is even more marked in "The Mask of Proteus and the Adamantine Rock." As an elaborate invitation to the dance, a mask finds its true end when the art quite literally turns into reality and the maskers go out into the hall, choose partners from among the spectators, and invite those partners to dance. The moment is described by the chronicler of *Gesta Grayorum* in precise detail. The iconic centerpiece of the mask is the Adamantine Rock that Proteus has miraculously transported from the magnetic north pole of the earth to the court of Elizabeth, the "*trew adamant of Hartes*" (83). It is out of that symbolic rock that the Prince of Purpoole and his Knights of the Helmet make their appearance before the queen:

> the Prince and the seven Knights issued forth of the Rock, in a very stately Mask, very richly attired, and gallantly provided of all things meet for the performance of so great an Enterprize. They come forth of the Rock in Couples, and before every Couple came two Pigmies with Torches. At their first coming on the Stage, they danced a new devised Measure, &c. After which, they took unto them Ladies; and with them they danced their Galliards, Courants, &c. And they danced another new Measure; after the end whereof, the Pigmies brought eight Escutcheons, with the Maskers Devices thereupon, and delivered them to the Esquire, who offered them to Her Majesty; which being done, they took their Order again, and with a new Strain, went all into the rock. (86)

In this ritualized act of homage, the make-believe court of the Prince of Purpoole not only defers to the real-world court of

Queen Elizabeth, it dissolves into it. In the very last act of the
two months and more of revels, the nonce Prince of Purpoole is
invited to leave the fiction behind and to join actual knights of
the realm in an actual exercise of military honor:

> The same Night there was fighting at Barriers; the Earl of *Essex* and
> others Challengers, and the Earl of *Cumberland* and his Company
> Defendants: Into which number, our Prince was taken, and behaved
> himself so valiantly and skillfully therein, that he had the Prize
> adjudged due unto him. (88)

The effect of such an ending, for *Gesta Grayorum* as a liminal
space measured in months and for *The Comedy of Errors* as a
single "grand night," is to reify the artifice, to reveal that the
artifice is, after all, reality itself. Play has all along been doing
social *work*. That especially seems true when we consider those
more conspicuous "others" against which the gentlemen of
Gray's Inn defined their identity—women, foreigners, and
merchants.

In the end, both play and pageants find a place for women that
supports rather than threatens male identity. Surprisingly, that
happens not through a gesture of denial or denunciation that
would distance men from women once and for all, but through
an act of deference and homage to a powerful female authority
figure, whose sudden and dramatic appearance signals the end
of the entire rite of passage. The Lady Abbess presides over the
ending to *The Comedy of Errors* no less magisterially than Queen
Elizabeth does over the ending to *Gesta Grayorum*. Why should
that be so? Why should the Lady Abbess and Queen Elizabeth
allay rather than aggravate the ambivalences and anxieties that
so insistently have been registered before? The very power of
these female authority figures stands as a measure, perhaps, of
how successful play and pageants have been as rites of passage
that enact, vis á vis the female body, the separation-individuation
process that Erickson, Mahler, and Gilmore all see as essential to
the formation of male identity. In Coppélia Kahn's analysis, *The
Comedy of Errors*, with its narcissistic mirrorings and multiple
losses of identity, performs just such an act of ego formation.[21]

Under the aegis of these powerful female figureheads, the play
and the revels work out somewhat difference stances toward
women more generally. *The Comedy of Errors*, like all of Shakespeare's comedies, ends in a celebration of multiple marriages.
The Lady Abbess is reunited with both her real name, Emilia,

and her husband, Egeon; Adriana is reconciled with her way-
ward husband, Antipholus of Ephesus; in Antipholus of Syracuse Luciana finally finds a husband to match her sister's; even
Nell, the kitchen wench, gets her man. The characteristically
romantic couplings of The Comedy of Errors could hardly be less
like the characteristically unromantic conjugations of Plautus's
Menaechmi. Since all the men in question (Nell's Dromio ex-
cepted) are merchants, the ending of The Comedy of Errors affirms values, ethical and monetary, that belong quite solidly to
urban burgesses in the social hierarchy of early modern England.
It is no tournament, but "a gossips' feast" (literally, a feast of
godparents, a christening party) that is supposed to follow the
play's last lines. For all the exoticism of Ephesus as a setting,
The Comedy of Errors celebrates the code of commerce. In the
code of chivalry that marks the end to Gesta Grayorum, women
figure not as marriage partners, but as the inspiration for heroic
deeds—deeds that happen not at home, but in the arena of action
that Egeon and his sons are preparing to leave behind. The
Prince's speech on Twelfth Night sets the scenario in place:

> Gentle Ladies, be now benign and gracious to your Knights, that
> never pleased themselves, but when their Service pleased you; that
> for your sakes shall undertake hard Adventures, that will make your
> Names and Beauties most famous, even in Foreign Regions; let your
> Favour kindle the Vigour of their Spirits, wherewith they abound;
> for they are the Men, by whom your Fame, your Honour, your Vertue
> shall be for ever advanced, protected and admired (70).

If The Comedy of Errors ends in private, with family and
friends retiring into the shrine of the Mother and shutting the
door behind them, Gesta Grayorum ends very much in public,
with a vision of the entire globe paying tribute to Elizabeth, true
adamant of hearts, and to England, the new lodestone of the seas.
Attended by "a Tartarian Page" taken in the late wars of the
Emperor of Russia, a Squire of the Knights of the Helmet tells
how the Prince of Purpoole and his Knights dispersed themselves after the wars "in many sundry quests" all over the world.
One of them, "in token of his duteous love,/And for a Trophe of
his victories," sent to the Prince "a Commoditie/of Pigmeys taken
in his private quest" (79–80)—a "commodity" who soon appear
in person as torch-bearing escorts when the knights make their
triumphal entry out of the Adamantine Rock. How that rock
came to be situated in England is the real subject of the Squire's
speech. It was no less a personage than Proteus, outsmarted in

his tricks by the Prince of Purpoole, who agreed to translate the rock from the Arctic pole to England, "assuring him,/That the wide Empire of the Ocean,/(If his fore telling spirit faild him not,)/Should follow that, wheare ere it should be sett" (82). When Proteus himself steps forward, he promises Elizabeth and her courtiers wealth and imperial power to rival Spain's:

> Thus hath this Load-stone by his powerful touch
> Made th'Iron Load-star of the world,
> A Mercury to point the gainest way
> In watry wildernes and the desert sands.
> In confidence whereof . . . th'assured Mariner
> Doth not importune love for sin or stars[.]
> By this Attractive force was drawne to light
> From depth of ignorance that new-found world
> Whose golden mines Iron found and conquered
>
> (83).

Here, in nine short lines, are not only a proclamation of the world-wide empire England indeed went on to assume, but its justification as well: whether the "depth of ignorance" in which America lay waiting to be found and conquered belonged to Europeans or to the peoples of America is not altogether clear from the syntax.

Merchants and merchandising in *The Comedy of Errors* take on, then, truly heroic dimensions in "The Mask of the Adamantine Rock." The imperial project proclaimed in Proteus's speech offers, in economic terms, a way of shoring up a feudal economy with newfound capital; in ethical terms, a way of combining the code of chivalry with the code of commerce; and in personal terms, for certain of the gentlemen of Gray's Inn, a way of maintaining their self-image as gentlemen by finding the financial means to support it. Here, indeed, lies "the gainest way." In effect, Proteus's vision of empire consolidates into one the two "arenas of action," business and arms, that Segar marks out for males in early modern England. The distinction between the two economies of power, and the possibility of their being combined into one, are both apparent in the words the chronicler uses to describe how Queen Elizabeth rewarded Henry Helmes. After he had fought at barriers alongside the Earl of Essex and the Earl of Cumberland and had been judged the winner, Elizabeth herself handed him the prize, telling him, that it was not her Gift; for if it had, it should have been better; but she gave it him, as that Prize which was due to his Desert, and good Behavior in those Exercises; and that hereafter he should be remembered with a better Reward from her self. The Prize was, a jewel, set with seventeen Diamonds, and four Rubies; in value, accounted worth an hundred Marks (88).

To chivalry belongs the prize; to business belongs the price. The code of honor bestows a "Reward" or a "Gift"; the code of commerce inventories seventeen diamonds, four rubies, one hundred marks. A visual equivalent of the chronicler's report can be seen in the design of Sir Thomas Gresham's steelyard, or weighing beam, now in the collection of the Museum of London. Possibly made for the Royal Exchange, which was built at Gresham's personal expense, this iron device for calculating how much things weigh, and hence how much they are worth in money, is enriched with bronze icons of chivalry. Three winged dragons from the coat of arms of the City of London dart out menacingly from the head of the hook on which goods to be weighed were hung, lizards and snakes out of illuminated manuscripts form all the hooks and handles, and on the mount two knights do battle across a beast with a putto on its belly. (Does this Renaissance putto, stranded amid images of chivalry, allude to the banking wealth of Italy?) In the design of Gresham's steelyard, merchandising becomes a knightly enterprise.

"So great an Enterprize" (86): the chronicler's synonym for the concluding tasks can aptly stand for the entire Gesta Grayorum and for the imperial vision it sets in place. In its ethical as well as in its economic senses, "enter-prise" is not just a "taking up" of something, but an "among-taking," a specifically group endeavor. The enterprise of manhood in The Comedy of Errors and Gesta Grayorum finds and proclaims a male identity that satisfied, for early modern England, the same three needs that codes of manhood continue to fulfill in cultures all over the world. With respect to the material environment, it establishes an imperial project that expands the emerging capitalist economy at the same time that it satisfies the particular economic needs of unlanded gentlemen. With respect to controlling ideology, it articulates that material project in terms appropriated from the traditional code of chivalry. With respect to individual psychology, it gives men a cautiously negotiated distinction from women and a group identity as brothers in arms. For the brothers of the Adamantine Rock, the fraternal fantasy of The Comedy of Errors

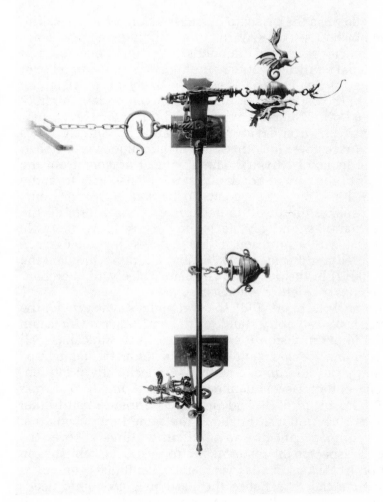

Steelyard or Weighing Beam (Hook inscribed "Thomas Gresham" and dated 1572). Courtesy of the Museum of London.

Thomas Gresham's Steelyard (detail of mount). Courtesy of the Museum of London.

inaugurated an imperial epic whose end has been reached only now.

NOTES

1. *Gesta Grayorum: Or, The History of the Prince of Purpoole, Anno Domini, 1594*, ed. Desmond Bland (Liverpool: Liverpool University Press, 1968), 31–33, italics added. Future quotations from *Gesta Grayorum* are taken from Bland's edition and are cited in the text.

2. See, for example, Louis Adrian Montrose, "The Purpose of Playing: Reflections on a Shakespearean Anthropology," *Helios*, n.s. 7 (1980): 51–74, and Stephen Mullaney, *The Place of the Stage* (Chicago: University of Chicago Press, 1988).

3. This essay had its beginnings in the graduate seminar on "Constructions

of Masculinity in Early Modern England" that I convened at Georgetown University during spring 1992. I want to thank the members of that seminar for their adventurousness in signing up for such a topic (at the time, it didn't seem to exist), for the ideas they put forward in discussion, and for the encouragement they bestowed on this essay: Amy Appleton, Renee Brehio, Scott Brennan, Tina Chen, Joyce Choate, Stephanie Kim, Suzanne Sullivan, Peter Taylor, and Leslie Yezerinac.

4. *Iron John: A Book About Men* (Reading, Massachusetts: Addison-Wesley, 1990). A particularly full and perceptive account of the men's movement is provided in Diane Johnson's review article on Bly's book and others in "Something for the Boys," *New York Review of Books* 39:1 and 2 (16 January 1992): 13–18.

5. Erik H. Erickson, *Identity and the Life Cycle* (New York: W. W. Norton, 1980), 51–77, and Margaret S. Mahler, *Selected Papers*, (New York: W. W. Norton, 1979), 2: 147–65.

6. E. O. Wilson, *Sociobiology* (Cambridge, Massachusetts: Harvard University Press, 1980); Lionel Tiger, *Men in Groups* (New York: Random House, 1969); and Luce Irigary, *This Sex Which is Not One*, trans., Catherine Porter with Carolyn Burke (Ithaca, New York: Cornell University Press, 1985).

7. David D. Gilmore, *Manhood in the Making: Cultural Concepts of Masculinity* (New Haven: Yale University Press, 1990).

8. On the impossibility of "scientific objectivity" in the study of other cultures—and the necessity for an observer of accepting his or her rootedness in his or her own culture—see James Clifford, "On Ethnographic Allegory," in *Writing Culture*, ed. James Clifford (Berkeley: University of California Press, 1986), 98–121, and Richard A. Shweder, *Thinking Through Cultures: Expeditions in Cultural Psychology* (Cambridge, Massachusetts: Harvard University Press, 1991), 1–23, 27–72.

9. The literal sense of the Latin *errare* is to move about in something other than a purposeful straight line. It is beyond that literal sense that the verb shades off into the figurative senses "to go astray," "to fall into error," "to sin."

10. Demographic information, as well as accounts of the social and intellectual life of the inns, is provided by Philip J. Finkelpearl, *John Marston of the Middle Temple: An Elizabethan Dramatist in his Social Setting* (Cambridge: Cambridge University Press, 1969); Wilfrid R. Prest, *The Inns of Court Under Elizabeth I and the Early Stuarts 1590–1640* (London: Longman, 1972); and Arthur F. Mariotti, *John Donne: Coterie Poet* (Madison: University of Wisconsin Press, 1986). On the age of newly admitted members, see Prest, 9; on the ages of the men in residence, see Finkelpearle, 6.

11. According to Walton, John Donne was educated at home until the age of nine, when he was sent to Hart Hall, Oxford. At age fourteen, he was "transplanted" to Cambridge, where he remained three years. "About his seventeenth yeare he was removed to London and entred into Lincolnes Inne, with an intent to study the law, where he gave great testimonies of wit, learning, and improvement in that profession, which never served him for any use, but onely for ornament." He left Lincoln's Inn two years later, when he decided to abandon the law and take up divinity. (Izaac Walton, *The Life and Death of D*ʳ *Donne, Late Deane of S*ᵗ *Pauls London* [1640], reprinted in John Donne, *Poetry and Prose*, ed. H. W. Garrod [Oxford: Clarendon Press, 1946], xix–xx.)

12. Gilmore, 5.

13. The chronicler prefaces the script of the masque enacted before the

Queen on 4 March 1595 with this disclaimer: "there was no other Performance, by reason of want of the Stage and Scaffolds, till *Shrovetide* [4 March 1595], that they went to the Court: And the things that were then performed before Her Majesty, were rather to discharge our own Promise, than satisfie the Expectation of others. In that regard, the Plot of these Sports were but small; the rather, that Tediousness might be avoided, *and confused Disorder, a thing which might easily happen in a multitude of Actions*" (76, italics added).

14. See R. A. Foakes, "Introduction" in *The Comedy of Errors*, The Arden Shakespeare (London: Methuen, 1962), xvi–xxiii.

15. Arnold van Gennep, *Rites of Passage*, trans., Monika B. Vizedom and Gabrielle L. Caffe (Chicago: University of Chicago Press, 1960), 10–12, 15–25, and Victor Turner, *From Ritual to Theatre* (New York: Performing Arts Journal Publications, 1982), 20–60.

16. Erickson, 97–100.

17. To apologists who claim that stage plays contain "good examples," Stubbes in *The Anatomy of Abuses* (1583) offers a rejoinder that could be taken as the *Urtext* of the Prince of Purpoole's proclamations: "truly so there are; if you will learn falsehood; if you will learn cozenage; if you will learn to deceive; if you will learn to play the Vice, to swear, tear, and blaspheme both heaven and earth; if you will learn to become a bawd, unclean, and to devirginate maids, to deflower honest wives; if you will learn to murder, flay, kill, pick, steal, rob and rove; if you will learn to rebel against princes, to commit treasons, to consume treasures, to practise idleness, to sing and talk of bawdy love and venery; if you will learn to deride, scoff, mock and flout, to flatter and smooth; if you will learn to play the whore-master, the glutton, drunkard, or incestuous person; if you will learn to become proud, haughty and arrogant; and finally, if you will learn to contemn God and all His laws, to care neither for Heaven nor Hell, and to commit all kinds of sin and mischief, you need to go to no other school, for all these good examples may you see painted before your eyes in interludes and plays" (quoted in Leonard R. N. Ashley, *Elizabethan Popular Culture* (Bowling Green, Ohio: Bowling Green State University Press, 1988), 170.

18. Foakes, "Introduction," xxxiv–xxxix and Bruce R. Smith, *Ancient Scripts and Modern Experience on the English Stage: 1550–1700* (Princeton: Princeton University Press, 1988), 83–84, 162–64.

19. William Segar, *Honor Military, and Civill* (London: Robert Barker, 1602), iii.

20. Keith Wrightson, *English Society: 1580–1680* (New Brunswick, New Jersey: Rutgers University Press, 1982), 17–30.

21. Coppélia Kahn, *Man's Estate: Masculine Identity in Shakespeare* (Berkeley: University of California Press, 1981), 199–205. Marjorie Garber offers a wider-ranging account of separation and individuation in *Coming of Age in Shakespeare* (London: Methuen, 1981), 30–51.

The Two Gentlemen of Verona on Stage: Protean Problems and Protean Solutions

Carol J. Carlisle and Patty S. Derrick

In the theater, as in the study, The Two Gentlemen of Verona, possibly Shakespeare's earliest comedy, has traditionally been one of his least popular plays. By our present count, there have been just twenty-four productions of it on the London stage since Shakespeare's time, and seven of these were first seen elsewhere.[1] At Stratford-upon-Avon there have been only ten since the annual Festivals began there in 1879. Most of the productions in these two major centers have been in the twentieth century, the greater number in the second half. The play has also been produced three times by the BBC, twice on radio and once on television. In New York, as one would expect, Two Gentlemen has had a much slighter stage history than in London,[2] and at the "other Stratford" in Ontario it has had just four productions in a forty-year history. Curiously enough, however, a surprising number of British provincial theaters and American regional or festival companies have been willing, at least once or twice, to tackle the problems of this "flawed but endearing play."[3]

Two Gentlemen does have its charms, but they are largely offset by its peculiar weaknesses. To evoke its magic, a production must overcome these weaknesses or somehow turn them to advantage. Although the same basic problems have confronted producers of the play in all post-Shakespearean periods, some have loomed larger at one time than at another because of differing social and theatrical conventions, and the solutions that actors and directors have found for them have therefore varied considerably. Since such solutions (or attempted solutions) have influenced interpretation of the play, not singly but in varying combinations, it is best to consider them within the contexts of particular productions. Accordingly, we shall discuss here some salient productions from each period in toto, giving our fullest attention to

126

seminal ones and occasionally mentioning others to illustrate trends.

First, the problems. For the average reader, *Two Gentlemen*, with its formula-ridden plot, outdated conventions, sketchily drawn characters, and absurd conclusion, is probably too simplistic and too incredible to be very interesting; at the same time, it may have an oddly disturbing effect since the apparent simplicities prove, on examination, too slippery to catch hold of with assurance. This combination of characteristics is not a hopeful one for effective stage production.

The dramatic action of *Two Gentlemen* is largely illustrative of either faithfulness or disloyalty to the potentially conflicting ideals of heroic friendship and courtly love—impossibly rarefied ideals for everyday human life, as the action demonstrates, yet far better than none at all.[4] The concept of ideal friendship, grounded in a medieval blend of classical and scholastic ideas with the lore of blood brotherhood, was prominent in Elizabethan retellings and dramatizations of old tales like *Titus and Gisippus*, glorifying two men of equal endowments and mutual interests who were so united in love that each became the other's *alter ego*—a relation that could transcend love between the sexes.[5] The ideals and conventions of courtly love, a Renaissance descendant of medieval literature portraying love as an all-consuming power and the lover as humble "servant" to a religiously worshipped lady, were found in the Petrarchan lyrics and the romances of the Renaissance, including Jorge de Montemayor's *Diana*, the source (direct or indirect) of Shakespeare's Julia-Proteus plot.[6] Although love and friendship are ageless, these particular concepts had lost their familiarity before any post-Shakespearean revival of *Two Gentlemen*; thus, the heroes' language and actions might well seem a little strange to later audiences. But, even within the context of their own world, Valentine and Proteus are hard to take seriously as romantic heroes.

The naive Valentine is (or becomes) a devotee of both ideals. He exalts Proteus's merits (2.4.62–74), identifies his friend with himself (2.4.62), and feels Proteus's treachery as if his own right hand had turned against his heart (5.4.67–68). Originally he scorns love as an underminer of manly accomplishments, but, once he meets Silvia, he becomes the conventional courtly lover: he recounts the sufferings inflicted by the "mighty lord" Love (2.4.128–42); he resorts to outrageous hyperbole in praising Silvia (2.4.151–53, 156–63) and shows his veneration of her in terms like "heavenly saint," "divine," and "sacred" (2.4.145, 147;

3.1.212); he calls her "myself" and says that without her, his "essence," he will "cease to be" (3.1.172, 182–84). In the courtly game of Milan's aristocratic society, a lady may have publicly acknowledged "servants," whose chivalrous devotion need not be—though it can be—erotically inspired. Valentine becomes Silvia's "servant" in both senses. Though fleetingly aware that Silvia has usurped Proteus in his thoughts (2.4.172–73), he never questions that each of them is his very "self" or wonders what would happen if love and friendship should collide. He persuades Silvia to accept his friend as a "servant" socially, never suspecting that he will make an amorous claim as well.

Proteus, though less idealistic than his friend, is obviously attached to Valentine at first, and he is passionately in love with Julia. He knows all along, however, that his emotions are in conflict: thus he simultaneously approves and rejects his father's command to join Valentine in Milan, since he must leave Julia to do so (1.3.90–91). When he falls in love with Silvia, Valentine's lady, he notes the loss of "zeal" toward his friend as well as toward Julia; he adopts an amusingly pragmatic attitude, promising to master his new passion if he can, but vowing to win Silvia for himself if he cannot (2.4.192–214). His sophistry in rationalizing infidelity to both friend and love (2.6.1–32) is almost disarmingly juvenile, but with self-love as guide, he plunges into ever-increasing treachery. His villainy causes little concern, however. He cuts a poor figure in wooing "holy" Silvia, and he is plainly enmeshing himself in a tightening net.

The crux of the play occurs when the demands of love and friendship finally clash, and Valentine, after his long absorption in love, chooses friendship without the blink of an eye—without, in fact, showing any recognition that he is making a choice. Faced with the shocking evidence of Proteus's treachery, quickly followed by a brief speech of repentance, he instantly pardons his friend, and to demonstrate the restoration of his affection, surrenders to Proteus his own claim to Silvia's love (5.4.77–83). The only response to this astonishing offer is Julia's swoon, and the disclosure of her real identity is sufficient to restore the heroes to their abandoned true-loves. Conflict has not been resolved, just ignored.

Some scholars defend Valentine's offer by associating it with the noble self-sacrifices of the friendship tradition or the "courtly virtue of Magnanimity."[7] But if Shakespeare means the audience to sympathize and admire, he does little to elicit this reaction. He hints at no motive for Valentine, no sense of regret over losing his "essence," no sign of consideration for Silvia herself. Even worse, dramatically speaking, he gives Silvia no response when her ideally constant lover proposes to turn her over to her would-be ravisher (indeed no speech at all for the rest of the play). To treat her as a passive "prize," aside from giving the actress a thankless task and (in modern times) offending feminist sensibilities, would contradict the effect of her previous speeches and actions—defying her father's will about Thurio, going after Valentine, denouncing Proteus. Muriel Bradbrook, once a "prize" adherent, later suggested a different interpretation: Valentine, holding Silvia by one hand, "invites" the kneeling Proteus to kiss the other, as he offers him "all that *was* [not is] mine in Silvia." What he offers is not Silvia herself, but reinstatement as her courtly servant, a position which he and Proteus had formerly shared but from which he has now risen to be Silvia's betrothed.[8] Although the interpretation of Valentine's words seems too subtle for the theater, the suggestion is appealing. Another "Elizabethan" interpretation—one which has actually been tried on the stage—construes Valentine's offer as a "courteous gesture that will give Proteus a chance to be his best self" by declining it. To implement this, Valentine must signal his real purpose somehow, most easily by exchanging meaningful looks with an approving Silvia.[9]

Read and played without sophistication, however, the climactic scene seems to cast ridicule on all three members of the love triangle: on Valentine, whose mechanical adherence to one code makes him an unwitting traitor to another or (for spectators unacquainted with these codes) whose sudden shift in attitude suggests a more-than-Protean instability; on Proteus, whose clever scheming has led only to disgraceful exposure; and even on Silvia, the paragon for whom three men have striven, who finds herself forsaken by the winner. Only Julia, who loves not an ideal but a particular man, who loves him steadfastly, if foolishly, despite his well-known flaws, escapes absurdity.

These effects are partly the result of unskillful plot development, but there are hints that the two gentlemen at least—idealist as much as villain—were meant to appear comic. One hint is the comic exposure of Valentine himself in an earlier scene, caught by the Duke with a rope ladder under his cloak. Another is the incongruous behavior of that other idealist, Sir Eglamour, whose valor, wisdom, and compassion are praised by Silvia (4.3.11–13), but who takes to his heels when confronted by the outlaws, leaving Silvia unprotected (5.3.6–7). Most notable is Shakespeare's use of the comic servants to comment on or reflect their masters' behavior: Speed satirizes Valentine's romantic excesses (2.1.18–32, 42–78), and Launce unwittingly parodies the aristocrats' behavior in several passages—for example, his account of the family farewell (2.3.1-32), which exaggerates to absurdity the pathos of Proteus and Julia's parting.

It has been suggested that *Two Gentlemen*, which presents many problems as romantic comedy, makes perfect sense when considered as burlesque.[10] There are burlesque elements, certainly; but, although Shakespeare sometimes ridicules his young friends and lovers, he does not ridicule friendship or love. To turn the whole romance into burlesque is to lose some of the play's qualities that can be particularly attractive in performance: the lyricism, the passion (often moving, despite the exaggeration), and the youthful spirit, which makes the adolescent lovers appealing without obscuring their follies and vices. Shakespeare's method, so notable in later comedies, of balancing romance with deflating humor yet without destroying its charm, seems to have been attempted in this early play, though less firmly and skillfully: it is hence more puzzling in its effect and more difficult to translate into theatrical terms.

In addition to major problems in interpretation and tone, there are minor ones in simple "factual" matters due to confusing or inconsistent references: to "Verona" and "Padua" in passages seemingly related to Milan: to an Emperor who turns out to be a Duke; to two different Sir Eglamours, only one of whom actually appears on the stage; and so on. These are comparatively easy to deal with, but the mere listing of an Eglamour among Julia's suitors has occasionally colored the representation of the one we see, a sworn celibate who befriends Silvia. There are also failures in dramatic technique, such as an undue reliance on monologue and duologue, the latter even when a number of characters are on the stage.[11] Casual readers may overlook such lapses until the end, when they are suddenly shocked by Silvia's silence; in the theater, however, even the minor awkwardnesses must be dealt with in some way.

The three earliest productions of *Two Gentlemen* that can be described with any confidence tried to cure the play's ills by radical textual revisions; the third used, in addition, a more potent medicine. Being closely related, they can be discussed together: (1) David Garrick's production at Drury Lane, using an adapted text by Benjamin Victor, introduced on 22 December 1762—the first production of the play now known, though there had probably been one in the 1590s; (2) John Philip Kemble's production at Covent Garden, using his own version (based on Victor's but with alterations), first seen on 20 April 1808; and (3) an "operatic" production at Covent Garden, opening on 21 November 1821, with libretto by Frederick Reynolds and music by Henry Bishop—the text evidently based on Kemble's but with extensive cuts to make way for the interpolated songs and for new passages of dialogue to justify them.[12] (Two other London productions of this period, seen just four times in all, may have had texts closer to Shakespeare's, but the evidence is sparse.)[13]

Some of the changes that Victor made and Kemble adopted were typical of that period's theatrical editing of Shakespeare: cuts (mainly in out-of-date wordplay and some indecorous references) and rearrangement of scenes to tighten structure and suit the convenience of the scenic stage. But their other alterations were more drastic. In addition to numerous verbal substitutions, there were many new passages, some to clarify motives left obscure by Shakespeare, others to fill gaps in his action, to strengthen or modernize characterization, to give greater prominence to the comic roles, or to bolster a new interpretation. The rearrangements and amplifications of scenes did give the play a greater sense of coherence and drive, but at the sacrifice of Shakespeare's subtler dramatic effects: for instance Launce's monologue about his family's farewell was no longer paired with Julia and Proteus's parting, and Julia's decision to follow Proteus, now placed immediately after his departure, was no longer in ironic juxtaposition with Proteus's determination to win Silvia. Among Victor's additions were two scenes for the comic players; Kemble retained (with a softening touch) the first one, in which a badly frightened Launce and a phlegmatic Crab are captured by outlaws, but not the second, in which a disguised Speed plays a callous joke on Launce. Reynolds evidently followed Kemble's lead.

The characters most affected by Victor's additions were Lucetta and Thurio, each of which was economically but effectively remodeled into a contemporary stage type. Shakespeare's Lucetta, a lively but sketchily drawn waiting woman of the Nerissa type, became a pert, intriguing chambermaid, who vowed that Julia shouldn't "think . . . to carry on even an honourable intrigue" without her (Victor, 9); Jane Pope, known for her saucy and hoydenish roles, was Garrick's Lucetta. Kemble returned to the original version of this character, but he followed Victor in giving a new personality to Thurio—that of an affected devotee of the arts, absurdly vain of his ability to write sonnets, set them to music, and sing them himself. In one passage, Thurio, instead of joining the search for Silvia, lingers to practice his new song; when he hears that Proteus has already galloped off, he promises to "gallop after him—fal, fal, fal": he exits singing and, one imagines, "galloping" mincingly (48). On the stage this character may have become progressively more ridiculous: Garrick's Thurio, Joseph Vernon, a gifted singer as well as an actor of some comic parts, is depicted in a contemporary engraving as an elegant figure gracefully posing with a lute (he sang "Who is Silvia?" himself); in Kemble's production, John Liston, famous for his "vain, rich, cowardly, stupid" characters, probably repeated his parodies of the *corps de ballet*'s dancing, which he had recently used successfully as Caper in a farce by J. T. Allingham; William Farren, in the Reynolds-Bishop production, reportedly made Thurio a "sportive coxcomb," and a drawing of him in the character, wearing an elaborate, finicky costume and holding a looking-glass, suggests that he did heavily emphasize Thurio's vanity and foppishness.[14] One character that Victor left as he found it was Eglamour. Kemble, however, smoothed out the Shakespearean wrinkles: to avoid confusion, he substituted "Altamont" for "Eglamour" in Julia's list of suitors, and to redeem Silvia's friend Eglamour from the ironic inconsistency between reputation and deed, he had him fight manfully and, after being struck down and left for dead, revive in time for the denouement.

The most important changes, however, affected the interpretation of the whole play. Evidently the adaptors saw nothing comic in Valentine's worship of Silvia but found his climactic offer to Proteus incredible; accordingly they concentrated upon the love story, elaborating the relationship of Valentine and Silvia by additional passages (for example, mutual declarations of love in Act 2 and a tender reunion after Silvia's rescue from Proteus). They completely reformed the climactic scene: Valentine, instead of forgiving Proteus immediately, threatened him with death; this precipitated Julia's swoon and, ultimately, the revelation of her identity; Silvia, not Valentine, joined the hands of Proteus and Julia, then persuaded Valentine to be reconciled to his friend. Victor ended the play by having the reformed Proteus speak a moralizing couplet, which Kemble expanded into seven lines, ending with "A lover must be constant to be bless'd." The love interest must have suffered when stately, fifty-year-old Kemble played Valentine: he was heroic and, in his best scene (the last) very energetic, but, according to the *Morning Chronicle* (22 April

1808), "cold and unimpressive" where love was the "immediate impulse."

The operatic production went well beyond its predecessors in expedients for popularizing *Two Gentlemen*: its revised and much-cut text was embellished with a great deal of music and spectacle. In addition to a newly-set "Who Is Silvia?", there were an overture and eleven elaborately-arranged vocal pieces—solos, duets, glees, choruses, and a grand finale. The words for the new songs were based, with considerable freedom, on passages from other Shakespearean works, mostly sonnets and other poems, but also four plays. The music was obviously more important than the drama, though Maria Tree, a good Shakespearean actress as well as a fine mezzo-soprano, seems to have given an effective portrayal of Julia despite the slender text. None of the male characters except the outlaws had singing parts, and none except John Liston as Launce got much attention from reviewers. Most of the praise went to the two heroines and a young singer who played the interpolated role of Julia's page. The staging was extravagant, with "wonders of scenery and machinery." Especially "gorgeous" was the final scene of Act 4, set in the Great Square of Milan, with grotesque groups of dancers and merrymakers celebrating Carnival. It featured a series of spectacles, notably a huge model of Cleopatra's galley and "an artificial mountain transformed into the Temple of Apollo, by the singular process of conflagration." This "noble pageant," half an hour long, would seem irrelevant to the play, but apparently the distractions of Carnival enabled Silvia and Eglamour to leave Milan unnoticed.[15]

This was the first popular production of *Two Gentlemen*: Garrick's had been seen only six times, Kemble's only three, but the operatic version had twenty-nine performances in its first season and six in its second—an excellent record at that time. Audiences obviously preferred less of the play (even in revised form) and more of the embellishments. As the *Examiner* explained, the passages omitted for the sake of music and spectacle were not "*dramatically* beautiful," and there was nothing a modern audience appreciated less than mere blank-verse recitation.

The first documented production of *Two Gentlemen* that restored Shakespeare's text was William Charles Macready's, which premiered at Drury Lane on 29 December 1841.[16] "Restoring," of course, did not mean returning to Shakespeare's complete text or strictly adhering to his arrangement of scenes. Macready took the usual liberties in both respects. In fact, he cut more lines than either Victor or Kemble, his most noticeable omissions being the whole of 3.2, in which Proteus hypocritically advises Thurio how to woo Silvia (though he transferred seven of its lines, with some verbal changes, to 4.2), and the most vulgar passages of Launce's monologue about Crab's misbehavior. In making structural changes, however, he was more sensitive to the dramatic consequences than the adaptors had been. For example, he preserved the ironic relationship between Julia's plan to join Proteus and the latter's defection to Silvia.

Textual restoration, as Macready understood it, consisted of purifying the original text from "the gross interpolations that disfigure it": in this case, ridding it of all the adaptor's additions and refraining from making any new ones.[17] In preparing his version of *Two Gentlemen*, he came close to this ideal: he cut out all previous accretions to Shakespeare's text; he made far fewer verbal changes within the lines than his predecessors had done; and he added only one full line of his own. But he not only purged the text, he also restored the long-abandoned lines in which Valentine forgives Proteus and offers him "all that was mine in Silvia" (5.4.83). This revived emphasis on friendship reflected a current interest of Macready's: later in the same season he produced Gerald Griffin's *Titus and Gisippus*, a blank-verse dramatization of the old story.

Macready's comparatively slight changes in characterization were made through cuts rather than additions: for example, he made Eglamour seem more consistent by omitting Silvia's praise of his valor rather than by making his behavior conform to it. Several cuts made the two heroes appear in a somewhat better light, but performance, more than textual changes, revealed his interpretation of these roles.

As Valentine, Macready was a noble hero—frank, kindly, warm-hearted. (At forty-eight he was too old for Shakespeare's inexperienced, slightly ridiculous idealist, but he would have rejected that interpretation anyway.) He and James R. Anderson, a "gallant" Proteus, "more picturesque than villainous," played well together; they were better, according to one critic, in their "manly cordiality" as friends than in their "boisterous ardor" as lovers. Another critic found fault with Macready, however, for his "overly-fervid" demonstration of friendship when bidding farewell to Proteus; his "perilous sighs" seemed too emotional for male friends in England's "'cauld clime.'" Young Miss Fortescue, as Julia, was the center of the audience's sympathetic attention, charming them with her warmth, passion, and pathos.

Robert Keeley, a fine comedian, played Launce effectively despite his missing vulgarities. Thurio, though now deprived of a chance to sing and caper, was by tradition a fop; Compton created a new identity by combining "foppishness" with "surliness."[18]

The difficult climactic scene was played like this: As Proteus advanced on Silvia, threatening rape, Valentine rushed forward, sword in hand, commanding him to "let go." Proteus drew his own sword and was about to attack, but when he recognized his opponent, he dropped it and staggered back in horror. The actors froze in their positions, creating the effect of a "fixed group" by an artist or sculptor, before Proteus fell to his knees and begged for forgiveness. The applause was "tumultuous." Proteus's horror-struck attitude, which epitomized his shocked self-conviction, seemed to one critic "worth a life's repentance." Idealizing the encounter as a work of art gave the moment of first remorse a symbolic importance, countering, as much as possible, the commonplace demands of probability. Valentine's rebuke was "delivered with manly grace, which was enhanced by the generosity of his forgiveness." Not everyone was reconciled to his offer of Silvia, but critics made surprisingly little objection— perhaps because Miss Ellis's dignified but cold Silvia aroused little sympathy. What did she do? We have only a negative clue: the remark that she had not yet mastered "the mystery of by-play."[19]

Among the most effective features of this production were the artistic scenes of characters in Renaissance dress moving against carefully-detailed, authentic-looking Italian backgrounds. Macready had chosen the year 1500 as the approximate time of the story and had consulted the antiquarian authority Colonel Hamilton Smith about the costumes. He had new scenery painted (less common for legitimate plays than for opera at that time) with emphasis on specific, identifiable places. For example, the opening scene, in which Valentine parts from Proteus, was located not simply on "A Street in Verona" (as in Kemble's promptbook), but before the "Tombs of the Scaligeri," and there were several views of the Duke's palace, with differing Milanese landmarks in the distance—the Duomo in one, the City Gate in another, and so on.[20] Reviewers approved the "attention to the local scenery and uses of the period," and they praised the "succession of beautiful and animated pictures," noting that the decor, rather than "overlay[ing] the drama," was "in fine keeping with [its] effects."[21]

Audiences and critics were enthusiastic. The latter praised not only the production but (equally complimentary to it) the play itself. The *Argus*, which called *Two Gentlemen* "charming," said that it was "so admirably got up and so deliciously acted" that it produced "a quiet and continual succession of pleasurable sensations." For the *Times* critic, the atmosphere of "Southern warmth" evidently turned what were usually-considered flaws into part of the play's charm: excessive use of conceits became the "freshness and recklessness" with which *concetti* are "sprinkle[d]" over everything, and the lack of strong characterization hardly mattered with this "company of graceful sonneteers." Such reviews were a pleasant change from some earlier ones, which had condemned the play as dull and not worth reviving.[22] The new appreciation seemingly reflected not only the appeal of the Italian Renaissance decor and the fine acting, but also—for the *Morning Chronicle*'s critic, at least—the liberating effect of the rediscovered Shakespearean text. Macready's revival, he wrote, was "in the simple form" intended by Shakespeare, something that had been previously misunderstood by adaptors and managers. Neither an elaborate work of art nor "a collection of . . . stage effects," it is a "careless, graceful, romantic piece" from Shakespeare's earliest years. Treated that way, "what beauty, what inimitable grace, what freshness and buoyancy" it had! The audience could laugh, sigh, and sympathize with the characters without bothering very much about "character": they need not even feel unhappy about Proteus's perfidy, for it was "clear from the first that everything must come right in the end."

Macready's production had thirteen performances—as many as all preceding ones put together, except for those of the "opera." Unimpressive as the number sounds, it was a very good showing for a minor Shakespearean play at that time. For *Two Gentlemen* without textual or musical embellishments it was remarkable. This production, whose promptbook was used again by Charles Kean (New York, 1846; London, 1848), established the theatrical use of Shakespeare's text with few, if any, additions and often, though not always, with Valentine's offer intact. Stage versions of later years would vary in the amount of liberty taken with the original text (Augustin Daly's in 1895, for example, was heavily edited), but they would, on the whole, conform more closely to it, not less so, than Macready's did.

The next productions of particular interest were William Poel's, important for radical innovations in staging. Unlike the other directors in this study, Poel gave his attention not to making the play more stageworthy, but to revealing its own qualities, which were currently obscured by elaborate sets, artificial breaks in the action, and slow, overly-emphatic speech. His search for "some means of acting Shakespeare naturally and appealingly from a full text"[23] led him back to the original staging as he envisioned it—continuous action on a thrust platform and rapid speech accented only on key words. His involvement with the New Shakspere Society was an early example of cooperation between stage and study. Although Poel was at first ridiculed, his influence and that of more flexible followers revolutionized Shakespearean production.

Not counting a dramatic reading in 1892, Poel directed two London productions of *Two Gentlemen*, both for the Elizabethan Stage Society: at the Merchant Taylors Hall on 28 November 1896 and at His Majesty's Theatre on 20 April 1910 during Beerbohm-Tree's annual Shakespeare Festival. (Each was repeated at other locations). For both he used a conservative text, with no changes except occasional cuts (the only notable ones being the references to Eglamour's running away), and he tried to create the theatrical conditions of Shakespeare's day.[24] The costumes were authentically Elizabethan, if not always appropriate to character and situation: the women wore ruffs and farthingales, the gentlemen's clothes were based on some sixteenth-century frescoes in the Hall of the Carpenters' Company, and the outlaws' on a costume design for a halberdier in the Fishmongers' Pageant of 1609. (A semi-military group, the outlaws marched with banner and trumpeter.)

The first production was not successful, largely because the "stage," an open space at the upper end of a large hall, was too flat to allow good visibility and the amateur actors had difficulty making themselves heard. The second one, however, though seen only once in London, was, in Robert Speaight's opinion, one of Poel's "most important contributions to the Elizabethan Revival." Poel had an apron built out over the orchestra pit of Tree's theater, thus gaining something like a platform stage. The acting seems to have been generally good. Critics approved the distinct enunciation and the use of the old pronunciation when the verse required it; they also noticed some "Elizabethan" gesture. One of Poel's eccentricities, occasionally casting women in men's parts (a reverse reminder of the boy-actress), was used successfully in this production: Valentine and Panthino were reportedly played well by actresses, though Valentine (Winifred Rae) was chided by her director for lack of "virility." Individual perfor-

mances were less impressive, however, than the mood or atmosphere created by the whole group. Thus Speaight recalled the
"innkeeper nodding over his lantern," not as an example of the
actor's art, but as one of the production's "beauties which lin-
gered in the memory," and the *Times* mentioned the "'right'
Shakespearian" fooling of the "two clowns" without naming the
actors or noting any details of performance. In this production,
declared the latter, the "puerile complications and improbabili-
ties" of the plot, which would have been "more glaring" in a
realistic setting, "became of little account," and the play's best
qualities were clearly brought out—the "verve of its dialogue,
the lyric beauty of many of its passages," and "the atmosphere
of warm, romantic amorism."

During virtually the next half-century, productions of *Two
Gentlemen*, in both London and Stratford, generally used Elizabethan costumes, or something like them, though at least one
used medieval Italian decor; the settings varied from pictorial
to simplified and suggestive. But on 22 January 1957 Michael
Langham broke the trend with a production at the Old Vic set
in the early nineteenth century, the first *Two Gentlemen* at either
major center in a period later than Shakespeare's.[25] The acting
text was Shakespearean except for a good many cuts, occasional
brief changes in wording, and some (not many) additional lines.
Valentine's famous offer in the last act was retained. Changes in
interpretation were effected mainly through innovative decor
and greatly amplified stage business.[26]

A vaguely Italian permanent set, suggestive of a garden in neo-
Gothic style, had flower-entwined pillars, an ivy-covered ruin,
and, in the foreground, a small, ornate structure, from whose
high window Silvia looked down in the serenade scene; different
backcloths indicated changes of location. The "mock-Regency"
costumes pleased both eye and fancy with their romantic flair—
the gentlemen in brightly-colored jackets, close-fitting trousers,
caped coats, and velour top hats, the ladies in full-skirted dresses
with lace parasols. Valentine and Proteus, "attractively posturing
juveniles," looked like Byron and Shelley. The outlaws (stretch-
ing chronology) resembled the Pirates of Penzance.[27] The Romantic period, closer to the present than the Renaissance, yet remote
enough to evoke a "make-believe" atmosphere, seemed to most
critics an inspired choice: it sorted well with the play's sighings
and swoonings, its poetic fervor and idealism, and its Byronic
philandering. Turning the two gentlemen into "a couple of
bucks" heightened the absurdities of the plot and, at the same

time, "almost conjured away" one's impatience with them. Reviewers disagreed about the amount of burlesque Langham used, but most thought he managed it delicately (at least, until the climax): as one of them remarked, his production succeeded because the play's "naively young but passionate poetry . . . survive[d] the drastic treatment."[28]

The acting created the effect of irony balanced with sympathy. Robert Gale, a Valentine of "dashing 'true-blue' simplicity," was both lovelorn and valorously spirited. Keith Michell as the Byronic Proteus was "so fiercely driven by passion" as to be "unaware that he was turning into a knave"; at times he seemed "astonished at his own behavior," his attitude varying from humorous ruefulness to "Keatsian melancholy." Barbara Jefford's "shiningly sincere" Julia was praised for "genuine fire and eloquence." Ingrid Hafner's Silvia, though comparatively colorless, was a lovely-looking, nobly-bred heroine. Dudley Jones gave a "brisk" performance of the word-mongering Speed. Robert Helpmann, with comic precision and "ingratiating audience-contact," portrayed Launce as a squeaky-voiced, vacant-looking, but likable Cockney, "funny with pathos." A clever yellow Labrador named Duff was "engagingly miscast" as that dirty dog Crab: he "shook hands," carried parcels, and behaved so decorously as to belie his master's vulgar account of him (all its vulgarities intact).[29]

The most notable aspect of Langham's production was its constant and ingenious use of stage business which, though not implied by Shakespeare's text, seemed to grow naturally out of it. It endowed the most archaic verbal conceits with a modern spirit, and it often won laughs with the ironic touches it gave to the speaker's words. Since the actors rarely said anything without doing something too, they gave the illusion of a fuller, faster-moving plot than the play actually has. Among other embellishments were an artist painting Silvia's portrait, archery practice, and dancing in the candlelit palace garden. Stage business, combined with distinctive costumes, was also used to "develop" minor characters: Antonio, apparently a country squire, came in with bag and gun, fresh from hunting; Thurio, vain as ever but now a "superannuated rake," was shown being shaved; the Duke, wearing a splendid uniform with epaulettes, strode about, smoking cigars and seeming "always on the edge of sending a gunboat to subdue rebellious tribesmen." Eglamour was uniquely reinterpreted: the "two Eglamours" were combined into one, an ineffectual but dapper old beau, who first courted Julia in Verona, then turned up at Milan, paying his addresses to Silvia. (Chaste devotion to a dead lady was not mentioned.) Stage business, added to scenes where Eglamour did not originally appear, carried out the new interpretation; at one point he was visually paired with Thurio—two silly old fops together.[30] The portrayal, as the *Guardian* suavely remarked, was "not quite perhaps what Shakespeare meant," but it "fitted well in this 'Vanity Fair' treatment of the tale."

The most striking use of stage business, however, was in the climactic scene, where it gave a new explanation of Valentine's notorious offer. Proteus's rescue of Silvia was heard offstage (not merely referred to, as in Shakespeare), with Proteus demanding Silvia's release and, when an outlaw refused, threatening force. The outlaws having fled, Silvia hurried on stage, closely pursued by Proteus, armed with a pistol and followed in turn by Julia-as-Sebastian. Silvia, trying to escape from Proteus, who had gained hold of her, succeeded in taking the pistol from his pocket and, presumably pointing it at him, broke loose and backed away from him, down the shallow steps. He wheeled down after her, took the pistol away, and threatened to force her; he then swung her to him, laying the pistol down for freer action. When Valentine advanced from behind a rock, ordering, "Villain, let go . . . ," Proteus released her, exclaiming, "Valentine!" Silvia fell in a faint, and Valentine and Julia knelt to help her. Julia stayed with her as Valentine confronted Proteus and denounced him. At one point Proteus put his hand on his old friend's shoulder, but Valentine ignored this overture. Proteus, after begging forgiveness, picked up the pistol; Silvia, who had revived, took cover behind a pillar, Julia (drawn toward Proteus?) behind Valentine. Proteus, however, was bent on suicide, not murder. Valentine hastily forgave him, then, taking the pistol from him, made his offer of Silvia "on the spur of an emotional moment."

Critics joined in the audience's merriment over the transformation of Shakespeare's puzzling finale into nineteenth-century melodrama—"a sort of abridged version of . . . 'The Corsican Brothers.'" Nothing could "finally disguise" Valentine's lunatic forbearance, wrote one, "but the players' confidence survived the inevitable laughter"; another said that the mask of light romance, which had been kept in place until now, dropped under the strain of this scene, and "the repressed burlesque [burst] out." The tongue-in-cheek response was, no doubt, exactly what Langham wished. His "brilliant" solution to the problem of Valentine's offer was praised as the best example of his inventive talent.[31]

Langham's successful treatment of the play influenced both critical attitudes and some later productions. Its springlike gaiety was remembered and favorably contrasted with the autumnal mood of Peter Hall's production (Stratford-upon-Avon, 1960), with its decor in the deep, rich tones of an Italian Old Master. And its long-lived influence was felt in Richard Digby Day's productions (Open Air Theatre, Regent's Park, London, summers of 1968 and 1969) with their nineteenth-century costumes, their light-hearted lyricism, and their sharply-defined minor characters (including some anachronistic ones—outlaws in Robin Hood suits and Sir Eglamour in cobwebbed armor like an ancient Quixote).[32]

Among the most interesting of other productions with latter-day settings was Robin Phillips's contemporary *Two Gentlemen* at the Royal Shakespeare Theatre, Stratford-upon-Avon, 23 July 1970 (revived in December for a brief run at the Aldwych in London). Its permanent set, which served for both Verona and Milan (and for the forest, with the help of dangling ropes and dappled light), depicted a scene at an Italian resort, featuring a miniature swimming pool with real water; the lovers were wealthy, golden-tanned adolescents, wearing trendy leisure clothes and huge sunglasses. Antonio, a cigar-smoking tycoon, or perhaps a Mafia boss, doffed his monogrammed beachrobe for a quick swim; the Duke, who sometimes appeared in an academic gown, looked like a vice chancellor of a university. The outlaws were hippies, and Eglamour was an aging scoutmaster, dressed in bare-kneed uniform, who arrived on a bicycle, brought along his camping gear and ordnance map, and laid a bridge across the pool for Silvia to escape on. Launce (Patrick Stewart) was a dour, North-Country workman, dressed in black, who stood apart, a grave, unmoved observer of the others' follies.

The production reflected the current emphasis on a search for identity—it began and ended with an echo-song "Who is Silvia? Who is Valentine? Who is Proteus? Who is Julia?"—and also a modern concern with psychological motivation. Proteus, more cerebral than the handsome, athletic Valentine but relatively puny physically, seemed to be moved to treachery by envious admiration and a sense of his own inadequacy. Simply as interesting characters, the lovers were well played: Peter Egan's Valentine, sincere and naive, a little conceited but maturing under the influence of love and its troubles; Ian Richardson's Proteus, "coldly impassioned," subtle, and self-aware; Helen Mirren's Julia, "delightfully spirited and endearing," at times a "tigress" or "whirlwind," at times an agonized adolescent, sucking her thumb for comfort; Estelle Kohler's Silvia, a graceful socialite, but capable of taking the initiative and acting with spirit. The reconciliation scene was effectively played: as he wound up his expression of forgiveness, Valentine kissed Silvia; then, crossing to Proteus, he ended "And that my love may appear plain and free" (5.4.82) by kissing him. The crucial line that followed ("All that was mine in Silvia I give thee") evidently meant, "The love I have given to Silvia I also give to you." Even so, the play ended on an uncertain note, as Valentine spoke its final line with a doubtful pause before the last word, "One feast, one house, one mutual—happiness." The sound of a cuckoo underlined the ambiguity.

Some critics deplored the effects of the modernization: "incongruities," substitution of irony for lyricism, loss of the lovers' innocence, sacrifice of serious Shakespearean themes. (Once again the Langham production of 1957 was wistfully recalled as the contrasting ideal.) Others insisted that the play had gained by the contemporary treatment of timeless truths. Most reviewers, however, like most audiences, simply enjoyed the production.[33]

An unusual amount of experimentation with *Two Gentlemen* has taken place in North American regional and festival theaters: the play has had settings, for example, in Little Italy of 1900; on a 1920s campus of "Millen University," where Valentine had an athletic scholarship; and in a farcical Wild West, with Silvia doubling as a teasing Mae West and the disguised Julia wearing a ten-gallon hat over her enormous beehive hairdo. It has been given in the style of circus, *commedia dell'arte*, vaudeville, and a combination of all these.[34] In 1984 the American Repertory in New York even revived Kemble's 1808 adaptation.

Among other experiments have been several musical ones. The most famous was the award-winning "rock musical" (which also used other popular rhythms like jazz and Latin American dance), directed by Mel Shapiro from his and John Guare's text, Guare's lyrics and Galt MacDermot's music. It was produced in the summer of 1971 for Joseph Papp's New York Shakespeare Festival in Central Park, had a successful run at the St. James, Broadway, in 1971–72, and was revived (with a different cast) at the Phoenix, London, in 1973. This *Two Gentlemen* was much more, and much less, than an adaptation. Fewer than 450 Shakespearean lines survived, some of them from sonnets and other plays, and

a good many new lines were added, besides those of the numerous songs (nearly forty, finally). Some striking character changes
produced a pregnant Julia, a lusty Silvia who hated to be idealized, a tough-looking Duke in dark glasses who was a sleazy
politician as well as a tyrant, an Eglamour (Silvia's old boyfriend)
who had been drafted into the army, a Lucetta who paired off
with Thurio, and metadramatic servants (Launce and Speed)
who bemoaned the plight of the working man with no time for
love and wished to be a "hot lover . . . like the kids in the play."
There were references to contemporary concerns—war, abortion,
the environment. A racially mixed cast made the point of brotherhood. But the chief emphasis was on the songs, the dances,
the mood of lively abandon—and the theme of love, love, love.
It was a long way from Shakespeare, but it had some of the same
youthfulness, vitality, and, in its own way, innocence.[35]

Some modern directors have attacked the problem of anti-
feminism in *Two Gentlemen,* usually by reinterpreting Valentine's offer so as to remove its callousness toward Silvia. As we
have seen, Robin Phillips tried this solution, yet a critic of his
production remarked that this play could "provoke a demonstration by the Women's Liberation Movement." Some North American productions have simply made the offer ridiculous, for
example by using double-takes or having the men walk off together and then turn to see with comic dismay the women leaving in the other direction. The most effective expedient, however,
has been to involve Silvia in the forgiveness of Proteus.[36]

The *Two Gentlemen* that best illustrates this method—the
Royal Shakespeare Company's latest production of the play—
also offers examples of other strategies for bringing audience and
play together. Directed by David Thacker, it opened at the Swan
Theatre in Stratford-upon-Avon on 6 April 1991, transferred to
the Pit at the Barbican in October 1992, and later went on tour
with a largely different cast, finally closing at the Haymarket
Theatre in London in January 1994.[37] Its most obvious features,
the choice of period and the related use of music, proved interpretive as well as entertaining. The play was set in the 1930s,
when "Coward dressing gowns . . . Lonsdale evening dress and
Wodehouse tennis gear" were fashionable—a period whose combination of elegance and shallowness revealingly reflected the
same qualities in the play's characters. The atmosphere was established during the quarter-hour before the play began: a palm-
court orchestra, ensconced in a bandstand, played hit-parade
songs by George Gershwin, Cole Porter, Irving Berlin, and others,

while couples in evening wear danced downstage. Between the scenes of the play, a blonde *chanteuse* crooned songs like "Blue Moon," "Night and Day," and "Love Is the Sweetest Thing"—all "cunningly chosen to point and counter-point the action." The evocation of a past distinctly different from today, yet familiar as Bertie Wooster on TV, brought the audience into tune with the play. As Benedict Nightingale explained in the *Times*: "When lovers appear in doublet and hose, we expect them to behave in conventionally romantic ways. Transpose them to places we more easily associate with youthful skittishness and folly, and they can seem perfectly plausible." The actors never mocked or patronized their characters, but their innocent yet artificial world was one whose adolescent passions might well be the subject of fun. The tone was close to Shakespeare's own. Interestingly, a critic who disapproved of the chosen setting—an unusual response—admitted that a post-Shakespearean period makes sense but preferred the early nineteenth century, with a Byronic Proteus. Langham's production and its imitators were hard to forget.[38]

Another notable feature of the production was its success in giving Shakespeare's sketchily drawn characters some sense of development or depth. Valentine (Richard Bonneville), though never profound, progressed from "an awkwardly ingratiating lover" to "an impressively bold one." Even Thurio (Henry Guy) was no mere fop or "silly-ass wooer," but "a stilted prig desperately trying to hide his intellectual and emotional limitations"; unlike the Thurios with literary pretensions, he was depressed by Proteus's suggestions that he woo Silvia with poetry. As usual in modern productions, however, the chief interest was in Proteus (Barry Lynch) and the motivation for his treachery. Here the use of potentially symbolic stage business was striking, though the interpretation depended on the spectator's own bent. The introductory scene showed the two friends in adolescent horseplay, wrestling on the floor, which, for some viewers, would inevitably connote latent sexuality. Paul Nelsen, who was struck by the strange mixture of devotion and rivalry he saw here, has described Lynch's Proteus in some detail, emphasizing the actor's "subtext." For Nelsen, this Proteus was "sullen ... and Iago-like," and his treacherous actions stemmed from ambiguous feelings toward Valentine rather than erotic desire for Silvia. This dark interpretation was not widely shared, however. Some critics, indeed, saw a boyish charm in Lynch's Proteus: they found him "likeable and inexperienced," even "more naive and impressionable" than Valentine, before he became obsessed with Silvia. And one critic noticed a "curious sense of baffled innocence" (much in line, we think, with Shakespeare's text) even as he argued his way into treachery. Yet there was also something in the actor's manner—a "nervous intensity," a slight instability, a "disturbing little flicker of a smile"—that suggested, even to sympathetic viewers, introversion and suppressed emotion. Lynch's psychological suggestiveness obviously did not clarify Proteus's motivation, but it did result in an intriguing portrayal.

The other roles were acted well, but there was nothing unusual about them psychologically. Julia (Clare Holman) had a "jaunty boyishness" as Sebastian but also a touching pathos; Silvia (Saskia Reeves) was cool, elegant, but determined. Richard Moore's shuffling, bowler-hatted Launce, with his "hangdog dignity" and deftly executed "takes," was, with his lugubrious-looking lurcher, Woolly, among the memorable pleasures of the production. Small parts were given sharp or colorful touches: the wisecracking Speed (Sean Murray) in his cheap suit had the personality of a traveling salesman; the Duke (Terence Wilton), an amateur cook, zestfully dismembered a lobster.[39]

The use of symbolic stage pictures was most effective in the climactic scene of the final act: Valentine stopped Proteus from raping Silvia by wrestling him to the ground, "echoing, now in desperate earnest, the playful rough-housing of act one." The parallel visually marked the change that had occurred in the relationship, with perhaps a suggestion that the comradely closeness had always included some potential hostility.[40] The actual violence might be interpreted as cathartic. When the change from conflict to reconciliation occurred, the pictorial elements remained strong. After Valentine's denunciation, spoken with "a moving sense of heartfelt grief," there was a lengthy pause before Proteus bowed his head, knelt, and made his short speech of confession. Critics were generally impressed by the poignancy of Lynch's acting here: he "[caught] very well the conflicting emotions of Proteus's final onset of guilt," "flesh[ing] out the character's woefully underscripted moment of shame most realistically." (Nelsen, however, questioned Proteus's sincerity, and indeed, as Smallwood has explained, Lynch's interpretation varied from one performance to another, according to whether he let "that enigmatic flicker of a smile" appear.) The most difficult part of the scene—and the most illuminating example of pictorial acting—followed. As Proteus begged forgiveness, Silvia stood beside him, facing Valentine, and silently but eloquently seconded the plea by her attitude and expression; as Valentine pardoned his friend, she crossed over and stood with him while he offered Proteus "all that was mine in Silvia"—meaning, perhaps, a share in "the mutual love and trust" between himself and Silvia. The exact interpretation of the words was not important; what mattered was Silvia's participation in the forgiveness and the gift of restored love.

Response to this production was joyously enthusiastic. A number of critics, both journalists and scholars, praised Thacker's handling of the difficult climax: his approach made "such perfect sense" that the "'crux' was not evident," and the "near-impossible" scene became both "riveting" and "plausible." But even critics who still found the ending either "risible" or "outrageous" applauded the production. As for the audiences, in Smallwood's euphoric words, "Shakespeare's so-called failure, his apprentice work, his unplayable flop, became the hit of the season."[41]

Reviewing these theatrical attempts to popularize *Two Gentlemen*, one sees some salient trends. Rewriting the text to improve it, never successful, has long since been abandoned, though using it as a framework for new creations has occasionally resulted in popular productions (opera, rock musical). In every age nonverbal elements have been determining factors in making the play's simplicities attractive or, alternatively, in creating the impression of additional depth and development. Extra music has been used, not just in outright musicals, but in a good many regular productions. Decor and style of performance have often been important, especially when a new look has revealed certain aspects of the play more clearly than before—for example, Macready's meticulous Italian sets at a time when stock scenery often sufficed for Shakespeare, Poel's return to simple Elizabethan staging for an audience accustomed to visual illusion, and Langham's evocation of the Byronic period when Elizabethan productions had become the norm. The search for novelty has led to a variety of unusual and inventive treatments. It seems, indeed, that some directors have been willing to undertake this play largely because its reputation for unpopularity serves as a license to experiment without giving much offense. Other things being equal, however, the most effective productions have been those whose staging had some special affinity with the youthful mixture of passion, artifice, lyricism, and folly in the play itself.

In all periods there has been a noticeable attempt to give life and color to Shakespeare's minor characters. In early productions certain roles were transformed into contemporary stage types by textual additions, and even after the adaptations had been discarded, some influence from the memory of previous portrayals probably remained, at least for Thurio. About the middle of the present century, directors began, through inventive use of decor and stage business, to give more distinctive personalities to other mainly functional characters. The types of roles assigned to them have, of course, been suitable to the chosen setting, but they have also reflected the interests and concerns of the period when the production occurred. Eglamour's transformations are particularly interesting in this respect: he has moved from Kemble's perfect knight, to Macready's coward, to Poel's representative of spiritualized love, to modern portrayals as a figure of fun— an elderly beau, an anachronistic Don Quixote, a childish do-gooder. Directors have never quite known what to do with Eglamour, but their different ways of dealing with this absurd but poignant figure reveal him as a touchstone for a production and its time.

Some interesting analogies are found in the climactic scene as staged in otherwise dissimilar productions, widely separated in time. In the earliest ones, using adapted texts with a heavily revised climax, Silvia persuaded a formidably reluctant Valentine to forgive her would-be ravisher; in the latest one (Thacker's), using Shakespeare's version with a more amenable Valentine, she silently did the same. A closer parallel links Macready's production, using a restored text, with Thacker's: in both, Proteus froze for a long moment after Valentine's denunciation, his attitude and facial expression suggesting the emotions he felt at the sudden disclosure of his treachery; in both, the stage picture helped to fill in what was lacking in the short repentance speech.

One aspect of the play noticed by modern scholars, the satirical and parodic function of Launce and Speed, has often been overlooked in the theater. Indeed, some reviewers have remarked that Launce, entertaining as he is, has nothing to do with the main part of the play.[42] The Phillips production called attention to his metadramatic function with a Launce silently brooding over the antics of his social superiors, but although one critic was impressed by this conception of the play's "dark angel," another thought it was merely pretentious. Less blatant was the extra stage business in Thacker's production that showed Launce making clownish use of facilities designed for more elegant purposes (like putting dogfood in the Duke's fruitbowl); thus, as

Robert Smallwood observed, "mov[ing] in the hinterland between the audience and the fiction."[43] While less scholarly reviewers, writing to deadlines, did not notice the implications,
that hardly matters. Provided Launce is not allowed to overwhelm the romance completely, it is just as well simply to laugh
at him, responding unconsciously to his subversive ironies and
leaving anything more to afterthoughts.

A notable recent change is the increasing interest in the two
gentlemen themselves. In 1808, Leigh Hunt wrote that they came
and went, talked or were silent, without exciting sympathy for
the one or contempt for the other; in 1842, reviewers commended
Macready for taking such a slight role as Valentine in the interests of art.[44] Proteus has always been condemned, of course,
though he has frequently seemed less villainous on the stage
than in the study; in more recent times Valentine, too, has been
denigrated. But some stage productions, in dealing with the
problems of Proteus's motivation and Valentine's callousness,
have so developed these characters that their central importance
in the play goes unquestioned. While the friends' relationship
has not reflected the *alter ego* conception (indeed, quite the opposite), Shakespeare himself shows a reality that does not conform to Valentine's ideal.

Again and again over the years some reviewer of a successful
production has asked why *Two Gentlemen* has been so neglected; then it has been neglected again for awhile. Today, however, the play is becoming better known in the theater. With
Thacker's production to brighten its reputation, with revivals by
regional companies to test its wilder possibilities, and with the
BBC's stylized work of television art to be viewed on demand,
this trend will probably continue. *Two Gentlemen* will always
be a special challenge, though. All dramatic productions are
collaborations between author and theater—director, actors, designers, and so on. In productions of this play, Shakespeare's
collaborators are more than usually responsible for a significant
part of the "text."

NOTES

1. This does not include any with amateur actors, except for William
Poel's—too important to leave out.

2. Even counting a rock musical, we know of only five full-length productions (one of which had a single performance) in New York; three of these were
later seen in London. Short entertainments based on *Two Gentlemen* included

two skits (one with black minstrels) and a farce. See George C. D. Odell, *Annals of the New York Stage*, 15 vols. (New York: Columbia University Press, 1927–49), 8:219; 11:549; 12:104, 312.

3. Charles Spencer's phrase, in his review of David Thacker's production, *The Daily Telegraph*, 19 April 1991.

4. Other concerns (education, the courtly code of behavior, the qualities essential to 'a gentlemen), though important, do not impress a spectator as driving impulses of speech and action for the major characters. Kurt Schlueter, in the introduction to his edition, *The Two Gentlemen of Verona*, The New Cambridge Shakespeare (Cambridge: Cambridge University Press, 1990), 2–6, gives a good, condensed discussion of the play's themes. In addition to the scholarly articles he cites, see Ann Jennalie Cook, "Shakespeare's Gentlemen," *Shakespeare Jahrbuch* (West) (1985): 9–27.

5. Gervase Mathew, "Ideals of Friendship," *Patterns of Love and Courtesy: Essays in Memory of C. S. Lewis*, ed. John Lawlor (Evanston: Northwestern University Press, 1966), 46–50; Laurens J. Mills, *One Soul in Bodies Twain: Friendship in Tudor Literature and Stuart Drama* (Bloomington, Indiana: Principia Press, 1937), 259 et passim; Geoffrey Bullough, ed. *Narrative and Dramatic Sources of Shakespeare*, 8 vols. (London: Routledge and Kegan Paul, 1957–75), 1: 204.

6. Bernard O'Donoghue gives a good review of courtly love's various features and its influence on English Renaissance literature, in *The Courtly Love Tradition*, Literature in Context (Manchester: Manchester University Press; Totowa, New Jersey: Barnes and Noble, 1982), 5–6, 15. He defends the term "courtly love" against modern attacks (14).

7. See Mills, 258; Muriel C. Bradbrook, *Shakespeare and Elizabethan Poetry: A Study of His Earlier Work in Relation to the Poetry of the Time* (New York: Oxford University Press, 1952), 151.

8. Bradbrook speculates that the play was written for a private performance by boy actors. See "Love and Constancy in *The Two Gentlemen of Verona*," *Shakespeare in His Context: The Constellated Globe*. The Collected Papers of Muriel Bradbrook, vol. 4 (Totowa, N.J.: Barnes and Noble, 1989), 47–49, 55. In *Shakespeare and Elizabethan Poetry* (152) she had declared that Silvia "should not react at all. She is the prize, for the purpose of argument, and must not call attention to herself. . . . "

9. Camille Wells Slights, "*The Two Gentlemen of Verona* and the Courtesy Book Tradition," *Shakespeare Studies* 16 (1983): 27. A 1974 production had already used a similar interpretation. See note 36.

10. See, for example, William Rossky, "*The Two Gentlemen of Verona* as Burlesque," *English Literary Renaissance* 12 (1982): 210–19.

11. For the "minor oddities" in the play, see Clifford Leech's introduction to his edition, *The Two Gentlemen of Verona*, The Arden Edition of the Works of William Shakespeare (London: Methuen, 1969; University Paperback, 1986), xv–xxi. For a discussion of its technical failures, see Stanley Wells, "The Failure of *The Two Gentlemen of Verona*," *Shakespeare Jahrbuch* 99 (1963): 162–66.

12. Discussion of the Victor and Kemble versions will be based on these published texts: (1) [Benjamin Victor, adaptor], *The Two Gentlemen of Verona. A Comedy Written by William Shakespeare. With Alterations and Additions. As it is performed at the Theatre-Royal in Drury Lane* (1763; London: Cornmarket, 1969); and (2) John Philip Kemble, *John Philip Kemble's Promptbook of William Shakespeare's Two Gentlemen of Verona. Revised by J. P. Kemble*.

In Vol. 9 of *John Philip Kemble's Promptbooks*, ed. Charles H. Shattuck, 11 vols. (Charlottesville: University Press of Virginia, for the Folger Shakespeare Library, 1974). Reynolds's dramatic text has not been preserved, but words of the interpolated songs, along with Bishop's music, are available in a rare volume: Henry R. Bishop, *The Overture, Songs, Duetts, Glees & Chorusses. In Shakespeare's Play of the The Two Gentlemen of Verona. as Performed at the Theatre Royal, Covent Garden. The Words Selected entirely from Shakespeare's Plays, Poems & Sonnets. The Music Composed (with exception of Two Melodies) . . . by Henry R. Bishop . . .* (London, [1821]). The songs, together with reviews, give a good idea of the operatic production. For Reynolds's probable use of Kemble, see Schlueter, 31–33.

13. These were a single performance at Covent Garden, 1784, and a first attempt by Kemble, at Drury Lane, 1790. Although stage historians have said that these used the original text, or the original with slight alterations, Schlueter argues persuasively (22, 24, 25) that the alterations were probably more substantial than previously supposed.

14. Vernon: Engraving by J. Roberts, published for Bell's Edition of Shakespeare, 7 March 1776 (copy in the Folger Shakespeare Library; also reproduced by Schlueter, 20). Liston: Jim Davis, *John Liston, Comedian* (London: Society for Theatre Research, 1985), 104; 16–18. Leigh Hunt, in *Examiner*, 24 April 1808: 266–67, accused Liston of turning Thurio into Caper. Farren: *Morning Herald* 30 November 1821; contemporary drawing published by J. Smart, London, 29 January 1822 (copy in the Folger Shakespeare Library).

15. Reviews used in discussing music and spectacle: *Times*, 30 November 1821 ("noble pageant"); *Morning Post*, 30 November; *Morning Herald*, 30 November ("artificial mountain"); *Examiner*, 2 December. Relevance of spectacle: Kemble's version, the basis for Reynolds's, ended Act 4 with Silvia and Eglamour preparing to flee.

16. Discussion of Macready's production is based on his promptbook (Folger Shakespeare Library PROMPT Two Gent. 11) and the following reviews: *Morning Chronicle*, 30 December 1841; *Morning Herald*, 30 December; *Morning Post*, 30 December; *Theatrical Observer*, 30 December; *Times*, 30 December; *Spectator*, 1 January 1842: 9–10; *Argus*, 1 January; *Athenaeum*, 1 January: 19; *Theatrical Journal*, 8 January: [9]–10; *The Age*, 9 January: 5–6.

17. *The Diaries of William Charles Macready*, ed. William Toynbee, 2 vols. (London: Chapman and Hall, 1912) 2: 18–19.

18. *Athenaeum* ("gallant"); *Morning Chronicle* ("more picturesque"); *Spectator* ("manly cordiality"); *Morning Herald* ("overly fervid"); *Times* ("foppishness and surliness").

19. CONFRONTATION: Promptbook, 254 and opp.; *Times* ("fixed group" and applause); *Morning Chronicle* ("a life's repentance"); *Theatrical Observer* (rebuke and forgiveness). NOT RECONCILED: *Times*. SILVIA: *Spectator* (dignified); *Times* and *Theatrical Journal* (cold); *Morning Herald* (lack of byplay).

20. Details of scenery are based on a printed flyer that was handed out at the theater, a copy of which is bound with Macready's promptbook in the Folger Library. Apparently the Reynolds-Bishop production had also used some localized Italian scenes, but with less correctness in both place and detail. See Schlueter, 33.

21. Quoted phrases are, in sequential order, from *Theatrical Observer*, *Athenaeum*, *Times*, and *Morning Chronicle*. The only dissenting voice, as far as we know, was from *John Bull*, 10 January 1842, which praised the scenery but

said the costumes were "in some particulars almost grotesque, and as a whole apparently hardly in unison." "Historically accurate" costumes did sometimes strike viewers as strange, but the appropriateness and harmony attributed to Macready's decor by other critics were characteristics generally associated with his productions. See Alan Downer, *The Eminent Tragedian* (Cambridge, Massachusetts: Harvard University Press, 1966), 225–26; 252.

22. See, for example, *Morning Chronicle* 22 April 1808 and *Examiner* 24 April 1808: 266–67.

23. Quoted by Robert Speaight, in *William Poel and the Elizabethan Revival* (Cambridge, Massachusetts: Harvard University Press, 1954), 90.

24. See Poel's promptbook for *The Two Gentlemen of Verona*, now in the Theatre Museum, London. Though obviously made for the 1896 production, it was almost certainly used for both. For descriptions of the first production see reviews in the *Times*, 30 November 1896, and *Sunday Times*, 29 November; also George Bernard Shaw, *Our Theatres in the Nineties*, 3 vols. (1932: London: Constable, 1948), 2: 284; and Speaight, 119–20 (note his quotation from a favorable article by the French director Lugné-Poe). Our description of the second production is based mainly on Speaight, 120–22, and *Times*, 21 April 1910: 12, but see also *Sunday Times*, 24 April 1910: 6.

25. A production using modern dress had been seen much earlier in the provinces, at the People's Theatre, Newcastle, on 17 May 1930. See *Observer* (London), 18 May, and *Shields Daily News*, 19 May 1930.

26. Discussion of Langham's production is based on his promptbook, now in the University of Bristol Theatre Collection, and the following reviews, clippings of which are found in the Shakespeare Library, Birmingham Reference Library: Stephen Williams, *Evening News*, 23 January 1957; *Times* 23 January; J. C. T. [Trewin], *Birmingham Post*, 23 January; Anthony Carthew, *Daily Herald*, 23 January; Alan Dent, *News Chronicle*, 23 January; Patrick Gibbs, *Daily Telegraph*, 24 January; D. H., *Bristol Evening Post*, 24 January; Philip Hope-Wallace, *Manchester Guardian*, 24 January; A. M., *Stage*, 24 January; Patrick Keatley, *Montreal Star*, 26 January; *Western Independent*, 27 January; W. G. McS., *Scotsman*, 28 January; *Daily Worker*, 29 January; *Punch*, 30 January; Derek Grainger, *Financial Times*, 23 January; George Scott, *Truth*, 1 February; P. R., *Kensington News*, 1 February. See also Richard David, "Actors and Scholars: A View of Shakespeare in the Modern Theatre," *Shakespeare Survey* 12 (1959): 76–87.

27. SETTING: *Times, Punch, Western Independent, Daily Telegraph.* COSTUMES: Men—*Montreal Star, Times, Western Independent*; Women—*Financial Times*; Byron and Shelley—*News Chronicle.* Outlaws: *Birmingham Post.*

28. QUOTED PHRASES: *News Chronicle* ("make-believe"); *Scotsman* ("bucks," etc.); *Daily Worker* (the rest). AMOUNT OF BURLESQUE: *Daily Herald* (much); *Birmingham Post* ("shiver[ed] on the knife edge"); *Stage* (resisted the temptation); *Daily Worker* (just the right touch). RESERVATIONS ABOUT THE REGENCY TREATMENT: *Stage*; Richard David, 85.

29. VALENTINE: *Kensington News.* See also *Times* and *Punch.* PROTEUS: *Times, Punch, Financial Times, Kensington News.* JULIA: *Times, Evening News.* (*Kensington News* deplored her boisterousness, but *Financial Times* said she later muted it.) SILVIA: *Stage, Truth* (colorless); *Bristol Evening Post* (lovely); *Kensington News* (nobly-bred). SPEED: *Times*; see also *Kensington News.* LAUNCE: *Financial Times* ("comic precision," "squeaky"), *Stage* ("audience-contact," vacant expression), *Evening News* (Cockney), *Punch*

("funny with pathos"). CRAB: *Bristol Evening Post* ("engagingly miscast"), *Daily Herald* ("shook hands").

30. EXTRA STAGE BUSINESS: *Daily Worker* (reinterprets archaic conceits, passion survives treatment); *Times* (ironic touches); *Financial Times* (action always accompanies speech; archery, artist, dancing); *Stage* (many realistic touches). ANTONIO: promptbook, 14, 16. THURIO: quoted phrase from *Daily Telegraph*; shaving scene, promptbook, 92. DUKE: *Punch*. See also *Kensington News* and *Daily Telegraph*. EGLAMOUR: see descriptive phrases in *Daily Worker* and *Manchester Guardian*; stage directions in promptbook, especially in 1.2 (8) and in 2.4 (30, 32, 34—Eglamour and Thurio retire upstage together when Proteus arrives).

31. ACTING OF CLIMAX: See stage directions in the promptbook, pp. 95–100. One vital stage direction is lacking—Proteus' actually pointing the pistol at himself,—but the implications of the stage directions, together with Patrick Gibbs's reference to Proteus's suicide attempt (*Daily Telegraph* review), leave no doubt about the performance. The quoted phrase is from Gibbs. CRITICS' RESPONSE: *Manchester Guardian*; *Financial Times*; *Bristol Evening Post*; *Daily Telegraph*; *Truth*.

32. HALL: *Education*, 15 April 1960. DIGBY DAY: *Times*, 18 July 1968; *Daily Mail*, 18 July 1968; *Birmingham Post*, 20 July 1968 and 4 June 1969 (Eglamour). Putting Eglamour in armor might have been inspired by the bearded and helmeted Eglamour of Hall's production.

33. This discussion is based on the promptbook, in the Shakespeare Centre Library, Stratford-upon-Avon (see stage directions, opp. 123 for climactic scene), and on the following reviews, many from the *Two Gentlemen* clippings, Birmingham (see note 26): Irving Wardle, *Times*, 24 July 1970 (decor, Antonio, Eglamour, Proteus, some disapproval), but see more positive review in *Times*, 25 December 1970; B. A. Young, *Financial Times*, 24 July (Julia, Silvia); Pearson Phillips, *Daily Mail*, 24 July (Julia, Valentine); *Evening Standard*, 24 July (Julia); J. C. Trewin, *Birmingham Post*, 24 July (decor, deplores Eglamour); Harold Hobson, *Sunday Times*, 26 July (Launce [enthusiastic], Proteus, production shows ancient truths); Wendy Monk, *Stage and Television*, 30 July 1970 (decor, Eglamour, Silvia, loss of innocence, preference for Langham): J. A. P., *Warwick Advertiser*, 31 July (Eglamour, Julia, approves modern treatment); W. T., *Nottingham Evening Post*, 24 July (Eglamour, outlaws, loss of innocence); *Oxford Mail*, 25 July (incongruities, Launce [negative]); Neville Miller, *South Wales Evening Argus*, 25–26 July (Valentine, Silvia, approves "fable on the uncertainties of adolescence"); Eric Shorter, *Daily Telegraph*, 23 December 1970 (serious content "jettisoned") *Glasgow Herald*, 28 December 1970 (theme subtly underlined); Peter Thomson, "A Necessary Theatre: The Royal Shakespeare Season 1970," *Shakespeare Survey* 24 (1971): 120–21 (decor, Antonio, Eglamour, Launce [dubious], psychological analysis, Proteus, Silvia).

34. These settings were, in the order of their mention, for productions at the Champlain Shakespeare Festival, 1977, at the Pittsburgh Public Theater, 1981, and by the Acting Company on tour, 1990–91. A circus setting and style were combined with Byronic romanticism by the San Diego National Shakespeare Repertory in 1980; the *commedia* style was used at the Odessa Globe Shakespeare Festival (Texas) in 1977, the Utah Shakespeare Festival in 1983 (for some scenes and characters), and the Kentucky Shakespeare Festival in 1988 (in adapted and modernized form); a combination of vaudeville with other

styles was used for the heavily burlesqued production of the Acting Company in 1990–91.

35. John Guare and Mel Shapiro, *The Two Gentlemen of Verona. Adapted from the Shakespeare Play . . . Lyrics by John Guare, Music by Galt MacDermot* (New York: Holt, Rinehart and Winston, 1973). For details of both American and British productions, see reviews by Walter Kerr in *New York Times,* 12 December 1971, Foster Hirsch in *Educational Theatre Journal* 24 (1971): 194, and Irving Wardle in *Times,* 27 April 1973.

36. PHILLIPS: Milton Shulman, *Evening Standard,* 23 December 1970. DOUBLE TAKES: Alabama Shakespeare Festival, 1991. MEN GOING OFF TOGETHER: started to do so, Folger Theatre Group, 1977; did so, Great Lakes Shakespeare Festival, 1978. SILVIA'S APPROVAL: At the Oregon Shakespeare Festival, 1974, the offer was made as a ruse, conceived by Valentine and Silvia. In the BBC television production, 1983–84, although the camera focused solely on Valentine and Proteus during the offer, Silvia had silently shown approval of forgiveness before that. For varying interpretations of the BBC scene, see Patty S. Derrick, "*Two Gents*: A Critical Moment," *Shakespeare on Film Newsletter* (December 1991): 1, 4.

37. The promptbook for this production was lost after the provincial tour had ended; if it is found, it will be housed in the Shakespeare Centre Library, Stratford-upon-Avon. Reviews used in discussing the production are: Benedict Nightingale, *Times,* 19 April 1991 and 15 October 1992; John Peter, *Sunday Times,* 21 April; Michael Billington, *Guardian* 19 April; Rex Gibson, *Times Educational Supplement,* 3 May: 25; Paul Nelsen, *Shakespeare Bulletin* 9, no. 4 (Fall 1991): 15–17; Thomas Clayton, "The Climax of *The Two Gentlemen of Verona*: Text and performance at the Swan Theatre, Stratford-upon-Avon, 1991," *Shakespeare Bulletin* 9, no. 4 (Fall 1991): 17–19; Robert Smallwood, "Shakespeare at Stratford-upon-Avon, 1991," *Shakespeare Quarterly* 43 (1992): 350–53. Also passages from the following, as quoted by Clayton from the *London Theatre Record,* 9–22 April 1991: Paul Taylor, *Independent,* 19 April; Claire Armistead, *Financial Times,* 19 April; Carole Waddis, *What's On,* 19 April; Charles Spencer, *Daily Telegraph,* 19 April; Rod Dungate, *Tribune* 3 May.

38. SETTING AND MUSIC: *Times,* 19 Apr. ("Coward dressing gowns," "cunningly chosen,"); Smallwood, 351, and *Sunday Times* (appositeness of period to play); Nelsen, 15 (prelude of music, etc., reference to Masterpiece Theatre); *Times Educational Supplement* (musical interludes); *Guardian* (dislikes interludes, prefers nineteenth-century setting).

39. VALENTINE: *Times,* 1992. Thurio: *Times,* 1992; Smallwood, 351–52. PROTEUS: Clayton ("likeable"); *Financial Times* ("naive"); Smallwood, 351 ("puzzled innocence," "disturbing . . . smile"); *Times,* 1991 and 1992 (intensity, secrecy, passion); *Independent* ("nervous intensity"); *Sunday Times* (slightly unstable). JULIA AND SILVIA: Smallwood, 351; *Guardian* (Julia, "jaunty"); *Sunday Times* (considers both women warm, lively); Nelsen, 16 (emphasizes "deconstruction"). LAUNCE: Smallwood, 352 (detailed description); *Sunday Times* ("hangdog dignity"). SPEED: Smallwood, 352. DUKE: *Sunday Times;* *Times,* 1991; Nelsen, 17. Note that the second *Times* review was for the revival at the Barbican; descriptions of Valentine, Proteus, and Thurio are similar to those in the original review but fuller, possibly reflecting further development in the acting.

40. A similar parallel had been used the previous year in the Acting Company's touring production (U.S.A.), but, in our opinion, the unrestrained bur-

lesque of the production as a whole canceled out (at least for the average spectator) any serious effect beyond a momentary shock. See, however, Jean Peterson's interesting review in *Shakespeare Bulletin,* 9, no. 1 (Winter, 1991): 33–34.

41. CLIMAX AND ENDING: Nelsen, 16 ("echoing . . . act one," "outrageous"—he still considered the women victims); *What's On* ("great poignancy"); *Guardian* ("conflicting emotions"); *Independent* ("flesh[ing] out"); Clayton, 18 (description of Silvia's actions, abstruse interpretation of Valentine's offer, "crux" not evident); Smallwood, 352–53 (description of scene, Lynch's smile, simple interpretation of offer—the one we accept); *Tribune* ("near-impossible," "riveting," "plausible"); *Sunday Times* (previous skeptic persuaded by actors); *Daily Telegraph* ("risible"); HIT OF THE SEASON: The popularity continued next season at the Barbican in London. By the end of the tour, however, the production had evidently lost its sparkle. See Jeremy Kingston, *Times,* 16 December 1993.

42. *Manchester Evening News,* 20 April 1938; *Times,* 3 April 1958; Peter Lewis, *Daily Mail,* 18 July 1968.

43. PHILLIPS: Harold Hobson, *Sunday Times,* 26 July 1970 (approves "dark angel"); *Oxford Mail,* 25 July 1970 (pretentious). THACKER: Smallwood, *Shakespeare Quarterly* 43 (1992): 352.

44. HUNT: *Examiner,* 24 April 1808: 266. ABOUT MACREADY: *Argus,* 1 January 1842: 10; *Theatrical Journal,* 8 January 1842: [9].

The Disappearance and Return of
Love's Labor's Lost

MIRIAM GILBERT

I count myself fortunate that my first real memories of *Love's Labor's Lost* derive from the theater, rather than from the classroom. As a freshman at the University of Manchester in 1961–62, I took notes from Frank Kermode lecturing on the comedies (and dutifully wrote down as the conclusion "Oaths cannot be so easily forsworn"), but nothing else about the play really surfaces from the past until I come to 1968. Then, at the American Shakespeare Festival in Stratford, Connecticut, I encountered *Love's Labor's Lost* in all its extravagance and high spirits. Michael Kahn's production made the play daringly up-to-the-minute by portraying the King of Navarre as an Indian guru, and the three young courtiers as versions of the Beatles; the sonnets were sung to various musical accompaniments (the King accompanied, of course, by his ever-present sitar player); and the French women were dressed in form-clinging pants suits, fake fur hunting togs, or, finally, evening dresses. The satire on affectation that Shakespeare's play expresses through a wide-ranging display of verbal styles Kahn presented through contemporary fashions in dress and music. As one might expect, critical reaction varied from those who felt that Kahn had travestied the play to those who enjoyed the free-wheeling satire. What matters most to me is that the play seemed alive, exciting, relevant.

But the play I so enjoyed, and which I continued to enjoy in production after production (1974 at the Guthrie; 1975, with the RSC performing at Omaha in David Jones' 1973 production; 1978 at Stratford-upon-Avon) was, I found out, one that rarely got taught and that often merited only a brief mention in books dealing with Shakespearean comedy. Even more stunning, when I embarked on a study of the play in performance,[1] was the discovery that *Love's Labor's Lost* was the *only* play of Shakespeare's not performed during the eighteenth century. Why did *Love's*

155

Labor's Lost disappear from the English stage for over two hundred years? And what has brought it back, both to the theatrical stage and the pages of critical scrutiny?

THE DISAPPEARANCE

The problems with *Love's Labor's Lost* are, in fact, the central defining features of the play: the slightness of the play's plot, the verbal extravagance of the style, and the defiantly non-comedic ending to a comedy. One of the easiest ways to see what theater people found difficult is to look at the only adaptation of the play written, though not produced, in the eighteenth century. *The Students,* 1762, whose author remains anonymous, is considerably shorter than *Love's Labor's Lost,* with approximately 1625 lines compared to Shakespeare's 2785. Though most of the lines are from Shakespeare, some new ones are added, and some scenes rearranged.

The adaptor's blue pencil strikes, most obviously the scenes of wit and wordplay between the non-courtly characters. Most of Armado's punning with Moth vanishes. Holofernes and Sir Nathaniel disappear completely, with some of Holofernes' lines spoken by the Player (a new minor role), who confers with Armado about the pastime to be presented to the Princess. Dull puts in a brief appearance and gets a memorable line when, in answer to Armado's question about his profession, he replies "I am by trade a constable, and by profession a rat-catcher" (4.1.).[2] Since Holofernes, the deviser of the Pageant of the Nine Worthies, is gone, so too is the Pageant; instead the Player suggests a "new comic dance." But even the court characters are not safe from major cuts. The one surefire scene in *Love's Labor's Lost,* the scene in which Berowne discovers that the King, Longaville, and Dumaine are also in love, has disappeared, perhaps because the scene depends on hearing each of those characters read aloud a poem that lacks originality as well as sincerity.

While reducing the amount of wordplay, the adaptor increases the level of plot intrigue by adding scenes in which Biron (Berowne) appears as Costard. That disguise leads to various comic episodes: Biron-as-Costard flirts with Jaquenetta; Biron tries to convince the real Costard that he is not Costard, but someone else and even offers to find him another name; Dumaine meets Costard, asks about the letter that Dumaine sent to Catherine (which has, of course, been taken by the disguised Biron), and beats up the real Costard until he admits having taken the letter. The latter scene replays one of the mistakes in *The Comedy of Errors*, a play as full of plot as *Love's Labor's Lost* is lacking in one.

Since the overhearing scene is gone, and with it the moment when the men renounce their vows, *The Students* makes further use of Biron's disguise as Costard to accomplish that necessary action. Biron/Costard finds the sonnet of the King, is given sonnet-letters by Dumaine and Longaville, and takes all three of these to the women. He hears the women read the sonnets aloud, and at the same time hears the women confess their love for the young men. But the Princess decides that they should return the sonnet/letters, since "'Tis wisdom to conceal, where knowledge wou'd / Betray our weakness" (3.2). Biron/Costard thus receives the men's letters again; and in 4.2 he comes in, still as Costard, and hands the letters back, making sure, however, to give the letters to the wrong men so that each realizes that the others have broken their vows. Thus the adaptor uses the Biron/Costard disguise to expose the King, Dumaine, and Longaville, but keeps Biron's power supreme because his love is never exposed in the same way.

More importantly, the shift in the plot whereby Biron overhears the women's confessions is but one instance of the rewriting of the complex balance of power that Shakespeare's play presents. *Love's Labor's Lost* makes clear that Rosaline, Maria, and Katharine have heard about Berowne, Longaville, and Dumaine, and are presumably interested in them, but *The Students*, after using the relevant speeches (2.1.40–76 in Shakespeare's play), then adds new ones in which the women mock the men's studies. Moreover, Catherine suggests, "Suppose, we practise all our little arts, / To raise them from this legarthy [sic]" (1.3.), and Rosaline adds that they should flirt with the men and then disappoint them. Later, in 3.2 (a revision of Shakespeare's hunting scene, 4.1), Rosaline exults in her power over Biron: "Biron is my slave, / He has no will, but I have power to guide; / He has no joy, but when I deign to smile, / He has no oath, but what he swears to me." Her pride receives an immediate comeuppance when the disguised Biron enters with letters for the Princess, Maria, and Catherine, but none for Rosaline—and the other women throw her boastful phrases back at her.

By rewriting the scenes with the women to suggest first that they *plan* to flirt with the men, then that they are pleased to receive the sonnet/letters (or, in Rosaline's case, disappointed not to get one), and finally that they are in love but will pretend not to be, the adaptor eliminates the moral, intellectual, and emotional superiority that Shakespeare's women so strikingly possess. Shakespeare's women do not set out to capture the men, and when they receive presents and poems, they wittily comment on them, suggesting an emotional detachment from the situation. Their disguises for the Muscovite scene represent, as Shakespeare's Princess puts it, "mock for mock" (5.2. 140). And when the women finally receive what sound like sincere proposals from the men, they insist that such sincerity be tested by time— the year of trial. But the final scene in *The Students* rewrites the events of Shakespeare's play even further to set up a happy ending. Biron steps forward to reveal that he heard the women confess their love: "as Costard I o'erheard them." Rosaline still holds out, insisting that he will have to wait for her, "A man, my lord, who cannot love a year, / Is ne'er entitled to a woman's love," only to meet with Biron's threat to leave her entirely. So she pleads with him to stay, trapped by Biron's knowledge of the earlier scene and by her own desires into a quick capitulation, "Perhaps—I was but joking." The closing lines go to Biron and offer a tidy conclusion in place of Shakespeare's open ending:

> Our wooing now doth end like an old play;
> Jack hath his Jill; these ladies' courtesie
> Hath nobly made our sport a Comedy.

Thus, the adaptor manages to "solve" all of the problems of Shakespeare's play. *The Students* is tighter, less verbally extravagant (or obscure), fuller of comic incident—and offers no challenge to the notion that men do, and should, dominate all romantic relationships. But Shakespeare's play insists not merely that the young men have made a major mistake in taking a vow to leave the world, but that they will have to *take time* in which to rethink their ways. In this sense, *Love's Labor's Lost* is unique among the comedies, as the only one that fails to end with at least one marriage. It thus challenges both comedic and social decorum with an ending that at once gives the women a chance to dictate terms to the men, separates the men and the women, and takes "too long for a play."

THE RETURN: VESTRIS, PHELPS, AND GRANVILLE-BARKER

Interestingly enough, the very absence of *Love's Labor's Lost* from the London stage in the eighteenth century may have eventually contributed to its return. In 1839, Madame Vestris, the singer, actress, and theater manager, presented it as her opening production at Covent Garden, a venue previously managed by the eminent tragedian William Charles Macready. *Love's Labor's Lost* was not only her first production at Covent Garden but also her first production ever of a Shakespeare play. A recent biographer, Clifford John Williams, speculates on the motivations that may have led Madame Vestris and her husband, the actor Charles John Mathews, to undertake *Love's Labor's Lost*:

> Somewhat overplaying their hand in trying to prove that they were fitting custodians of the National Drama, the Mathewses chose *Love's Labor's Lost*. The choice of Shakespeare is understandable if not inevitable. The choice of play is rather insanely commendable, and anyone can see the arguments that led to it: a play not performed since Shakespeare's own time; a play not calling for a leading actor that they had not got; a play depending on the team work that they had always fostered and worked for, and a play giving Planché a fine opportunity for some costume lessons.[3]

What Williams implies is that by producing *Love's Labor's Lost*, Madame Vestris and Charles Mathews simultaneously moved into the "big leagues" while avoiding serious competition. While anyone could compare, perhaps unfavorably, their production of a better-known work to one of Macready's, no one would be able to hark back to an earlier production of *Love's Labor's Lost*. But even more important is Williams' speculation that they chose the play because it "depend[ed] on the team work that they had always fostered and worked for," an insight leading directly to one of *Love's Labor's Lost*'s salient qualities as a theater piece— its need for ensemble playing rather than a star.[4] Even though Berowne's role *is* a long one (591 lines, according to the Pelican Shakespeare, including his 54-line peroration about the value of loving a woman at the end of 4.3), he is still always "one of the group." Even though he appears twice in soliloquy (confiding to the audience his love for Rosaline and his difficulties in expressing that love) and even though he separates himself from the other men both by his questioning of the oath at the beginning and by his early realization that he has broken that oath, he nonetheless participates in their vow, in their Muscovite masquerade, and in their mockery of the unworthy Worthies.

The lack of a starring role for a major actor seems not have deterred Samuel Phelps, the Victorian actor-manager whose 1857 production of *Love's Labor's Lost* firmly rescued the play from obscurity. Madame Vestris had brought the play back to

London, but her elaborate production ran for only nine performances. Phelps had taken over Sadler's Wells Theatre in 1844,
producing a wide variety of theatrical fare. In his fourteenth season, with a company of actors used to working together, and
with roles such as Christopher Sly, Bottom, and Malvolio as part
of his repertoire, Phelps took on *Love's Labor's Lost*—and played
not Berowne, but Armado.

The subtlety of Phelps's production is apparent in the detailed
commentary reviewers gave to the actors, with Phelps's Armado
naturally attracting the most attention. Henry Morley commented on the resemblance between Malvolio and Armado,
"both fantastical and foolish men" and then praised Phelps for
defining "the essential difference between the two."[5] Morley records for us the facade of Armado as well as the pathos Phelps
evoked:

> He affects finery of speech, and is so utterly destitute of ideas, that
> to count three he must depend upon the help of a child who is his
> servant, and his master in all passages of wit. He carries a brave
> outside of clothes, but cannot fight in his shirt, because, as he is
> driven to admit, "the naked truth of it is, I have no shirt." This is
> the view of his character to which Mr. Phelps gives prominence by
> many a clever touch, such as the empty drawl on the word love,
> whenever Armado uses it, or the lumbering helplessness of wit dis-
> played by the great Spaniard when magnificently and heavily con-
> versing with the tiny Moth, in which part little Miss Rose Williams
> has been taught to bring out very perfectly some telling points.[6]

John Oxenford of the *Times* also praised Phelps, but extended
his observations to other roles as well; his review sees the play
as one "over which a great deal of good acting may be diffused,
for even the smallest parts are marked characters and some of
them very strongly and very strangely defined. . . . [Mr. Phelps]
has so well applied the talent of his company that there is not a
single weakly acted part."[7] The emphasis on what might be
called the "ensemble" effect of the play and the praise for the
director's ability to create a strong company are noteworthy because they point to an awareness, however implicit, that the
play's strengths lie not in bravura roles but in the inter-
relationship of all the roles, even the small ones.

The reviewers' delight in the comic characters may have begun
with their attention to the actor-manager playing Armado, but it
also indicates one of the main differences between reading the

play and seeing it performed. Lines that seem obscure on the page become clear when spoken, as Oxenford's review suggests:

> Holofernes, the schoolmaster, a fop of the pedantic sort, as exceptional in his way as Don Adriano, is most carefully and naturally rendered by Mr. Williams, who happily combines the scholastic sensitiveness with a fund of internal good nature. The line, 'boné for bené: Priscian a little scratched; 'twill serve,' he gives with marvellous effect, showing at once the magnitude of the crime committed by the ignorant curate and his own magnanimity in passing it over.[8]

To find not merely the pedantry of Holofernes, but the engaging quality of such Latinate details, argues an actor of skill and a production that did not condescend either to the characters or to the audience.

I dwell on these two nineteenth-century productions of *Love's Labor's Lost* because they reveal the interest generated by the play in performance. Indeed, it is through performance that *Love's Labor's Lost* has returned to us today. Critical opinion of the play was, until the middle of this century, much less favorable than that of audiences. But what is striking about critical opinion is how even the most negative comments nonetheless acknowledge, albeit unwillingly, qualities of the play that have led to its stage success. Samuel Johnson's closing summation is well-known, and in many ways typical, since he first criticizes the play's defects, finding "many passages mean, childish, and vulgar" but then notices the play's delights: "there are scattered through the whole many sparks of genius; nor is there any play that has more evident marks of the hand of Shakespeare."[9] In individual notes, Johnson often points to passages that seem "entangled and obscure," but even as he does so, he returns persistently to a topic of substance: "Biron, amidst his extravagancies, speaks with great justness against the folly of vows. They are made without sufficient regard to the variations of life, and are therefore broken by some unforeseen necessity. They proceed commonly from a presumptuous confidence, and a false estimate of human power."[10] A similar dichotomy occurs almost two hundred years later when H. B. Charlton labeled *Love's Labor's Lost* Shakespeare's "least substantial" comedy, and then, two sentences later, spoke of its "exuberant assertion of the high claims of romance."[11] Proposing that "its peculiar gaiety almost frustrates itself by the formlessness and the spinelessness of the thing as a play,"[12] Charlton clearly struggles with his intellectual perception that *Love's Labor's Lost* seems not to work, either on the level of substance (meaning) or structure (plot), while still responding to the play's "exuberance" and "gaiety." Just as Dr. Johnson found "many sparks of genius" in the play, so Charlton, after insisting that the male courtiers "lack personality" and that the women are "as empty and as uniform as are their wooers," goes on to find in Armado "more truth to human nature than in all the court society." And, in Nathaniel, Charlton discovers "a masterpiece in miniature. Every line expresses both his native quality and his professional habit."[13]

Charlton's ability to recognize the appeal of such characters as Armado and Nathaniel, in spite of his insistence on the play's "spinelessness," leads us to the heart of the dilemma about Love's Labor's Lost. On stage, the play works superbly, and the comic characters, so difficult to follow in the reading, reveal themselves immediately and charmingly to an audience. But without an appreciative critical tradition, directors may choose not to stage the play at all, preferring to work instead with plays they know and with plays they feel sure their audiences will both know and like. Critical disdain leads to theatrical neglect.

Fortunately for Love's Labor's Lost, the opposite is also true: theatrical success leads to critical awareness, perhaps even critical acclaim. We do not know if Harley Granville-Barker saw any of the late-nineteenth-century productions of the play, but we do know that he brought to Love's Labor's Lost all his instincts as a playwright, an actor, and a director. His Preface to Love's Labor's Lost, first published in a limited edition in 1924 and then reissued more widely in 1927, is one of the first critical pieces to acknowledge fully its theatrical vitality, while recognizing its literary obscurity. Indeed, some of Granville-Barker's most helpful notes are about "difficult" passages, such as the Armado/ Moth dialogues. Repeatedly, Granville-Barker gets the reader to visualize the action, or to hear the words as music. Thus, he quotes the exchange between Armado and Moth beginning "Is not lead a metal heavy, dull and slow?" (3.1.59) and insists:

> We must picture the long black barrel of a man, slow-gaited even in talk, and the little page, daintily at fence with him, and then off the stage at a bound. The art of it is akin to the artifice of a ballet.[14]

When struggling with the much longer passage that follows soon after in 3.1, with its seemingly endless puns on "enigma" and "plaintain" and "envoy," Granville-Barker sounds for a moment almost desperate: "What is a producer to do? How much of the stuff can any modern audience be brought to understand—even to understand, enjoyment apart?" His solution is both visual and aural:

Here is an effect gained by the resolving of the long Armado-Moth duet into a trio, by rounding off the sententious folly and nimble mockery with the crude humor of the clown. The dialogue passes from prose to rhymed couplets; then becomes gay with jingle, which Costard jollily burlesques in that long lolloping meter. *We must think of it all in terms of music, of contrasts in tone and tune, rhythm and breaking of rhythm* [italics mine]. There is the value of the picture too, set before us and held for its minute or two; of the egregious dignity of Armado, Moth delicately poised, and Costard square-toed and cunning, not such a fool as he looks.[15]

Though Granville-Barker's work on the play frequently illuminates some of the more "obscure" passages, he seems surprisingly unwilling to dwell on the dissonances of the play, especially at the end. He is aware of the sudden shift in tone, and with his usual ability to evoke the stage picture in just a few words, he creates for us the "pictorial values in the pageantry of this last scene":

Yesterday Navarre and his friends were recluse philosophers; splendid even so, no doubt, but with a pallid splendor. Today they are in love and glowingly appareled, in which symbolism their ladies can match them; and against this delicately blended coloring the village pageant tells crude and loud. Into the midst there suddenly steps Marcade, in black from head to foot. He hardly needs to speak.

The king your father—

Dead, for my life!

Even so, my tale is told.

Berowne takes order.

Worthies, away! The scene begins to cloud.

And it must seem to cloud; the gay colors fading out, the finery folding about its wearers like wings. But this is not the end, for the end must not be melancholy.[16]

Though Granville-Barker sees, and makes us see, that figure, "in black from head to foot," he still insists "the end must not be melancholy." Perhaps his emphasis on the play as dance, masque, ballet, music, makes him—for this moment, at least— slightly deaf to the other sounds of the play's ending. But his insistence on the play's liveliness was crucial to its theatrical success, since Tyrone Guthrie read his *Prefaces* and staged a production of *Love's Labor's Lost* in 1932 that clearly separated the two groups of court personages (the King's tent was red, that of the Princess green) while creating the masque-like world that Granville-Barker had described. Reviewing Guthrie's revival of his production in 1936 at the Old Vic, Audrey Williamson noted the "iridescent lightness that kept the wit buoyant, mobile as quicksilver; and the gay-patterned movement flowed through the play with a stylised grace that avoided artifice."[17] That this play should appear in London twice in four years is, in view of the play's infrequent productions, something of a record, and suggests just how enchanting Guthrie's production must have been.

THE RETURN: PETER BROOK, ANNE BARTON, JOHN BARTON

From the mid-thirties on, *Love's Labor's Lost* has appeared much more consistently on the British stage, and its appeal seems to lie in a series of factors. The "ensemble" nature of the play is crucial, whether we mean by that the lack of starring roles, its appeal to a relatively small acting company (the play can easily be done without any attendant "supers"), the presence of *five* speaking roles for women (only in *The Winter's Tale* are there more), and the attraction of many of the smaller roles, particularly those of Holofernes, Nathaniel, Jaquenetta, Dull, and Costard. The most famous production of *Love's Labor's Lost* in the twentieth century, the 1946 production directed by Peter Brook at Stratford-upon-Avon, seems directly related to the perception of the play as an ensemble piece, especially if one reads the amount of discussion at the beginning of the 1946 season about the lack of "stars" in that year's Stratford company.

But Brook's production became famous not for its lack of well-known actors, but for the haunting effect of its ending. Brook's central response to the play, as he puts it in *The Shifting Point*, was his recognition

> that when, at the very end of the last scene, a new, unexpected character called Mercade [sic] came on, the whole play changed its tone

entirely. He came into an artificial world to announce a piece of news that was real. He came on bringing death.

Death is not unknown in Shakespearean comedy, but it normally occurs either at the beginning (Egeus' threat to Hermia, the presumed death of Sebastian) or midway (the presumed deaths of Hero, Helena, and, later, Hermione); no Shakespearean romantic comedy announces the death, albeit of an offstage character, so near the end of the play. But in Brook's production, as Armado and Costard elaborately challenged each other in preparations for a duel that took them up and down the staircase that dominated stage left, Marcade entered from up center, virtually unnoticed; as he moved down center, space cleared around him. As Brook described it in *The Shifting Point*: "The man in black came onto a very pretty summery stage, with everybody in pale pastel Watteau and Lancret costumes and golden lights dying. It was very disturbing and at once the whole audience felt that the world had been transformed."[18] J. C. Trewin's description put the contrast in terms of weather: "the company remained stricken into absolute stillness, a fall of frost in the summer night, in the context both daring and just."[19]

To focus on the ending, rather than to obscure it as the elaborate procession staged by Madame Vestris had done, to insist that the shift in tone is not quirky, but rather central to the play's meaning, was the lasting achievement of this production. Some seven years after Brook had successfully demonstrated the power of the ending, a major scholarly article by Anne Barton (then Bobbyann Roesen) reiterated that idea so powerfully that it has become standard in the understanding of *Love's Labor's Lost*. I do not know if Anne Barton saw Brook's production in 1946 or in its 1947 revival, or Hugh Hunt's 1949 production at London's Old Vic, which similarly emphasized the darkness of the ending. The crucial issue is not influence, but the coincidence of thought—a critical article and theatrical productions (including Angus Bowmer's 1947 production at Ashland that also "effected a profound change in mood" with Marcade's entrance[20]) all stressing the power of the ending. Barton's essay appeared in *Shakespeare Quarterly* in 1953, and its opening sentences seem at first to be describing a play unknown:

> In a sense the play has ended; an epilogue has been spoken by Berowne and that haunting and beautiful kingdom created by the marriage of reality with illusion destroyed, seemingly beyond recall. In

the person of Marcade, the world outside the circuit of the park has at last broken through the gates, involving the people of the play in its sorrows and grim actualities, the plague-houses and desolate retreats, the mourning cities and courts of that vaster country over-shadowing the tents and the fantastic towers of Navarre.[21]

But Barton fully demonstrates that the death-message of Marcade is one that we might well have heard at the beginning of the play, in the King's opening speech, "an expression of that peculiarly Renaissance relationship of the idea of Fame with that of Time and Death." Moreover, as she makes clear, the reality that the young men try to escape is finally the reality that impinges on their fantastic closed world, and the reality that they must confront "not in the half real world of the park, but in the actuality outside its walls."[22] If ever a play insisted on its own non-reality, it is this one, but it allows no comfort in the illusion of theater, with Berowne's explicit rejection of the King's attempt to cheer him up about their penances:

> King: Come, sir, it wants a twelvemonth and a day,
>   And then 'twill end.
> Berowne: That's too long for a play.
>   (5.2. 877–78)

In Berowne's sober (or is it rueful? resigned? defiant?) clear-sightedness about the limitations of theater, which harks back to his earlier clear-sighted perception that the whole academic enterprise is unrealistic ("O, these are barren tasks, too hard to keep, / Not to see ladies, study, fast, not sleep!" [1.1. 47–48]), lies one of the play's major appeals to the twentieth-century audience. While more and more productions of the comedies have stressed the "darker" side of the plays, the difference with Love's Labor's Lost is that the "darker" side is built explicitly into the structure of the play, and only by removing the appearance of Marcade (as the anonymous adaptor of The Students did) can one really ignore the play's insistence on death, penance, and separation.

That darker ending puts Love's Labor's Lost more firmly in the camp of the anti-romantic comedies and even links it to a much later play, The Winter's Tale. But while The Winter's Tale actually includes the time that will allow Leontes to repent at length for the great wrong he has committed and allows Shakespeare to change the theatrical weather from murderous winter to re-storative spring,[23] Love's Labor's Lost takes a harsher course.

Though the ending of *Love's Labor's Lost* likewise invokes "spring" and "winter," the play rightly sees that the problems of the young men, though much less violent than those of Leontes, are not ones that can be solved overnight or with a single penitent song (cf. Claudio in *Much Ado About Nothing*). Growing up, whether from arrogance to sensitivity, or from jealousy to understanding, takes time. It also takes work, which is exactly what Rosaline requires of Berowne. His work is not just waiting, which seems to be the case for Dumaine and Longaville, and not just a retreat from the world as it is for the King (thus pushing him to enact his original vow), but a more active penance:

> You shall this twelvemonth term from day to day
> Visit the speechless sick, and still converse
> With groaning wretches; and your task shall be
> With all the fierce endeavor of your wit
> To enforce the pained impotent to smile.
>
> (5.2.850–54)

Berowne must use the wit he values so highly, the wit he has turned against the relatively helpless Nathaniel, Holofernes, and Armado, not for self-aggrandizement, but to cheer up others. Rosaline hopes that Berowne will come to discover for himself that "a jest's prosperity lies in the ear / Of him that hears it, never in the tongue / Of him that makes it" (5.2.861–63). She calls his jests "idle scorns" and twice refers to his "gibing spirit" as a "fault," (5.2. 859–69), clearly indicating what she thinks of his characteristic behavior.

By insisting that all of the young men grow up—and by reminding us that such changes cannot always work *within* a play—*Love's Labor's Lost* avoids the "happily ever after" ending, which has, for some audiences and critics, come to feel not merely unrealistic but patriarchal as well. Getting immediate acquiescence to their wishes is what the young men want: "Now at the latest minute of the hour / Grant us your loves" (5.2.787–88). But it is not what the women want—and in this play the women's wishes prevail, even if that means overturning the conventions of audience expectation, masculine desire, and comedic form. Though the women are never unequivocally the possessors of right reason and clear thinking, they at least have the good sense, and the good manners, to use their wit against their equals (as in the spirited exchanges at the beginning of 5.2) or against others, such as Armado, in their absence. They suspect that the young men are but playing with them, and so mask themselves for "sport" (5.2.153), playing the battle of wits with expertise. But when the time for games is over, only the women seem to notice the change. Neither the King nor Berowne speak directly to the Princess about the death of her father. The King stumbles through a speech that briefly mentions "the cloud of sorrow" (5.2.748), but that is so convoluted that even the Princess must confess, "I understand you not" (752). Berowne takes up the cause, "Honest plain words best pierce the ear of grief" (5.2.753), but then goes on to argue that the women are really responsible for the men's failing to keep their vows. Both the King and Berowne assume that speaking of love is not only desired, but appropriate for a woman who has just learned of her father's death! The self-centeredness of such an assumption (matched perhaps by Capulet's assumption that the announcement of her marriage to Paris will cure Juliet's sorrow) is stunning. The Princess deals with it gracefully, first explaining why the women thought the men were simply engaged in "merriment" (5.2.784), and then reminding them that the bond they seek is for "a world-without-end bargain" (5.2.789), No "o'er-hasty marriage" here, no failure to observe the proper forms of mourning.

Though the denouement may seem to disappoint some of the characters, it does not frustrate the audience. We recognize that the Princess is right, that the men's love needs the trial she sets up and that the appropriate course is indeed to wait. Moreover, the play ends not only with the setting up of the conditions that the suitors must meet, but with "the dialogue that the two learned men have compiled in praise of the owl and cuckoo" (5.2.885–87). Many scholars have written beautifully and movingly of the two songs that end the play,[24] but let me comment on the theatrical effect of this ending. Those who reappear are, for the most part, those who have been scorned and embarrassed: Armado, forced to confess that he has carried around Jaquenetta's "dishclout;" Jaquenetta, revealed as pregnant; Holofernes and Nathaniel, both driven from the stage, one by taunts from the audience, the other by his own confusion. Only Moth and Costard might well relish the return, and we can only guess at Dull's feelings. The important point is that this time around, the onstage audience *listens*. They do not interrupt with wisecracks and insults, but remain silent—and in that silence, they offer the former Worthies a worthy tribute. The harmony created by the songs thus works on many levels: the balance implied by songs of both spring and winter; the balance within each song of images both pleasing and harsh; and the harmony implied by the music that may accompany the words or by the music of the words themselves. But there is also the harmony of a stage full of people who are, for the moment, willing to accept each other. The "actors" perform without mishap. The audience attends. Surely the theatrical moment offers an image of community, however briefly it may last.

Yet, however much one may praise the subtlety of the ending of *Love's Labor's Lost* and its resonances for today's audiences, the question of the play's verbal extravagance still remains an issue. Directors may still ask, as Granville-Barker did, "how much of the stuff can any modern audience be brought to understand—even to understand, enjoyment apart?" Granville-Barker leans towards cutting passages that he finds unplayable, such as "Moth's pleasantries about the five vowels and the horn-book" (5.1.) and suggests: "If ever a passage could serve in a competition with a prize given to the set of actors that extracted some legitimate effect from it, this could!" Or he proposes a kind of operatic treatment, noting "we mostly miss the words of the *aria* as a rule." In some cases, as Granville-Barker notes, the incomprehensibility seems to be the point: "As to Holofernes and Sir Nathaniel, it is a good part of the fun of them that neither the innocent Dull, nor we, can make out half the time what they are talking about."[25]

But there are stronger ways of defending the style of *Love's Labor's Lost*, one primarily in terms of theme and the other of character. The thematic reading has long been recognized, namely that this play is about the abuse of language as well as its use, that Armado and Holofernes and Nathaniel may well represent the horrifying extreme to which language may go when speakers think more of effect than of meaning. Certainly Berowne's offer in the middle of the last scene to forswear "Taffata phrases, silken terms precise, / Three-piled hyperboles, spruce affectation, / Figures pedantical" (5.2.406–8) and his promise to woo with "russet yeas and honest kersey noes" (5.2.413) imply that he sees the extent to which language may falsify through its own glittering surface. Ralph Berry has argued that the young men "undermine words, for they see words as projections of their personal whims."[26] While Berry distinguishes between the King and Berowne ("The King wants words to mean what he wants them to mean; Berowne has the opposite tendency, the star debater's readiness to deploy words in any cause, for or against"), he sees both sharing a "common penance," "to learn the meaning of oaths, hence of words in general, and to see re-asserted their status as symbols of reality."[27]

Another way to see the relationship of language and reality is to approach the issue from within the character, adopting Stanislavsky's central idea: "Inside each and every word there is an emotion, a thought, that produced the word and justifies its being there."[28] Thus, language reflects not only the self the speaker wishes to present, but also a hidden self. In *Love's Labor's Lost*, Armado seeks to show himself as refined and witty through his elaborate circumlocutions in the letter to the King and through his conversation with Moth, but when he attempts to speak to Jaquenetta, he falls into monosyllabic confusion. Holofernes and Nathaniel show off their educated, Latinate vocabulary, both for Dull (who cannot understand it) and for Armado (who can), but when they meet a hostile audience, as they do at the Pageant of the Nine Worthies, their vocabulary changes noticeably; Nathaniel can only falteringly repeat the opening lines of Alexander's speech, while Holofernes, after a few attempts to deflect the insults of Berowne, Boyet, Dumaine, and Longaville with wit, retreats into silence. When he finally leaves, he does so with a line that is utterly straightforward: "This is not generous, not gentle, not humble" (5.2.629). The sentence follows the tripartite repetition we have come to expect from Holofernes, but the simplicity of the language makes the rebuke much more telling. With all of these men, we hear moments when the elaborate language vanishes, and something more genuine is revealed.

Separating mask and reality is much more difficult with the four courtiers. But the various articles of the oath that Berowne reads out dwell so much on the exclusion of women that one begins to suspect avoidance as well. We never see the men attempt to study or to fast, but we hear much about their attempts to keep women away. Berowne's description of women, once he admits that he is "forsooth, in love!" (3.1.174), emphasizes the notion that one must watch them carefully to keep them in "frame" or "in order":

> A woman, that is like a German clock,
> Still a-repairing, ever out of frame,
> And never going aright, being a watch,
> But being watched that it may still go right.
>
> (3.1.190–93)

Furthermore, he calls Rosaline a "whitely wanton," and "one that will do the deed, / Though Argus were her eunuch and her guard!" (3.1.196–99). Thus, he imagines her propensity for sexual misconduct, no matter how closely she is watched, but it's difficult to know if this is sexual fear or sexual fantasy, or perhaps a mixture of both. Whatever his feelings, it is significant that he sees a love relationship as one in which he will be deceived and conquered, either by the woman herself or by the force of Cupid. The puns on hunting the deer/dear rebound on Berowne himself: "The king he is hunting the deer; I am coursing myself. They have pitched a toil; I am toiling in a pitch—pitch that defiles" (4.3.1–3). Most significantly, the men never seem able to speak to the women directly. They ask questions of Boyet, they write sonnets, they send letters and presents, and when they finally appear, they disguise themselves as Muscovites. Only Berowne is willing to initiate a conversation with Rosaline, and that begins with yet another mask as he pretends that he doesn't quite recognize her. The ploy is not successful:

Berowne: Did not I dance with you in Brabant once?
Rosaline: Did not I dance with you in Brabant once?
Berowne: I know you did.
Rosaline: How needless was it then
            To ask the question!
                                                          (2.1.114–17)

Only when Rosaline specifically refers to Berowne as masked, "Which of the vizards was it that you wore?" (5.2.385), and indicates that she knows they were the Muscovites, does Berowne accept that the women know the truth.

The men's behavior and their language can thus be read as disguises worn unconsciously to hide their feelings and fears. Such an interpretation became explicit in John Barton's 1978 Stratford production, a production in whose rehearsals Barton said "Think Chekhov."[29] What Barton meant was not that the play was really a nineteenth-century play, but that "the linguistic surface functions as a kind of verbal disguise, masking feeling and an ability to speak one's true thoughts."[30] To emphasize both kinds of disguise, he cast very different actors for the two leading courtiers. Michael Pennington's Berowne, clearly a "leading man," was slender, witty, deft in his language and his movements, whether swinging gracefully over a huge branch bent to form a rustic bench, or hiding his feelings from Jane Lapotaire's clever Rosaline. But Richard Griffiths' King was tubby, bespectacled, and unaccustomed to speaking blank verse: to hear the King dither his way through the minefields of his interchange with Costard about a wench-damsel-virgin-maid (1.1.281ff.) was to know immediately just how inept he would be when actually looking at a woman rather than merely talking about one—and to sense the fear of women that motivates the oath. Thus, in Barton's production, language was not artificial or decorative, but the characters' response to their impulses and feelings.

In the last fifty years, *Love's Labor's Lost* has found many reincarnations, on stage, in critical articles, and in the classroom; Felicia Hardison Londré notes "over ninety revivals"[31] during the period 1946 to 1986. Brook's production influenced later ones not only through the power of its ending, but also through the creation of a beautiful—and artificial—world into which the messenger of death would arrive with particularly devastating effect. Brook chose the elegant society depicted by Watteau and Lancret as the visual representation of *Love's Labor's Lost's* courtly world, a choice echoed by Elijah Moshinsky for the 1984 BBC television version, while Michael Langham's designer at the Guthrie (Minneapolis, 1974) dressed the courtiers in costumes based on Fragonard, an inheritor of the Watteau tradition. Other productions have similarly turned to painting, with Hugh Hunt (at the Old Vic, 1949) using a backcloth similar to those in Elizabethan miniature paintings. Barry Kyle (Stratford-upon-Avon, 1984) and Terry Hands (Stratford-upon-Avon, 1990) and their designers were clearly inspired by nineteenth-century French painting: the 1990 production began with a version of Manet's "Déjeuner sur l'Herbe," showing us the four young men lounging around a tablecloth laden with food, and dressed in costumes that evoke Manet's painting. And even when the design does not allude to particular painters, it has become almost "traditional" to set the play in some sort of glamorous world such as the Edwardian university setting of Albert Marre's 1953 production (New York City Center), or Ian Judge's 1993 production (Stratford-upon-Avon). The most contemporary setting of the play (Stratford, Connecticut, 1968), picturing Berowne, Dumaine, and Longaville as pop stars going off to study with an Indian guru (the King of Navarre), opened less than five months after the Beatles had flown to India to study with the Maharishi; costume designs came from recent issues of *Vogue* magazine; Costard sported a button, "Make Love Not War" and yelled "Police Brutality" when Dull and Berowne marched him offstage. Even in this interpolated comic moment, Kahn's production was strikingly contemporary; in August 1968, when I saw the production, "police brutality" was the sobering reality played out at the Democratic National Convention.

Just as modern productions have defined a recognizable social world for *Love's Labor's Lost,* so too they have revealed characters who are less "artificial" and more believable. John Barton's 1978 production extended serious attention not only to the four pairs of lovers, but also to the so-called "comic characters": if Michael Hordern's Don Armado had elements of Lewis Carroll's White Knight, he also reminded audiences of Don Quixote. The pomposity of Paul Brook's Holofernes was somehow lightened by the obvious admiration David Suchet's Nathaniel had for everything Holofernes said. And, most importantly, the wisecracks of the young men at the expense of the Worthies became the real, if unacknowledged, explanation for the separation of the men and the women at the end. To watch Berowne reach for Rosaline's hand at the end, after she had ordered him to make jokes in a hospital and to have her move away, was to understand, in silence, Berowne's failure of understanding and the rightness of Rosaline's demands.

By making the characters people we must listen to—not only in admiration of their rhetorical skill, but with an awareness of what that skill may hide—Barton's achievement was to make the play's language highly playable. John Oxenford's delight in Holofernes' pedantry in 1857 finds a contemporary echo when Michael Billington commented on David Suchet's Nathaniel: "the biggest laugh of the evening comes when the curate, Sir Nathaniel, is paying homage to the pedantic Holofernes and dubs him 'learned without opinion'."[32] Billington exaggerates slightly, since Suchet actually got the biggest laugh of the evening by descending slowly underneath the weight of the huge hobbyhorse he wore/rode as Alexander the Great, visible finally as only a pair of feet scrabbling under the horse and audible as a small plaintive voice repeating "When in the world I lived, I was the world's commander." The moment blended farce and pathos, a visual image totally at war with the heroic line—a mixture of emotions that the play seems able to evoke throughout. The rediscovery of those manifold possibilities within a play once thought so obscure that it disappeared from theater history for two hundred years surely suggests that love's labor is not lost.

NOTES

1. *Shakespeare in Performance: Love's Labor's Lost,* Manchester University Press, 1993.

2. *The Students* (reprint, London: Cornmarket Press, 1969). All quotations from the adaptation are from this edition.

3. Clifford John Williams, *Madame Vestris: A Theatrical Biography* (London: Sidgwick and Jackson, 1973), 155.

4. One might note that in the twentieth century, none of the three major British actors associated with professional productions of Shakespeare (Ralph Richardson, John Gielgud, and Laurence Olivier) ever acted in this play, though Olivier directed it for the National Theatre in 1972.

5. Quoted in W. May Phelps and John Forbes-Robertson, *The Life and Life-Work of Samuel Phelps* (London, 1886), 165.

6. Ibid.

7. Quoted in W. May Phelps and John Forbes-Robertson, *The Life and Life-Work of Samuel Phelps* (London, 1886), 165.

8. Ibid.

9. Samuel Johnson, *Johnson on Shakespeare*, ed. Arthur Sherbo (New Haven: Yale University Press, 1968), 287.

10. Similarly Johnson argues against Hanmer's emendation of the Princess's line, "'Tis deadly sin to keep that oath, my Lord; / And sin to break it" [Hanmer read "not sin to break it"] by insisting "The Princess shews an inconvenience very frequently attending rash oaths, which whether kept or broken produce guilt" (p. 269). The issue of oath-breaking was clearly one that Johnson took seriously and that he is at pains to point out in his notes, bringing up the point on three separate occasions.

11. H. B. Charlton, *Shakespearian Comedy* (London: Methuen, 1938), 45, 46.

12. Ibid., 47.

13. Ibid., 272, 273, 274.

14. Harley Granville-Barker, *Prefaces to Shakespeare* (Princeton, New Jersey: Princeton University Press, 1946), 20.

15. Ibid., 29, 30.

16. Ibid., 14.

17. Audrey Williamson, *Old Vic Drama* (London: Rockliff, 1948), 58.

18. Peter Brook, *The Shifting Point* (New York: Harper and Row, 1987), 11, 12.

19. J. C. Trewin, *Peter Brook: A Biography* (London: Macdonald and Company, 1971), 26.

20. Priscilla B. Shaw in *Shakespeare Around the Globe*, ed. Samuel L. Leiter (New York: Greenwood Press, 1986), 341.

21. Bobbyann Roesen, *Love's Labor's Lost*, Shakespeare Quarterly, 4 (1953), 411.

22. Ibid., 412, 425.

23. The fourth act of *The Winter's Tale* may be set in early or middle summer, but the metaphoric season of the ending is spring, as is evident in Leontes' greeting to Florizel and Perdita: "Welcome hither, / As is the spring to th'earth!" (5.1.151–52).

24. In addition to Anne Barton, I think particularly of the final chapter of William C. Carroll's *The Great Feast of Language in Love's Labor's Lost* (Princeton, New Jersey: Princeton University Press, 1976).

25. Granville-Barker, 33, 32, 33.

26. Ralph Berry, "The Words of Mercury," *Shakespeare Survey* 22 (1969): 69.

27. Ibid., 71.

28. Constantin Stanislavsky, *Creating a Role*. A Theatre Arts Book, ed. Her-

mine I. Popper, trans. Elizabeth Reynolds Hapgood (New York: Routledge, 1961), 94.

29. Quoted by Barbara Hodgdon, "Rehearsal Process as Critical Practice: John Barton's 1978 *Love's Labor's Lost,*" *Theatre History Studies,* 8 (1988): 16.

30. Ibid., 17.

31. *Shakespeare Around the Globe,* 335.

32. Michael Billington, Review of *Love's Labor's Lost, The Guardian,* 14 August 1978.

Kate, Bianca, Ruth, and Sarah:
Playing the Woman's Part in *The Taming of the Shrew*

Carol Rutter

> *Mess.* Your honor's players, hearing your amendment,
> Are come to play a pleasant comedy. . . .
> . . . .
> *Sly.* Is not a comonty a Christmas gambold, or a tumbling-trick?
> *Page.* No, my good lord, it is more pleasing stuff.
> *Sly.* What, household stuff?
> *Page.* It is a kind of history.
>
> (Ind. 2.129–30 and 137–41)

LIKE Polonius trying to pin down the play at Elsinore, *The Taming of the Shrew* makes several stabs at fixing its own genre. But while the self-appointed master of the Danish revels has a clear political interest in mastering those revels (since to contain a play inside a genre is in some way to authorize its reception and to limit the audience's options for interpreting it), *Shrew*'s indecisiveness seems innocent of politics. Maybe the play doesn't know what to make of itself. Maybe it needs to wait and see what the audience will make of it.

Now, *The Murder of Gonzago* plays a joke on the censor ("Have you heard the argument? Is there no offence in't?"— 3.2.232–33): it evades his authorization. Not even "tragical-comical-historical-pastoral" (2.2.398–99) covers the subversive farce *Gonzago* turns into as *The Mousetrap*. The play resists establishment attempts to license it, to make it safe for royal consumption as comedy or tragedy or history or even as fiction. And this is instructive. Always, everywhere, Shakespeare's play resists containment. His play is never safe. As Louis Montrose has argued, the purpose of playing in a theater that occupied the

176

margins of Elizabethan culture (its site the suburbs, the licentious liberties, but its site, too, a magic circle, a wooden O) was
reflexive and conservative, but certainly also revolutionary. A
"plaything" reproduces culture but likewise generates culture. It
plays out marginal experiences that invert or interrogate structural norms and so provokes thought, but more than that, through
the process of enactment, it offers patterns for action—alternative options—that can be projected and tested in the 'safe' space
the theater encloses. The play liberates audiences from their
usual constraints. It makes cultural innovation possible. And the
tension it explores between the conservative and the innovative,
the reactionary and the revolutionary, the orthodox and the dissident are not just fundamental to the theater, but to Elizabethan
society as well. For Montrose, "the Elizabethan playhouse, playwright, and player exemplify the contradictions of Elizabethan
society and make those contradictions their subject."[1]

It is just this contradiction-at-the-core that John Arden was
beginning to detect when he "wrote that there were so many
corrections to the view of Agincourt as a lovely war within the
structure of Henry V that 'one is forced to wonder if the author
had not written a secret play inside the official one.'"[2] Arden
might have gone further. Given the material conditions of their
original production, every authorized play by Shakespeare con-
ceals an anti-play, a Mousetrap to interrogate, subvert, and finally
perhaps erase Gonzago. And since Shakespeare's plays continue
to intervene in culture, to make new meanings impacting upon
new audiences in subsequent performances, the challenge for
subsequent performers is to be alert not just to Shakespeare's
original "secret" play, but to discover ways of disclosing its subsequent secret alternatives.

I want to relate these ideas to The Taming of the Shrew first
by looking at Shakespeare's original play and performance texts
to decipher the "secret" Shrew I think is encoded in his ambitious, dissident script of 1592 and then by considering how, four
hundred years later, a handful of today's actors, working at the
Royal Shakespeare Company, have interpreted its women's roles.
How does Kate negotiate her final speech when 1592 speaks in
1992? If Shakespeare's original subversions are lost to us because
we no longer recognize the play's interrogation of contemporary
cultural practice, does our remake of Shrew still have power to
provoke new interrogations born out of the agitated, not to say
abrasive, relationship between modern female consciousness
and Elizabethan text? Is this play in our time one that knows

more than it speaks: is it, as Fiona Shaw, who played Kate in 1987, thought "underwritten and overendowed"?[3]

I shall claim that it is the Induction that gives access both to Shakespeare's *Shrew* and to ours. The Induction invites the audience of 1592 to decipher an anti-play that is an Elizabethan subversion of the conventional shrew-taming story. But the Induction likewise cannily predicts the play's reproduction and reception four hundred years after its original performance: in our own time, under feminist scrutiny, the "pleasant comedy" announced by the Messenger in the Induction (authorized to call it a comedy, one supposes, by the players themselves) has increasingly been seen as a "kind of history," an intervention in and interrogation of women's history, and not at all innocent of politics. Indeed, I want to suggest that a modern actor—and I will focus this suggestion on Shaw's performance—may only survive the ideological consequences of Shakespeare's original text for Kate by finding a way of deconstructing her own performance by simultaneously playing a critique of it. For Kate and her sisters in 1992—Bianca, Ruth, and Sarah (of whom more anon)—*Shrew* has become a very serious play indeed.

This, of course, has not always been the case, and so, to set up my double project of putting our *Shrew* against Shakespeare's, I will survey some recent performance history that makes my radical claims for anti-plays and secret *Shrews* sound about as serious as Dormouse's chat at the Mad Hatter's tea party because for thirty years the postwar Royal Shakespeare Theatre (or Shakespeare Memorial Theatre as it was known until 1961) played the "official" *Shrew* as "a gambold." In 1948, directed by Michael Benthall with Anthony Quayle and Diana Wynward, it was "a farce," "a boisterous romp": the traveling players were a Crazy Gang dressed in costumes grabbed indiscriminately from their touring skips so that scenes from *Trelawney of the Wells* intercut with *Supper with the Borgias*, and Kate looked like a cowgirl. (This Wild West image, with the cultural license or apology it seems to have stereotyped in postwar Britain, would reappear in two subsequent productions of the play, twenty years later.) An aspidistra pot cracked over Petruchio's head, custard pies flew, the Pedant unwrapped fish and chips.[4] In 1953, George Devine's *Shrew* was a "rowdy, knockabout piece of puppet fun, fast and coarse and common." And Stratford-upon-Avon, "filled with American and Empire tourists" (certain cultural assumptions, with implications for theater production, evidently load that parenthetical remark) was "delighted to find such simple fun. . . .

slapstick in a gilded frame."[5] A year later, Devine's production was revived, "broader, racier, more rumbustious than ever," with a "vigorous Petruchio" (Keith Michell) and a "spitfirish and louring" Kate (Barbara Jefford) who, "truly tamed" at the end, spoke "her one lovely speech with splendid assurance."[6] Publicity photographs showed her biting Petruchio's arm in the wooing scene and flung surprised and perhaps delighted over his shoulder, making her exit from the wedding. "Love is the Winner" proclaimed one review headline. But another disagreed: "the play itself is certainly not Shakespeare's funniest. In fact, it is a rather unedifying farce showing how a spirited young woman may be beaten and starved into submission." Two sentences into what sounds like a commitment to a serious *Shrew* and to a realignment of its sexual politics, though, and this review collapses into facetiousness: "it is also a little out of date. Nowadays we do not tame our shrews; we make them waitresses or elect them to Parliament." The unexamined, indeed unconscious, class and gender assumptions embedded in that universalized, masculine 'we' betray the reviewer's politics. He is not, after all, so very different in his requirements for the play than his fellow critic who approved of the production's "sweet Bianca . . . full of melting ruth and maidenly wile . . . like a rose in June sun."[7]

Even when Peggy Ashcroft played Kate in 1960, *Shrew* was comically romanticized. (She was fifty-three, at the peak of her power with the Royal Shakespeare Company, and with a near-complete string of leading roles behind her from Juliet and Rosalind to Desdemona. Her twenty-eight-year-old Petruchio was a newcomer to the company, Peter O'Toole.) "Giving the impression that she is not minding her rough usage so very much," this "scold reluctantly in love" came, in the wooing scene, "within an inch of a kiss that would make the play's second part unnecessary."[8] John Barton, like directors before him, fictionalized the taming play, emphasizing its status as "merely" play-within-a-play. But where Benthall and Devine had made the traveling players farceurs and their taming gags remote from real matrimonial lives anywhere, Barton employed a different distancing strategy. His players, and so inevitably their play, belonged to a former time: "a great deal is made of the fact that we are witnessing strolling players." What they performed, "in lavishly comic detail," was "a gently amusing antiquarian spectacle."[9]

Still, whatever comic delicacy Barton's production may have achieved for the play was abandoned a year later. His production was revived, redirected, recast: Vanessa Redgrave played Kate, but reviewers found her too English a shrew. One critic wanted someone "outrageous" in the role and longed for Maria Callas, "a shrew worth taming," a shrew whose shoe, aimed at Petruchio's head, would be lethal, not caught. Here was another *Shrew* placed "firmly in the tradition of the Royal Shakespeare Theatre Company's policy of all laughing, all falling down, all slapstick, all good clean fun for the kiddies."[10]

Was there then a company production policy on *Shrew*? Never officially. But in practice? In 1967, Trevor Nunn, who the following year would be named Artistic Director of the Royal Shakespeare Company, directed the play. He set it "in Padua, Arizona." A "horse opera," "a lark gone whole hog," it had a "superbly virile [sic] Kate," Janet Suzman, whose shrewishness was "but a cloak to waiting love" and a Petruchio in a ten-gallon hat (the rather diminutive Michael Williams) whose ripe-as-an-apple face exuded "friendly mischievousness" and whose speech had a "happiness which makes Petruchio into a chastising angel." Clearly, this "most outrageously knockabout production ever staged" was doing nothing to unsettle the play's production history as "gambold."[11]

By the time the next Royal Shakespeare Company *Shrew* came along, in 1973, the world had clearly shifted one or two degrees: one headline noted (with incredulity? relief? sarcasm?) "And Never a Whisper of Women's Lib." Whether in support or in reaction, reviewers had in place a new set of assumptions, a new vocabulary to discuss a play whose meaning was in the process of being reconstructed. Eric Shorter in *The Daily Telegraph* referred to a performance history that had been written in theaters other than the one in Stratford over the previous five years when he began, "Most revivals of *The Taming of the Shrew* suppose that it is all about the vexed old question of the place of women in society." That "Clifford Williams' production . . . supposes nothing of the sort" showed the director ducking the new agenda.[12]

By making *Shrew* yet again into "an anthology of funny business," Williams was suspected of trying "to take the offensiveness out of the play." "The trouble is," said Michael Billington in *The Guardian*, "he has removed much of its point at the same time."[13] In *The Times*, Irving Wardle reviewed some of the well-worn strategies that had always served to contain what was now being seen as the issue of the play—its disruptive sexual politics: "by directors and reviewers alike, some apology always has to be made for this play. An unshakable popular favourite, it carries a moral repugnant to all except wife-beaters. There are several ways of getting around this. One old ruse was to pretend that Kate and Petruchio are in love from the start and that their fight is only a game. Then there was Jonathan Miller's interesting conversion of the comedy into a Puritan polemic; and the Wild West treatment it had last time round at Stratford." Williams' innovation was evidently to pretend that the past decade hadn't happened: his "approach is to brush the sexual politics aside. Whether you agree with male domination or not, the wife-taming scenes are fun to watch; so play those for all they are worth, and treat the whole thing as a joke unconnected with life outside."[14] Wardle's contempt is unconcealed.

"Life outside" was impinging ever more clamorously on Stratford's theater. Miller's reading of Puritan history, a *past* life outside, had informed his direction of *Shrew* (at Chichester in 1972, with Anthony Hopkins as Petruchio). By historicizing the Calvinist ideology of "sovereign authority" ordained to manage an earth made unruly by the fall of man, Miller was able to "represent Petruchio as a serious man," to "develop the implications of lines such as 'To me she's married, not unto my clothes,'" and to render the taming not as "the bullying and subordination of an otherwise high-spirited girl, but [as] a course of tuition as a result of which Kate learns the necessity of obedience."[15]

A more calculatedly shocking version of "life outside" came up against the play when Charles Marowitz opened his version of *Shrew* at the Open Space, one of the first London fringe theaters, barely a month after Williams' fatuous production opened in Stratford. Reviewing it, Nicholas de Jongh saw Shakespeare's version as "in some sense . . . [his] cruellest play; a Tudor vision of women as property and reduced to attitudes of submission and humiliation." Marowitz's remake "totally subverted and changed the tone of the original." Marowitz hijacked the Bianca plot, reworking it into a series of counterpointed scenes between a stereotypical '70s couple, a middle-class girl and her working-class bloke. Kate and Petruchio's story was played out on "a bare grey stage" in "quiet menace and uneasy silence." At first "sour and rigid," Kate "achieves a shuddering sexual tension, giving the idea of a woman who understands the game played and her attraction to him; scorn giving way to anxiety." This Kate's final submission was to rape. The sun and moon scene had brought her to mental meltdown: "a high-pitched crescendo whistle is heard inside her head which the audience also hears," says the stage direction. "It builds to an impossible pitch and then something snaps. All lights go red."[16] The text reverts to Sly's Induction. When Kate, speaking Bartholomew, the Page's, lines, excuses herself from the order to undress and come to bed, her father exclaims, "O monstrous arrogance!" and, as Marowitz's stage directions have it, "Kate is backed over to the table and then thrown down over it. Her servants and BAPTISTA hold her wrists to keep her secure. PETRUCHIO looms up behind and whips up her skirts ready to do buggery. As he inserts, an ear-piercing, electronic whistle rises to a crescendo pitch. KATE's mouth is wild and open, and it appears as if the impossible sound is issuing from her lungs. Black out." As de Jongh observed, this "climax" was "more legitimate than the original's uneasy reconciling mood." When the lights came up, Kate's final speech of "supposed joy [was] here a masterpiece of dramatic irony. She delivers it haggard and handcuffed in chains before an inquisitorial Petruchio, who prompts her words when grief and pain intermit. As she does this, the contemporary young couple who have played their seduction games emerge before us, smiling at the altar." Thelma Holt's Kate was "a major performance of astounding, tragic dimensions," and Marowitz's "gothic tragedy" adaptation made the shocking suggestion, by contemporary parallels, that violation, violence, power play, and class oppression were secretly situated in Shakespeare's original text.[17]

SHAKESPEARE'S PLAY AND PERFORMANCE TEXTS

From opposite ends of a time-line, Miller and Marowitz were requiring audiences to look at what had until then been a "secret" play, The Taming of the Shrew as "a kind of history." Coincidentally, a first wave of feminist academic writers were crashing the gates of the university's ivory tower, most clamorously in the United States, and part of their project in historicizing a patriarchal bard was to recuperate a historicized Shrew.[18] Subsequent Shrews were not unaffected. They imitated or reacted. In 1978, like Marowitz, Michael Bogdanov superimposed contemporary images upon the taming play; in 1982, Barry Kyle directed an amnesiac, not to say mindless, romp; in 1987, invited for the first time to direct for the Royal Shakespeare Company, Miller revived from 1973 (and from 1980) yet another Puritan-informed Shrew.[19] But neither Miller, who in three attempts with the play always cut the Induction as tedious and unplayable, nor

Marowitz, whose declared project was to deconstruct Shakespeare's play, took on the implications of the full playtext or the performance text it directs. By cutting, they isolated Kate from the very performance strategies that make the taming play subversive in the original.

I want to argue that that original contained its own subversions. Their abstract stands in the title, The Taming of the Shrew, which, like Shakespeare's other comic titles, begins by authorizing a view of the play that develops fault lines as things proceed, fissures for interpretation to pry into and maybe prize open the meaning of the play. A Midsummer's Night's Dream isn't a dream at all, unless, as Puck suggests, the audience reinvent it as their dream. The Tempest's tempest doesn't happen: it's only a conjuror's trick. But then so too is Prospero's wedding masque (and the wedding?) and the theater, the great Globe itself. The tale of The Winter's Tale is suppressed, whispered into Hermione's ear. Twelfth Night plays metaphorically with itself as does The Two 'Gentle Men' of Verona.

Equally, The Taming of the Shrew turns more and more inquisitively on its own terms. In the shrew-taming literature, and in the private domestic histories that are the sources of this play, the shrew is gendered female. Shakespeare's play supposes Kate to be the shrew (Gascoigne's Supposes is another of Shakespeare's sources). Then, in an astonishing displacement, the shrew is re-gendered. Petruchio is "more shrew than she": he "kills her in her own humour" (4.1.85, 180).

The scold is by definition a noisy woman. Her distinguishing attribute is "a chattering tongue," which, "headstrong," she refuses to "curb" (two equestrian images). To silence her, to manage (menage) her, the curb or bit is put into her mouth as into a horse's mouth. It sits upon her tongue (figuratively, but literally when a woman is punished by imposition of a scold's bridle[20]). But here again Shakespeare's scenario subverts convention. If "shrew" = "noisy one," Kate is an odd shrew, indeed an impossible shrew. She has almost nothing to say. And Shakespeare, making a theatrical point of her silence, turns the contour of her play back to front: a shrew is tamed when the scolding woman is beaten, starved, humiliated, brutalized into silence, as the contemporary Geste of a Shrewd and Curst Wife lapp'd in Morrell's Skin documents with relish.[21] But Shakespeare's play brings the silent shrew to speech. At the end, Kate' performance text places her at the focal center of the scene as her playtext has her talk and talk and talk and talk. It is her last speech in the play, and it is the longest speech in the play.[22] Moreover, she has been invited to speak it by the actual "noisy one," the shrew Petruchio, who has spoken nonstop throughout, but who here falls silent, himself speechless—the taming of the shrew? In short, the performance of Kate's submission speech challenges the orthodoxy of its content while occupying a theater space that allows both the conservative and the revolutionary to resonate simultaneously. Reading the theater, the scene becomes an anamorph: it confirms the patriarchal status quo if eyed head-on; eyed awry, it distinguishes a new form, a cultural innovation.

The "taming" of The Taming of the Shrew experiences the same renegotiation. Shakespeare puts violence into the play: violence is the language the tamer in the ballads speaks to silence the woman's tongue. It is a language Petruchio has at his disposal. He cuffs Grumio, biffs his servants, turns the meat plate into a discus, disembowels (off stage) bolsters, and dismembers (on stage) a dress. The violence is contrived but also real: the tailor, beaten, does not know he is playing a walk-on part in Petruchio's impromptu. But the violence is also displaced: Kate observes it, but unlike her sisters in the ballads, she never experiences it. It is almost as if the violence is introduced to whet then disappoint the original audience's expectations.[23] For the tamer is going to tame his shrew not by fighting her but by playing her, by appropriating her tongue. Petruchio doesn't use his fists. He uses words.

In the plays Shakespeare was watching while he was writing Shrew—Tamburlaine, Dr Faustus, The Spanish Tragedy—Marlowe and Kyd were inventing a theater language of "working words," a language of omnipotence, of magical self-creation, of imagination, of power, that could, in the playhouse, literally get things done. But they were also exploring the futility of words, the ways words don't work, the way the word is merely the articulation of Babel, as in the final apocalypse of The Spanish Tragedy, spoken "in sundry languages," which plays out the defeat of words, but the triumph of theater. In Shrew Shakespeare is exploring both the effectiveness and theatricality of speech by way of the cultural icon whose distinguishing attribute is her abuse of speech. He takes the shrew's tongue and puts it in the tamer's mouth ("my tongue in your tail/[tale]") while demoting the tamer's violence to "play" (2.1.218).

Petruchio turns language upside down:

> Pray, have you not a daughter
> Call'd Katherina, fair and virtuous? (2.1.41–43)

Say that she rail, why then I'll tell her plain
She sings as sweetly as a nightingale. (2.1.170–71)

'Twas told me you were rough and coy and sullen,
And now I find report a very liar;
For thou art pleasant, gamesome, passing courteous. (2.1.243–45)

'Tis bargain'd 'twixt us twain, being alone,
That she shall still be curst in company.
I tell you 'tis incredible to believe
How much she loves me. (2.1.304–7)

Unfixing signifier from signified, Petruchio invents new selves, new realities. He rewrites the past and proleptically constructs the future; he generates fictions that stand as truths; through assertion he achieves the omnipotence of a Tamburlaine. And through subversion he subverts her subversion: "Say that she rail, why then I'll tell her . . ." The anarchic shrew is contained by one more anarchically shrewd than she, and the taming is redevised as disorientation. Petruchio's opening gambit ("Good morrow, Kate") commits an act of violence upon her name ("They call me Katherine that do talk of me") by chopping it in half to construct first a dainty "Kate" and then, with a pun on wildcat, "a wild Kate" (2.1.181, 184, 277). But Petruchio's opening gambit may also initiate a process of linguistic realignment that will erase labels like "shrew." In the taming play, Petruchio tests the patriarchal privilege, assigned to Adam in Eden, of naming all the animals and so controlling them because he controls the words that fix them. His deconstructions look backward, to test the Lord's power, in the Induction, of making Sly a Lord because he calls him one. In the sun and moon scene, that test will grow extreme.

Disorientation is the methodology of Petruchio's taming play, and the scenario it plays out over and over is a scenario of subversions of patriarchal structures, wrecking the very rituals the culture conventionalizes to legitimate itself. There are many Petruchios in Shrew—the "madcap ruffian" wooer; the "grumbling groom" who appears in "monster" apparel; the "master of what is mine own," who declares his wife "my goods, my chattels" (3.2.230) and then draws a weapon not to remove her at sword point, but to defend her from "thieves"; the irascible head of the household, who literally breaks meat; and the "careful" husband who will "deck" the beloved's body, replacing her wedding dress, that was wrecked by her fall from her horse into the mud, with a gorgeous new wedding dress, to wear to her sister's wedding, that is then wrecked in his argument with the tailor. All these Petruchios are playing out violent scenarios that challenge not Kate but cultural practices—wooing, wedding, bedding—that contain Kate and that incidentally write her down as "shrew."

In the taming play, such scenarios are played out comparatively in the double-plot structure. There are two wooings, two husbands, two futures. One sister is desired, the other disdained. One is conformist: her silence registers her exemplary "mild behaviour and sobriety." The other is "froward," "mad," a "fiend of hell." The monstrous sister gets a monstrous wooing from that "madcap ruffian" who shows up for the wedding in "monster apparel." The approved sister gets an approved courtship. But in playing the monstrous against the normative in scenes that stand back to back and that require the audience to observe alternatively, comparatively, Shakespeare's theater takes these ideas and stands them on their heads. Which is monstrous? Kate's scenario, or Bianca's?

The trajectory of Kate's wooing is from the *fait accompli*, the clap-hands-it's-a-bargain settlement, in only seven lines, of her dowry and her future, to the witty, lewd, disorientating "chat" with Petruchio, to the statement of his prerogative that leaves her speechless: "will you, nill you, I will marry you" (2.1.271). Petruchio barely observes the frame of custom—and that so scantly that Gremio mutters, "You are too blunt, go to it orderly" (2.1.45)—even as, astonishingly, he seems subversively to be rewriting the content of that wooing custom. By contrast, the negotiations that immediately ensue over Bianca's settlement play out normative social practice. She is not on stage when her father opens the bidding in a marriage auction that makes her the "prize," and "deeds" (as in "title deeds") the mechanism of exchange. Where Petruchio's blunt wooing worked iconoclastically in that earlier scene to unsettle, invert, and possibly open up some options, in this wooing, no one interrogates social practice. But the stage picture does. Its bizarre composition critiques the performance. Not only is Bianca physically displaced—her father is the theatrical object of the scene—but the ritual's conventional materialism is made ironic by spiraling inflation. Anyway, the whole thing is a fraud. Lucentio is Tranio in disguise. What he promises is a lie. Isn't *this* monstrous?

Ironically, Bianca will be achieved neither by the decrepit nor the fraudulent: she will shortly kick over the traces of social practice by improvising her own wooing games with a series of "monster" suitors, all in disguise. And then she will elope. With her "tutor." The sisters are of course opposites, but also doubles: when Kate is "rescued" from her wedding, leaving a gap in the feast, Bianca stands in, playing bride with a play groom, the fake Lucentio. Later, Kate will displace then upstage Bianca at her wedding feast. Bianca watched the fiasco of Kate's opening scene; Kate watches the delicious disaster played out around her sister's indiscretions in 5.1. Kate is schooled in gentleness; Bianca is schooled in "the Art to Love," ventriloquized as Latin grammar and the musician's gamut. (But Bianca masters her tutors. She rips up her gamut and conjugates verbs only in the imperative.) Kate is made a "falcon," a "haggard." So is Bianca. But Petruchio's metaphor registers mutuality, Hortensio's registers disgust.[24] Finally, one sister exits to bed; the other lingers, "sped," a new shrew whose resistance writes the labours of "great Hercules" (so Gremio titled Petruchio in 2.1.255) as no less illusory than the triumphs of "Richard Conqueror," recalled by Sly in the Induction (1.5). Kate leaves. Bianca remains. The shrew is never tamed.

This theatrical fact is almost as shocking as the way Shakespeare's play and performance texts repeatedly travesty wedding as a "monster" ritual. First there is Petruchio's arrival at the wedding with Grumio, "a monster, a very monster in apparel" (3.2.69–70). "Methinks you frown," observes Petruchio of the assembled guests. "Wherefore gaze this goodly company,/As if they saw some wondrous monument/ . . . comet . . . prodigy?" (93–96). Baptista calls his "habit" "shame to your estate,/ An eyesore to our solemn festival!" (100–101). Tranio, in Lucentio's clothes, scandalized by Petruchio's "unreverent robes," invites him to "put on clothes of mine" (112–13). Petruchio is a wreck. "But thus, I trust, you will not marry her," exclaims Baptista (115). But he does—and wrecks the ceremony too, as Gremio reports:

> when the priest
> Should ask if Katherine should be his wife,
> "Ay, by gog-wouns," quoth he, and swore so loud,
> That all amaz'd the priest let fall the book,
> And as he stoop'd again to take it up,
> The mad-brain'd bridegroom took him such a cuff
> That down fell priest and book, and book and priest.
> "Now take them up," quoth he, "if any list."

. . . .
                                he stamp'd and swore
. . . .
He calls for wine. "A health!" quoth he, as if
He had been aboard, carousing to his mates
After a storm, quaff'd off the muscadel,
And threw the sops all in the sexton's face
. . . .
This done, he took the bride about the neck,
And kiss'd her lips with such a clamorous smack
That at the parting all the church did echo.
And I , seeing this, came thence for very shame
. . . .
Such a mad marriage never was before.

                                                    (3.2.158–82)

Then he wrecks the feast—"I mean to take my leave" (188)—
and travesties the biblical formulation of the ordained relationship between man and wife—"She is my goods, my chattels"
(230)—by reinventing the moment not as Kate's defiance but as
an imagined assault upon her: "Grumio,/ Draw forth thy weapon,
we are beset with thieves" (235–36). As we the audience inspect
the wreckage that leaves Padua's pretensions so cruelly exposed
("To me she's married, not unto my clothes" [117]), we are required to decide: is it Kate who is mocked, or is it custom?

Inviting Kate to speak at the end, Petruchio may be representing, recuperating the disrupted wedding ritual. Lynda
Boose has found in Kate's prostration imagery ("place your
hands below your husband's foot" [1.2.177]), an allusion to
standard practice in the (obsolete) pre-Reformation marriage
ceremony.[25] But the wager Petruchio plays out with the other
husbands on the obedience of their wives is itself another theatrical re-presentation of ritual practice. "Wed" began its etymolog-
ical history meaning "to wager, stake (e.g., money, one's life, one's
head)."[26] To wed is to wager. So Petruchio's wager is another
wedding. This wedding, like the Ganymede-Orlando wedding in
As You Like It, takes place "on the fragile boundary between
carnival and blasphemy."[27] The Taming of the Shrew works to
unsettle male authority in ordaining such practices by reprodu-
cing patriarchal ritual as game.

And that idea—of game—has been with this play from its
opening moments: the rules of Shrew's performance-game are
taught by the Induction when the Lord enters from hunting, proposes a wager on his dogs, replaces that with a jest upon a drunk-

ard, engages his servants "to play our part" in a "pastime," a "sport," and then employs the players, who arrive coincidentally upon the scene, to make his game a play (70, 67, 91). The play takes over, so assertively indeed, that it eventually erases the Lord. Notoriously, in Shakespeare's *Folio* playtext, the frame never closes: the Lord's *Gonzago* is *Mousetrapped.* But before that happens, the Induction introduces performance as a complex signifier. Performance is a metaphor for cultural practice: it is what we do. But theatrically, performance is enactment, one of whose consequences might be the interrogation of that cultural practice.

When Christopher Sly comes reeling from the alehouse threatening violence upon the Hostess ("I'll pheeze you, in faith") and throwing himself upon history to legitimate himself ("the Slys are no rogues. Look in the chronicles; we came in with Richard Conqueror"), the audience is hearing the beginnings of ideas that will culminate in the taming play. Here, a woman is on top: "A pair of stocks, you rogue" (Ind. 1.1–5). The legitimating context of male power is a fiction: there was no Richard Conqueror. Sly falls down drunk. Such a stage picture of prostration may be replayed at the very end, when Kate volunteers the wife's hand beneath her husband's foot. Here, it suggests the repulsive metamorphosis that inspires the play of transformations to ensue. "O monstrous beast," observes the Lord. "How like a swine he lies!" (Ind. 1.34–35). He sets in motion a reverse metamorphosis, not man to beast but beast to Lord, as the taming play makes the woman a shrew, then a wife.

Carried home and dressed in rich, if borrowed, robes, transvestite Sly stops being Sly: "I'm a lord indeed/And not a tinker" (Ind. 2.72–73). He has been tutored in persuasive new realities by those who themselves were tutored by the Lord (Ind. 1.44–68) in the details of a command performance: the tutorial, as we shall see, will emerge as a major strategy in the taming play.

Another transvestite is summoned to play the woman's part to Sly's Lord:

> Sirrah, go you to Barthol'mew my page,
> And see him dress'd in all suits like a lady.
>
> (Ind. 1.105–6)

The performance required of Bartholomew contains both the cultural and theatrical significations I referred to earlier. Like a boy player, he must put on a costume to enact a role. But this role is devised in imitation of cultural role-play, a part, as the Lord's instructions make clear, constructed and deliberately played as a strategy for enacting the public roles of lord and lady. The woman's part is one that can be observed, learned, imitated, played:

> Tell him from me, as he will win my love,
> He bear himself with honourable action,
> Such as he hath observ'd in noble ladies
> Unto their lords, by them accomplished;
> Such duty to the drunkard let him do.
>
> (Ind. 1.109–13)

It is that word "action" that connects my two senses of performance, for action is what soldiers and politicians and men of action do. And action is what actors do too. The "honourable action" the Lord orders is called "duty" and can be "accomplished" that is, performed, by particular choreographed rituals in "real" life. But it can also be simulated by a boy player performing it as a role. Subversively then, the status of "duty" in the real world may be undercut by this association with fraudulence, an "action" that is, after all, only actorly. This understanding of cultural practice as performance has proleptic implications for the taming play. Kate and Bianca, actors themselves, may act cultural conformity in the fiction while the acting itself writes the action as dissidence, an act.

In the Lord's speech, approval and love are linked not just to obedience and commandment, but to integrity of the deception. The role-play must persuade. The plot against Christopher Sly depends upon it. But the plot demonstrates how entirely persuasive play is, how play may appropriate or displace real life. The Lord's hall is transformed into a playhouse. True things are commissioned by the fiction. The silver basin full of rose water becomes a stage prop. Clothes become costumes. The Lord plays a servant and casts his servants as impostors. (Such fictionalizing is reproduced in the taming play when a hat is made into a porridge bowl and Petruchio becomes the shrew.) In this deception, identity is presented as an aspect of theatricality: what you play is what you are, an unstable view of the self that is immediately literalized. The Sly plot is hardly out of the Lord's mouth when noises offstage announce the arrival of a cry of players. They offer duty, a play. But then also real-ize what might, confined to Sly, remain a marginal idea. The players' identities are theatrical, their truest selves are fictions, and their persuasiveness is a play of lies. Pointing to one of the company, the Lord says:

> This fellow I remember
> Since once he play'd the farmer's eldest son.
> 'Twas where you woo'd the gentlewoman so well.
> I have forgot your name; but sure that part
> Was aptly fitted and naturally perform'd.
>
> (Ind. 1.83–87)

"I have forgot your name" might invite the player to supply it; significantly, when he does, he gives not his own name, but the role's: "I think 'twas Soto that your honour means" (Ind. 1.88). The reticent player has no name. He is what he plays. And this offers him an enormous freedom of comic self-invention. But to be what you play is likewise potentially tragic if the self is a blank for others to write a name upon, like shrew, or is crushed inside a role, like shrew, whose performance is a playing out of cultural inevitabilities with no space for the improvisations that would renegotiate the role.

The Induction, then, is something of a bizarre hall of mirrors. The Lord is like Petruchio, but so is Sly, while Sly mirrors Kate, as Bartholomew does too. The issues of gender, class, privilege, hierarchy, and power that modern viewers of the play see so prominently here can be located in Shakespeare's original play and performance texts. But the idea Shakespeare's theater advances most insistently in the Induction is the idea of theatrical performance. Visibly, to perpetuate the fiction of the lording of Sly involves perpetrating the fiction of the taming of the shrew. These fictions mirror and inform each other. They play out each other's metaphors. They fix and then unfix each other's contexts. They are meaningful because they question each other, and they can go to dangerous extremes because role-play is their methodology. On this stage the players are all men. The traveling comedians enter as an all-male company; engaged by the Lord to play to Sly, they leave the stage to change into their costumes. When they return, the stage is wholly transvestite: Sly watches as Lord, Bartholomew as Lady, the Lord as servant. The player-Lucentio enters as *commedia* juvenile lead; the virile player, whom the Lord approved as Soto, perhaps comes on to play Kate. This Kate, like Sly, will be denied a return to his real life in Shakespeare's playtext as itinerant player. As *Gonzago* is *Mousetrapped*, so the

Sly play is Kated. "Her" last exit will be in role, as Kate leaving the taming play, not as the professional player who impersonates her leaving the Lord's play. Still, like Bartholomew, who never gets completely enclosed in "her" role-play, Kate never fully erases the player, the man in the role-play beneath the woman's part. All the men and women here are men. And because that is so, the gendered actions they role-play in *The Taming of the Shrew* can be all the more acutely inspected as cultural performance.[28]

"KATE WOZ HERE"

To play Kate four hundred years later in a (however uncertain) feminist age is to throw oneself onto the horns of a dilemma. The role has been reckoned a lead: to be invited to play it for the Royal Shakespeare Company, the authorized producer of Shakespeare in Britain today, is perhaps a first step up some hierarchy of roles toward Rosalind and Cleopatra. And despite a whispered consensus among such theater critics as Michael Billington and Irving Wardle that *Shrew*, as Billington put it, is the one play by Shakespeare that "should be placed firmly and squarely on the shelf" because, in Wardle's words, "it carries a moral repugnant to all except wife beaters," audiences still love it.[29] How, then, does a modern actor square her politics to the taming play? What sense can the actor make of Kate's final speech?

In 1987, Fiona Shaw found one solution and found it in a genre unimagined by Christopher Sly's Induction. She played *The Taming of the Shrew* as a problem play. Three weeks into rehearsal she had already struck the ambivalent tone of emotional assent and intellectual dissent that would characterize her performance. The play, she had concluded, was "glorious and perhaps irredeemable."[30] She wanted it to be glorious, perhaps, in the performance opportunities she rather hoped it would offer her as an actor. She feared it was irredeemable in belonging irrecoverably to an ideological past that could neither be represented accurately on the modern stage nor updated by discovering a transhistorical analogue: the play "resists being dragged into the late twentieth century and yet, left in its own time, it looks murky and bleak, as if the intervening centuries have placed a grid between them and us."

It was also, she felt, "over-endowed" with ideas, ideas that pressed on its own culture's nerve endings and certainly on our culture's nerve endings as well. But as far as Shaw could see, the big ideas in *Shrew* were ones that never got written. Instead, the model of its discourse might be extrapolated from that exchange in 4.3 when Kate claims language:

> Why, sir, I trust I may have leave to speak,
> And speak I will. I am no child, no babe;
>
> . . . .
>
> My tongue will tell the anger of my heart,
> Or else my heart concealing it will break,
> And rather than it shall, I will be free,
> Even to the uttermost, as I please, in words.
>
> (73–74, 77–80)

Petruchio responds, "Why, thou say'st true, it is [a] paltry cap" (81). The scene moves on.

In rehearsal Shaw became a shrewd analyst of *Shrew*, discovering that the play didn't "survive the analytical scrutiny of the later plays." Its problem was that "its subject is the relationship of the characters on stage and not an ideal world; its morality is historical rather than philosophical." Other comedies have a forest of Arden or a Belmont or a wood near Athens to site "wonder," and physical or verbal transformations work to idealize what, in those plays, begins, merely *begins*, as gritty urban realism. So fairy-speak hijacks Athenian literalism; Belmont transmutes the Rialto. A weaver, translated into an ass, translates experience into dream mystery; transvestite Portia rewrites law; transvestite Rosalind rewrites myth. The pull of the wonderful against the real in those plays prevents the audiences from overhistoricizing their fictions: we would be ill-advised to work out normative Elizabethan marriage practices or laws of inheritance from these plays. But *Shrew* seems to invite a different level of engagement. The only wonder it has to offer is the duping of Sly. In Kate's play, fictions of bourgeois urban life are unperturbed by encounters with exotics or immortals. Merchant meets pedant meets fortune hunter; sister meets sister meets suitor. *Shrew's* scenarios almost dare us to take it for documentary. Not until the play's closing couplet is the issue of wonder raised again, and this time it is attached to Kate and her submission. Closure gooses this play in the backside. Kate's act of conformity has just validated the patriarchy's claim to legitimacy. Her final speech real-izes those claims, authorizing male supremacy as, after all, the *status quo*, the natural law. But for two of the newly married men listening to that speech, male supremacy is no more real than Sly's dream. So while Kate makes her submission into "natural" conformity, Hortensio and Lucentio simultaneously unmake it, rewriting it as "a wonder":

> Hor. Now go thy ways, thou hast tam'd a curst shrew.
> Luc. 'Tis a wonder, by your leave, she will be tam'd so.
>
> (5.2.188–89)

Is the play, then, making realism, ironically, a wonder?

Shaw devised strategies for constructing her own performance by deconstructing the play's discourse. She contested her director's "unwavering, unthreatened view" (raided from L. P. Hartley's *The Go-Between*) of the "past as a foreign country" where "they do things differently," a view that imposed upon the production the need "to re-establish certain late-sixteenth-century 'givens' now lost to us." What were those givens? "The notion of sovereignty" was "crucial." So was the idea of "a hierarchical society where the superior has duties to those beneath him as much as vice versa."

Shaw's director was Jonathan Miller, then having a third go at *Shrew*. She was only partly aware that he was (yet again) recycling both a settled attitude toward the playtext and a settled reading of it, which caused him to make (as always) his first interpretative decision: the cutting of Christopher Sly's frame play. But the "certain givens" Miller felt bound to represent as recuperating the authorized Shakespearean *Shrew* were the same "certain givens" Shaw, the actor outside the role, felt bound to interrogate:

> What the play doesn't seem to deal with is if the very structure [of hierarchical society] is questionable. It stands as the Elizabethan model; that is how they functioned and organised themselves. So women—reactive or not—are not seeking a change in that structure, only a redefinition of their place within it. Kate's journey is one which moves, albeit unorthodoxly, from a position of such violent reaction as to be dangerously near finding no place in this immutable structure to a final reconciliation with it.

But since her own consciousness was "irrevocably suspicious of that structure," Shaw found it hard to believe

> that some Elizabethan women didn't balk at the square circle theology of Eve as a rib of Adam and its resonance through to husbands

as mini gods in the microcosm of the family. I say this only because women no matter what century experience themselves as fully human and any kind of developed intelligence can observe intelligence or its absence in another. So the success of this system must have needed women to collude with the notion of their own inferiority aided by various deprivations in rights while surviving by manipulating men-folk based on their own sense of superiority—a bleak view of the sixteenth century . . .

Like Kate facing a Petruchio in the wooing scene who would invent her future by rewriting her speech, Shaw in rehearsal faced a director who would invent her Kate by rewriting her (and her) history: Miller countered Shaw's objections with "rich illustrations of happiness between men and women in that time—sixteenth-century portraits showing mercantile wives contented, steady, and secure: carvings on the graves of Cotswold churches of united husbands and wives; [and] general optimism . . . about the possibilities of companionship and mutuality in marriage."

Only Miller then evoked the pastness of this past promiscuously.[31] Having cut Christopher Sly, he denied the shrew-taming play its metatheatrical brush with that ontologically superior "kind of history." Setting the production in Elizabethan costume, around Elizabethan images, as if the play were a sixteenth-century domestic portrait, he declined to see that while the female face that stares out of the portrait is a woman's, the female face gazing out of the Elizabethan play is not. The boy player who first played Kate had a double layer of role-play (playing a player playing Kate to Sly) standing between himself and his performance. Fiona Shaw playing Kate did not. The role became personalized; Shaw began to see herself and Kate as inscriptions of each other as the actor's journey in rehearsal mapped itself onto the character's journey in the fiction. Shaw and Kate became *alter egos*:

I found myself feeling very protective of womankind in relation to the play, and in rehearsal, being watchful. Women have a regular crisis in rehearsal rooms because you're often the only woman there. The Kate I played saw things in monochrome. And my performance was partly due to the rehearsal period. I was conscious of wanting to radiate that terribly clouded confusion that overwhelms you when you're the only woman around. That was Kate's position. And it was mine. Men together sometimes speak a funny language. You don't

know what's happening, and you become one frown because you
can't see. Kate can barely see in front of her.

Shaw's Kate became, in performance, a master study in watching. From her first entrance, lagging behind her father, her sister,
and those clamorous suitors, tightrope walking down the steeply
raked, sheer-drop precipice into High Street, Padua, this Kate
roamed the back boundary of the scene, eyes fixed on it, flashing
a pair of embroidery scissors like a switchblade. The audience
watched the suitors wrangling with Baptista over Bianca; but
more, they watched Kate's face watching from behind, registering
disdain, humiliation, alienation, and rage. Hers was a performance that contested the conventional spectatorly pleasure in
Shrew, a perhaps specifically male pleasure in watching Kate
subjected, mastered, and tamed by a Petruchio who, privileged
with soliloquy (unlike Kate), equips the audience to see things
with his own eyes. In this production, the audience looked on.
But Shaw's Kate looked back. The play was locked between op-
posing gazes, an interplay that played one gaze off the other.
Kate's looking back claimed the look back for women's roles in
this play.[32] It also registered a continuous critique of those "certain givens" her scrutiny made uncertain. So it was in the tailor
scene (4.3). Having been thrust (as a stand-in tailor's dummy)
into the gown and hoisted onto the soap box (that might as well
have been a scaffold as a pedestal) only to be dismembered
("What's this?" Petruchio bellows. "A sleeve?" as it comes away
in his hand) and discarded, Shaw's Kate was stripped once more
to her smock. It now looked like a grubby gown of humility.
The scene had passed into male uproar: Petruchio's fake fury,
Grumio's noise, and the tailor's loud indignation. Kate sat behind, silently watching. She pulled off her wedding ring and
peered through the circle of its emptiness, momentarily ex-
tending her imaginary telescope to lock it onto the eyeball of the
audience. Like her, they saw the wedding band encircling
nothing.

The sun-and-moon scene (4.5) literally repositioned Kate.
Shaw collapsed downstage as the men trudged up the hill and
off behind her. Nothing stood between her wild-eyed face and the
audience when Petruchio played his outrageous line: "It shall be
moon, or star, or what I list,/Or ere I journey to your father's
house" (7–8). She had been peering straight out front—a visual
echo of that staring through the ring in the tailor scene—but

now she turned upstage in alarm, trapped between Petruchio and the audience—his lunatic obduracy behind, their laughter out front.[33] Hortensio ventured advice: "Say as he says, or we shall never go" (11). Shaw's Kate swung herself back to stare at the sun. A look of astonishment shared only with the audience passed across her face. Silently she tried out "sun, sun!" as she twisted her fingers into a cat's cradle. Nothing stood between her and her choice. She turned her look back to Petruchio, who was looking away, then moved to him and clapped him on the back. They stood face to face looking at each other to play out the final exchanges in their comic bonding ritual, finally in the same frame of perspective. It was a move into visual alignment that Shaw would reproduce in her final speech.

Shaw's watchfulness interrogated the taming of the shrew: it allowed her space to deconstruct her performance *in the act.* But it achieved more than that. For as an acting strategy, it effectively appropriated the production to Kate's point of view by writing a performance text out of her silence that shouted down Petruchio's lines. Shaw had been disconcerted to discover in rehearsal that Kate was no roaring girl. Generically, "shrew equals noisy one, but we never hear Kate speak. Along comes a man to tame the noisy one, and *he* speaks through the whole play. But the *noisy one* doesn't speak." Her Kate was driven to carving her name on Padua's city walls with her switchblade scissors because "she doesn't get to speak. Making her mark is trying to say who she is—'Kate woz here.'" But such inscription had also the subversive effect of claiming authorship for Kate: Shaw wrote onto the surface of her performance text the lines Shakespeare had failed to give her role. This series of maneuvers—claiming spectatorship, interpreting silence, inscribing authored copy with graffitti—dismantled male authority in this *Shrew.* Her playing of Kate's final speech finished the job. Her record of rehearsal comes close to the effect her performance had in the theater:

> In the run today, I made a hefty attempt at allowing the haltingness and choice of every word dribbling out while she constructs a new synthesis as yet unuttered. The room was deadly silent. The feast table of men looking hangdog and inadequate, clearly not the sovereigns worthy of the 'love, fair looks and true obedience' that the speech describes. The play ends unresolved and out of joint, even for its own time.

HITTING THE WHITE

The Taming of the Shrew does not end on Kate's speech. It ends on men's self-congratulation: "I won the wager, though you hit the white"; "thou hast tam'd a curst shrew" (5.2.186, 188). But it also ends on a quibble (the "white"), a taunt ("We three are married, but you two are sped"), and a measure of bemused or bitter skepticism ("Tis a wonder") (185, 189). The final stage picture is of misalliance, of comic couples uncoupled. As the tamed shrew is put to bed, new shrews spring up like dragon's teeth, and men, laughing-stock Richard Conquerors, shift and sidle away. Bianca's last word is to call her husband "fool," and when Kate exists, Bianca remains, standing in for her sister one last time, "more shrew than she."

It is a nice irony. In the theater, Kate makes the noise and grabs the notices, but all along Bianca is the play's closet subversive. Her big sister contests patriarchal stereotypes as a dissident; Bianca, as an exemplary conformist. She is the very embodiment of the patriarchal model of female excellence. "In [her] silence do I see/Maid's mild behaviour and sobriety" (1.1.70–71), says Lucentio, falling in love with that same silence that can be recruited to misogyny—women beware women!—in the reproof of Katherine: "her very silence flouts me" (2.1.29). But what Bianca's continuous play of conformity achieves is to isolate, without the complication of contradiction, the normative wooing practices this culture conventionalizes and to turn them over to detailed, increasingly ironic inspection. The taming play has its monstrous woman; the wooing play, its monstrous men, its unsuitable suitors.[34] Playing by the rules, Bianca might get Gremio. Or Hortensio. Or even Tranio. Her prospects are appalling.

The history of this role in performance is, in the 1950s and 1960s, of trivialization and marginalization; in the 1970s and 1980s, in parallel with the problematizing of Kate, it is of a gradual hardening of "sweet Bianca . . . delectable Bianca . . . pertly fey . . . charming . . . like a rose in June" Bianca, into something thornier, tougher.[35] In 1978, Zoe Wanamaker's Bianca was stylish and devious, a smart cookie whose brittle-looking platinum wig over big doe eyes and wide comic mouth parodied the theater tradition that has this role played blonde, dumb, and harmless. At her sister's wedding, she enjoyed Kate's humiliation: she couldn't *wait* for Kate to clear off and leave the social whirl for her to bustle in. At her own wedding, working off the mafiosi imagery this production invented, the newly married Bianca would finally discard all those premarital games: the wife holds the whip at her own threshold, and Bianca would from now on.[36] In 1987, Felicity Dean played a Bianca one imagined ultimately winding up on Falstaff's knee at the Boar's Head in Eastcheap, fumbling with his codpiece. She moved on ball bearings, but her slack voice could suddenly harden into Maggie Thatcher at the dispatch box. She was overripe, vulgar, genuinely put out that Tranio's Lucentio and Hortensio's music master could agree to jilt her. Her secret tippling, which Lucentio had found titillating over their Ovid, had settled into cheerless habit by the time she reached their wedding scene: hatched-faced, Bianca knocked back the dregs of the toast, glanced contempt at her twittish husband, then strode off unsteadily without him, wiping her mouth with the back of her hand.[37]

Wanamaker and Dean were able to claim some space for Bianca, but given the productions they were in, neither of their performances could do much to reverse an earlier reviewer's dismissive verdict on the theatrical irrelevancy of Bianca: "no one cares who marries Bianca."[38] Their directors evidently agreed. In both productions, rehearsal time was spent on Kate and Petruchio. The funny business surrounding Bianca was understood to be there to generate hilarious gags for the boys—and it did— but really all that was to be gotten out of the way as quickly as possible, for it only distracted from the main business of the taming play.

So without further thought to Shakespeare's structural design or to his comic strategies, they directed a Bianca who was a theatrical irrelevance.[39]

Then in 1992, along came Rebecca Saire's Bianca to re-invent the role.[40] Saire looks like Dresden porcelain but acts like carbon steel. In collaboration with a Tranio (Richard McCabe) whose innovation was to play the impostor playing the wooing scam for keeps, she discovered a Bianca whose marriage projects might seriously disrupt society, might, indeed, bring down the whole patriarchal house of cards.

As Saire saw the role, "Bianca doesn't become Kate at the end. She becomes more and more Bianca. Bianca's potential is all there in her opening speech":

> Sister, content you in my discontent.
> Sir, to your pleasure humbly I subscribe;
> My books and instruments shall be my company,

On them to look and practice by myself.

(1.1.80–83)

Saire points to the precision of "content/discontent" as revealing "Bianca the performer," her utterance constructed and maddeningly opaque. It might be anodyne. It might be caustic. While offering a humble subscription to her father's pleasure, Bianca is imperious and imperative: she constantly speaks in imperative verbs. "But what reveals Bianca is that the speech moves to 'myself': Bianca is going to please 'myself'; in the tutor scene she will 'learn my lessons as I please myself.'"

"Performance" was Saire's master metaphor to the role. Her Bianca got by by playing by the rules. But in this production, the metaphor had a double extension, for the taming play was performed by modern actors, a troupe that might have been the Royal Shakespeare Company on a small-scale tour, so Saire's first entrance established her as a professional player. Her role thereafter played upon playing.

In 2.1, with Kate, she played at childhood games, circuses perhaps, or dress-up, that showed the sisters they might have been. Bianca entered like a prancing pony, waving ribbons; Kate, like a lion tamer, carrying a chair and, in her mouth, a decapitated doll (she was lion, too). The ribbons for Bianca's hair got tied around her wrists instead: the new game was interrogation, and the sexual anxiety betrayed in the questions sat bizarrely against the imagery of play. Bianca was unperturbed by Kate's envy. But she thrashed in terror when Kate pulled a pair of shears big enough to scalp a sheep and menaced her hair. Saire saw Kate "threatening my external show: Bianca is a decorated woman, a woman on display, like some exotic bird in the animal kingdom." Her meticulous clothes, her jewels, her hair were all part of that display, props to a performance. This Bianca found her sister physically distasteful. It wasn't just that Kate was unruly but that, unruly, she was unkempt. Her hair fell about her face; her performance got out of control: she bit her fingernails; she sucked her thumb. Bianca was perfect, every feather in place: chopped-off hair would have spoiled the show and depreciated the merchandise. "Her suitors want her as a decorative fixture: she wants them in order to maintain her status. Like a prostitute she'll give herself away to the highest bidder."

This production showed a Bianca actively playing out that scenario: it put her onstage, center stage, for the contract bartering between Gremio and supposed Lucentio (2.1). But it likewise showed a Bianca literally seeing possibilities for unimagined improvizations. Moments earlier, the brawling scene of Kate's enforced betrothal got off to a start with a coyly adenoidal love-birds-at-first-sight look between Kate and Petruchio. Now that exchange of looks was echoed: Tranio-as-Lucentio began the line, "I am one that love Bianca . . ." (2.1.335), but Tranio-as-Tranio finished it, locking eyes with Bianca, who did not turn away. This look was bold, brazen; it made it clear that Bianca and Tranio would be birds of a far different feather, like Marvell's sexual carnivores, perhaps, his "amorous birds of prey." Meanwhile, still beaming at the realization that the "commodity" that lay fretting by him was finally disposed of, Baptista seated his saleable daughter between her two suitors. He put her hand into Gremio's. Gremio pawed it. He paddled it. Then, as his inventory of his wealth grew more excited, he groped his money bags with it. They hung from his waist, conspicuously stuffed, while the bags hanging next to them were just as conspicuously limp in his gold-embroidered codpiece. The massage climaxed. Disgust passed across Bianca's face, then a quick sweet smile of recovery. She did not remove her hand. Kate would have. Not Bianca. Bianca's detachment showed the woman's body to be an impersonal playground, a site this time to play out a commercial transaction. When she rose, though, and turned upstage to follow Baptista out of the scene, the auction over, she stopped. Tranio looked at her expressionless back. An arm extended. The fingers held out a lace handkerchief. Tranio moved to clutch it. Bianca's head turned. Her smile was dazzling.

Here was a Bianca capable of initiating her own secret play, a Bianca capable of walking out the stage door of the legitimate theater straight into a role on the fringe. She knew exactly who Tranio was. And she wanted *him*. Moreover, the kiss she gave him, stand-in bride to stand-in groom, as they exited to Kate and Petruchio's wedding feast, suggested that somewhere offstage she had been getting plenty of him. Watching the kiss, Lucentio stared in dismay. Instinctively he had stepped forward at Baptista's invitation: "Lucentio, you shall supply the bridegroom's place" (3.2.249). But a savage dig in the ribs from Tranio reminded him he had been replaced. He cast the beseeching look of the betrayed at Bianca. She gave him that sweet smile but turned into her role: nothing was going to disturb this performance.

This Bianca and this Tranio were natural allies, both performers authorized to play by a culture that licensed their performance: "I am tied to be obedient" (Tranio, 1.1.212); "To your pleasure humbly I subscribe" (Bianca, 1.1.81). They were like Bartholomew, the page, in the Induction. But they used their performance space to play out fantasies of subversion. Tranio, handed first Lucentio's trousers then his heraldic ring—the ring that authorized him master—was fascinated by it. He held it up to the light; his eyes narrowed. He was Tamburlaine considering Persepolis. Much later, in almost her final scene, Bianca would echo this gesture, but invert it. She, too, had considered Tamburlaine of the high-astounding line, but had settled instead for the mere translator of other men's daring ("Hic steterat Priami") into the prosaic ("I am Lucentio"). The stolen marriage with the unexceptionable Lucentio was the lesser, safer transgression. And there had been inklings of the collapse of fantasy as far back as 4.2, when Tranio had to watch what he genuinely found "despiteful," "beastly": Bianca in the role of "unconstant womankind" making love by the book to the real Lucentio (14, 34, 14). Tranio's sudden emergence from behind shocked her. "I have ta'en you napping, gentle love" (46) was blackly sarcastic. He snatched at her placket, then bent her hand back until she winced: the obscenity hurt more than her wrist did but this time Bianca was trapped inside her performance with Lucentio. She could not let that mask slip even long enough to explain. When the whole messy business of the "counterfeit supposes" was discovered to the fathers and the "marriage . . . [that has] made thy daughter mine" (5.1.117, 116), Bianca held out her hand appealingly, showing the wedding ring. Lucentio's family ring was back on his own finger: he had demanded it from Tranio in a gesture that the upstart, still insolent, had yet to obey. The transfer of rings was trebly significant: Tranio was trashed; Lucentio, restored; and Bianca, mastered, not manned. She held up the ring hand to the light. She had made the safe choice. And it was the wrong choice.

Here was a Bianca who had made "a god of . . . a cullion" (4.2.20). She played in earnest that fiction Hortensio supposes to be true in the "beastly" wooing scene when he watches Bianca kiss and court the Latin tutor—the cullion—whom he doesn't know is really a gentleman in disguise. Tranio was a cullion indeed. Making him a god, Saire's Bianca reanimated the visual and social subversiveness of Shakespeare's original disguised wooings. Making him a god, she reproduced sexually the class violations that had already occurred. (Baptista had fallen for Tranio too; the clothes were enough.) Making him a god, playing into his class fantasies, Bianca very nearly let this cullion get a leg over (and a leg up into) the gentry. But making him once again a cullion, she showed that since the patriarchal bastion is surrounded by walls that any spring-heeled jack can leap, the defense of the patriarchy must depend on the willing collusion of its exemplary conformists. But poor Bianca. She discarded the cullion who only, among all those unsuitable suitors, had hit her white.

RUTH AND SARAH

Ruth and Sarah don't figure in Shakespeare's *Shrew*. The director Bill Alexander invented them.[41] And his 1992 production for the Royal Shakespeare Company invented for them a world that rhymed, oddly, with the real world; every Ruth and Sarah sitting in the audience (for that was part of Alexander's project, to create spectator roles to double those on stage) recognized it instantly. It was a dilapidated world, a world whose structures (physical? ideological?) were under stress, a world requiring reconstruction, masked in builders' scaffolding and miles of paint-splattered canvas. On the downstage corner was a pub, "The Ugly Duckling," a sign of things to come: in the taming play the sign would switch to "The White Swan," the ugly duckling metamorphosed, only now with an elegant chain around her neck. But the sign was also another rhyme, a slant rhyme. All the Ruths and Sarahs of the audience had passed the real pub, Stratford's "Dirty Duck," on their way into the theater. Somehow, this world was our world, and maybe that meant that our view of Shakespeare's *Shrew* was going to be represented on this stage.

The "Duckling" was in full swing, pumping out disco music and then slinging out its door a drunken bum in a flat cap who managed to stagger to his feet long enough to declare his lineage, "the Slys are no rogues," before passing out. Whooping and whistling, a hunt in full cry got louder as its two-legged victim dashed in, a youth in jogging sweats. He stumbled over Sly. The "hounds" fell upon him: a friendly debag, or a bit of gay bashing? Then they got wind of Sly. "Don't touch him, Simon!" brayed the Sloane Ranger trenchcoat. "He's probably *working* class," honked the designer stubble. It was the leader of this upper-class brat pack, one Lord Simon Llewellyn, who hit upon the wheeze of carrying Sly home to daddy's country pile behind the gates (and, as it happened, behind the scaffolding and canvas), setting

him amidst the candelabra in the oak-paneled Elizabethan drawing room and, putting the family signet ring on his finger, making
him a lord. The project was distinctly nasty: "The drunk needs
to be taught a lesson. We'll just mess around with his mind for
a bit."

Lady Sarah Ormsby and the Honorable Mrs Ruth Banks-Ellis
(along with the other "Hons" who made up Lord Simon's party—
Peter, Hugo, and little brother Rupert of the jogging sweats) were
Alexander's device for recuperating Shakespeare's frame play, for
widening that frame and realigning it. Theatrically, the new
frame multiplied spectator relationships and politicized them—
gender, class, and power roles were re-imagined—while at the
same time locating on the stage a proxy audience, a double of
the audience out front, who, inside the fiction, might enter into
dialogue with the taming play and offer to interrogate it on behalf
of all those other Ruths and Sarahs. Thematically, the frame devised analogs several fictions deep that would play off each other.
So, as Hugo and Peter carried Sly off into Simon's psychosis, the
actors Simon had engaged for the evening appeared. They looked
like the Royal Shakespeare Company on tour. They also looked
like Sly, in actorly versions of working man's gear (leather
bomber jackets, suede boots), a species apart from the aristocrats
in baggy black and so self-conscious rumple. But, then, when
they returned in character to play their Shrew, the actors began
to look more than a little like doubles of their patrons. Petruchio
caught Simon's manic glitter; Bianca perched between two
suitors looked like Ruth with those parrots, Peter and Hugo, on
each shoulder. It became clear as things developed that this
Shrew's meanings were going to emerge by friction, not just between Kate and Petruchio, but between Simon and Sarah, between the aristocrats and the actors, and between Shakespeare's
taming play and Alexander's new-model Induction.

That Induction wrote contemporary colloquialism ("Hey, brilliant!") onto Shakespeare, even as it raided the authorized
playtext for fragments of "authentic" lines ("You're mad," said
Sarah, trying to beat off Simon's demand that she use her sexual
power over young Rupert to make him dress up to play Sly's
wife. "Just do it," he screamed. "Don't cross me. You're always
crossing me!"). This careful regard, and just as careful disregard,
for the authorized text in the Induction signaled Alexander's
double project. He wanted to find a way of playing the original
Shrew with its integrity intact while at the same time claiming
the right to rewrite a subsequent Shrew with a subsequent audi-

ence. While the actors played their Shrew in Elizabethan costumes, and in Lord Simon's Elizabethan hall, thus visually
locating its ideas in a historicized past where accommodation
either by irony or apology was unnecessary, the two Shrews
would eventually get superimposed when the taming play, the
one the actors were playing, literally reached out and grabbed
its spectators, recruiting them into the taming play as "extras."
Ruth and Sarah were handed scripts. Still in their evening dress,
they walked on as Nathaniel and Gregory. When they did, when
they stepped across the frame into the fiction, they closed the
gap that had made the play of 1592 (whose power games they
had watched with smug detachment) safe viewing in 1992; they
had recognized in that play none of their own power games represented. Now not only were they visually aligned with Kate,
they were trapped (like Kate) in a script that they had no power
to alter. Moreover, when Ruth and Sarah crossed the frame, they
brought Simon with them, and by a bizarre chiasmus of this
production's rhyme scheme—life with play—the actor Petruchio
then proceeded to use his role to require these recruits to experience Kate's fictive ordeal for real.

Emily Watson played Ruth, "a young widow, married at eighteen to a hugely rich Italian designer who died a couple of years
later"; she would step in to play the Widow at the end. Catherine
Mears was Sarah (in a red sheath that echoed Kate's red dress:
"we'd all been at Oxford together, privileged, emotionally desen-
sitized, living on the edge, and looking for excitement").[42] For
them, the core of Alexander's production was the interaction
between "the Watchers," as Lord Simon's party came to call
themselves, and the play they were watching. And they did
watch it, the whole of The Taming of the Shrew every night.
Watson felt that Alexander "wanted us to represent a contemporary element in society who would do to Sly what Shakespeare's
Lord did to his Sly—people who could be that cruel. For Bill,
the play is all about identity—changing identity, changing per-
ceptions of relationships, taking a positive view of the possibility
of change. What happens to Sly is a nasty version of that scenario. His forced change of identity is a deception perpetrated
upon him. He's victimized, and the Watchers start off thinking
it's a great hoot. But then we become increasingly uncomfortable
with it, because watching Kate's play changes the Watchers. We
watch the violence. We watch the kiss. The onus is put on us to
make sense of it all. The playing of the play turns the play on

us." Here was a version of "messing around with his mind for a
bit" that the Watchers hadn't anticipated.

Mears agrees. "The Watchers represent emotional bleakness.
But because we *are* models of emotional sterility, the audience
can see in us the capacity for change. That's how we function in
the plot. But on a strategic level, the Watchers embody if not the
limitations of *Shrew* for a modern audience, at least its difficulties. They represent a modern director's feeling that somehow
the play needs to be re-presented or clarified in some external
way. You can't get away from the fact that in this play Petruchio
chooses to meet Kate's violence of behavior with his own violence of behavior instead of doing something very twentieth-
century like saying 'let's sit down and work this through.' To
accommodate this play to a modern audience, or maybe to medi-
ate it, our director devised the Watchers. And he devised a scenario between Simon and Sarah that frankly imitated Petruchio
and Kate and that displayed the continuing problematics of gender power. Simon is *casually* violent to Sarah. He doesn't even
think about it. It's almost conversational, his vocabulary of violence. And it's sterile. Of course, what that's supposed to be
doing is to show up the Watchers' violence against Petruchio's,
so the 'sterility' of our violence demonstrates the 'con-
structiveness' of his. What that *doesn't* examine is the rather
frightening suggestion, in Shakespeare's *Shrew*, that violence *is*
constructive."

If Alexander's strategy was indeed accommodationist, Watson
felt it achieved something major for Shakespeare's taming play
in 1992: "Playing the frame play, putting an audience onstage
who were looking at Kate's play from the outside, meant that this
production did not have to find a solution to the problem of
Shrew within the central performance. It meant that Kate did not
have to resolve the feminist/political issues a modern audience
is going to see in the play. Kate could play her final speech
straight."

So it was the Watchers, not Kate, who were going to problema-
ticize this *Shrew*. Their reactions—"first laughing their heads
off," says Watson, then wincing, glancing at each other furtively,
and finally averting their eyes—continuously monitored the taming play and interrogated it, seemingly on behalf of all those
Ruths and Sarahs whose spectator roles they evidently were doubling. Putting such radical viewing in place, Alexander's production looked set to crack the core problem this play poses on the
modern stage. Playing the frame against the taming play, he had

devised a way of playing the 1592 *Shrew while at the same time* critiquing the 1992 *Shrew.*

But then it seems he lost his nerve. The on-stage audience was never really going to be a genuine double for the audience out front whose Sarahs were not "Hons" with double-barrelled surnames. And their critique was certainly not innocent, nor even representative: they were set up to be "more shrew than he" [sic], or as Watson put it more colloquially, "We were shits." So the effect of their watching was not ultimately to contest or dismantle Petruchio's playful policy "to kill a wife with kindness," but rather to achieve sympathy for it by representing it as infinitely more humane, more liberal than anything their own culture (or ours?) had to offer.

It might have gone the other way. There was a moment when, having nipped the hand that fed it once or twice, the taming play bit down hard on its audience and locked its jaws. Momentarily, the taming play looked very dangerous, when the audience saw Petruchio's play with Kate's eyes. Grumio staggered in from the journey home (4.1) in foul gear and fouler temper. He bawled for Curtis. He bawled again. On the plush sofa where he'd been lounging, watching the play, Hugo was handed a script. He was waved on. Grinning foolishly, stumbling over the lines, he entered the play. They came to Grumio's 'knock, knock' joke: "Lend thine ear," he tells Curtis; Curtis obeys: "Here" (60–61). So Hugo obliged. And Grumio cuffed him. Hugo reared back, livid, nonplussed. There was deadly silence. Grumio whistled, smiled, pointed blandly to the script. The box on the ears was in the script. The violence wasn't Grumio's, it was the text's. Suddenly, the script was committing an act of aggression upon the very spectators who had patronized it so condescendingly. And it disorientated Hugo, but he was trapped in the script. Was it a parallel text to the cultural text Kate was expected to perform? There was nothing he could do but play along with the (to him outrageous) logic of that script.

Grumio summoned the household. Hugo's mates, who'd been sniggering on the sofa, were put on their feet, scripts in hand. Petruchio appeared in the door. The change in him was shocking. He was no more the jolly, thriving wooer, but the husband psychopath. The eyes glinted. The voice jumped octaves. The new cast looked around, off balance, when he shrieked, "Where is Nathaniel, Gregory, Philip?" They didn't know their roles; they didn't know the script; Sarah stepped forward tentatively (was she meant to play Nathaniel?) to obey the command, "Off with

my boots, you rogues"; "you pluck my foot awry," screamed Petruchio. "Take that!" The kick in the stomach sent Sarah sprawl-
ing, but the script made her come back for more: "and mend the
plucking off the other." Simon and his cronies tensed. Suddenly
wary, Sarah picked herself up. Ruth-as-Gregory offered the basin.
It was knocked from her hands. "You whoreson villain!" roared
Petruchio, belting her across the face and upending the table.
Sarah fled. Ruth cowered. The men stood rooted. Grumio mo-
tioned toward their scripts (145–55).

When Petruchio exited to bed with Kate, it took the household
a long time to break the silence and get back to the script. "Peter,
didst ever see the like? He kills her in her own humour" (179–80)
were delivered in flat tones. It wasn't just the violence or its
unpredictability that shocked; it was the confrontation with a
culture of absolute authoritarianism that did not need to account
for its practices. The Watchers were experiencing a Shrew re-
scripted by, say, Kafka. Their confusions and disorientations du-
plicated Kate's and gave them immediacy as, looking through
the Watchers, the audience saw her play made unfamiliar and
therefore painfully new. The irony was, of course, that the Watchers were made to experience "for real" the violence that Petruchio orchestrates around Kate but that Kate never feels, and
not just because that violence is displaced onto, for one, the
tailor—because the tailor never feels it either. Kate and the tailor
are, after all, only actors; stage violence is staged. Not being
actors, the Watchers took Petruchio's blows on the chin.

Alexander's production might have kept this pressure up. It
didn't. The Petruchio who returned to speak "Thus have I poli-
ticly begun my reign" (4.1.188) not as soliloquy but to his sullen
household was a new Petruchio, neither the Elizabethan bucca-
neer of the wedding nor the slasher-film psychotic of the home-
coming, but here, literally, the "new man" of Germaine Greer
fantasies. He broke the speech, he walked over to Ruth, he ca-
ressed her cheek. How did the audience read that gesture? Petruchio apologizing to his servant? The actor apologizing for
getting too real? The gesture, the apology, made him ever such a
nice man, really, one who was stunned to discover the line "This
is a way to kill a wife with kindness (208)." But the gesture
likewise turned aside the challenge Alexander's production had
been constructing. Conducted by new man Petruchio, the taming
play as "a kind of history" that would force 1992 to look at itself
by looking at 1592 proceeded to deteriorate into "a gambold,"
"a tumbling-trick." The taming was after all mere play! How silly

of Kate not to notice. But how much more exciting if Alexander's production had kept its nerve, played out the logic of its transfictional framing device and, in the final scene, when the Watchers were re-recruited and Hortensio, script outstretched, summoned Ruth back to play the Widow, Kate had turned to Sarah, handed her the script, and left *her* to speak the final speech. Having watched this play, what sense could Sarah make of it? How, as the Watcher in 1992 pulled in to speak for the play, would *Sarah* negotiate those lines?

That is a question to be put to Emily Watson and Catherine Mears. Veterans of a year's worth of watching *The Taming of the Shrew*, they are experts on the play in performance. Both of them in their twenties, both of them in their first professional job, what do they—as actors, as women—see in this play that needs, still, to be performed?

Watson answers with more questions. "Are we, postfeminism, really any wiser than *Shrew*? Are we any more sorted? Any better off? In a way, feminism (in a very broad, coarse, unsubtle, and unintelligent sense) deprived women of their historic role; it had to, ideologically, if it was going to break apart those conventional female roles. But that means women of my age have grown up in a generation where there aren't any rules to this game. The interest in doing *Shrew* may be in exploring a world and its relationships where the rules are so strong. And where they find a witty way of playing the rules."

Mears observes, somewhat wryly, that "even in a postfeminist age, people still enjoy the play. I wonder if we could analyze in what way *Shrew* describes something that is way way way below intellectualization, below social conditioning, the way it describes what really goes on between men and women. What happens in the play is that, strangely enough, enormous freedoms are examined in order to arrive at a highly formalized resolution. I think possibly that is what makes Kate's final speech acceptable on an emotional level even when we can't accept it on an intellectual level. There's an enormous amount of exuberance in the strategies this play follows. There's play. There's highly emotional intensities. There's a great deal of humor. And a lot of cathartic violence. In a formalized, hierarchial, non-individualized society, what renders Kate so attractive is that she puts her individual snap on playing the play by her rules. And in the play, Shakespeare certainly gives the generic bag a shake. He could have made three obedient wives at the end. He didn't."[43]

NOTES

1. Louis Montrose, "The Purpose of Playing: Reflections on a Shakespear-ean Anthropology," Helios 7 (1980): 57, 64, 66, 68.

2. Benedict Nightingale, New Statesman, 12 May 1979. I am, of course, adopting the idea of the "subsequent performance" at the end of the paragraph from Jonathan Miller's Subsequent Performances (London: Faber and Faber, 1986).

3. Carol Rutter, Clamorous Voices: Shakespeare's Women Today (London: The Women's Press, 1988), 1.

4. Theatre Records 36 (7 May 1948) Shakespeare Centre Library, Stratford-upon-Avon.

5. Theatre Records 40 (9 June 1953).

6. Theatre Records 42 (1 June 1954).

7. Theatre Records 42 (1 & 2 June 1954).

8. Theatre Records 50 (21 June 1960).

9. Theatre Records 50 (21 June 1960).

10. Theatre Records 54 (13 September 1961).

11. Theatre Records 69 (5 April 1963).

12. Eric Shorter, Daily Telegraph, 26 September 1973.

13. Michael Billington, The Guardian, 27 September 1973.

14. Irving Wardle, The Times, 26 September 1973.

15. Miller, 122, 121.

16. Charles Marowitz, The Marowitz Shakespeare (London: Marion Boyars, 1978), 176, 178.

17. Nicholas de Jongh, The Guardian, 3 November 1973.

18. For an account of this storming of the citadel, see Lynda Boose, "The Family in Shakespeare Studies; or—Studies in the Family of Shakespeareans; or—The Politics of Politics," Renaissance Quarterly 40 (1987): 707–42.

19. These three Shrews are documented in Carol Rutter, Clamorous Voices.

20. Lynda E. Boose, "Scolding Brides and Bridling Scolds: Taming the Woman's Unruly Member," Shakespeare Quarterly 42 (1991): 179–213. It should be observed, to balance Boose's argument, that if women were bridled, men were harnessed: "harness" referred equally to armor or tackle worn by man or horse. Macbeth dies with harness on his back; Cleopatra must leap through "proof of harness" to embrace Antony's heart. As far as I can see there is not much to choose between the bridle and the harness as metaphors of human expressiveness.

21. In his Introduction to the Arden Shrew, Brian Morris summarizes this ballad. Once the shrew is married, she "starts to misuse the servants, and she abuses her husband when he admonishes her. She strikes him in her anger, and she rides off to give her time to cool down. When he returns she berates him and refuses him food. He orders his old horse, Morrel, to be killed and flayed, and his hide salted. He forces his railing wife into a cellar, beats her mercilessly with birch rods until she bleeds and faints, then fastens her naked body into the salted hide. The pain revives her, and he threatens to keep her tied up in the horse's hide for the rest of her life. With that, 'her moode began to sinke,' and when he releases her she becomes meek and obedient" (London: Methuen, 1981), 71.

22. When Barbara Hodgdon observes (in "Katherina Bound; or, Play(K)ating

the Strictures of Everyday Life") that "once Kate ventriloquizes the voice of Shakespeare's culture and lets it colonize her body, she never speaks again," she is, implicitly, directing one politicized version of Kate's final speech, the key elements of which are "ventriloquizes," "lets," and "colonize," all of which inform the further observation that she "never speaks again." My observations point to different, but no less politicized, performance opportunities. Hodgdon is cuing her direction of the speech mainly from its content, its playtext; I am cuing mine mainly from its performance text, its theatrical site and strategies. I see a Kate whose performance text puts her at the center of the scene, focuses on her, and empowers her with speech. It is of course true that Kate never speaks again. But then nobody else does much either: there are only ten more lines of the Folio playtext. But it is also true that, except for Rosalind in her epilogue (where she is ambiguously gendered, sometimes as female role, sometimes as male actor), Portia in her five-line promise to answer "inter'gatories," and Mistress Page in her four-line accommodation to Anne's stolen marriage, Kate comes closest to the male privilege of speaking the speech that silences the play, the last speech. Hodgdon, perhaps, would like Kate to say more, to recant, or, Emilia-like, to situate this representation of patriarchal supremacy inside an interrogation of it (*Othello*, 4.3). But Hodgdon knows very well (because she is teaching us all to read Shakespeare's theater as well as his words) that even where Shakespeare's playtext may be constructing some orthodoxy, his performance text may be busily dismantling it. We do not have to depend on the famous Pickford wink ('Play(K)atig, 544) to make the ending ironic when so evidently the stage picture is doing just that. The ventriloquized voice of the patriarchy is clearly falling on deaf ears. And the patriarchs themselves— Lucentio and Hortensio—have just demonstrated publicly their spectacular failure as "lord ... king ... governor" to extract "love, fair looks [or] true obedience." The ending of *Shrew* is the most desultory of Shakespeare's comic endings. Astonishingly, the comic couple around whom the "new order" should crystallize, especially given the "authority" evidently inscribed in Kate's last speech to formalize that order, abandons the play. Kate and Petruchio simply walk out. What they leave behind deconstructs Kate's speech. Not only does their exit leave a gap in the feast, but twelve other characters must subsequently make *their* exits. How do they go? What does their going say about the culture Kate's speech has invented? Is it, on the emptying stage, literally a utopia? The ending of *Shrew* is much more subversive to an audience who reads the scene than to the critic who reads only Kate. See Barbara Hodgdon, "Katherina Bound," *PMLA* 107 (1992), 538–553.

23. For a different reading of violence in *Shrew*, see Lynda Boose, "Scolding Brides." By invoking absence—"the scold's bridle that Shakespeare did not literally include in his play ... the fist-in-the-face that Petruchio does not use and the rape he does not enact in the offstage bedroom we do not see" (200)— Boose contrives to make that absent violence present.

24. In Elizabethan England there was only one method for taming the haggard (the full grown falcon captured in the wild as against the eyas, the unfledged nestling, removed from the nest and hand-reared). The procedure was known as "waking." The bird was tied to the falconer's wrist. She would not sleep until she trusted the keeper. He could not sleep until she was "broken" to his trust: a falcon is powerful enough to kill a man. By this (mutual) process of sleep and food deprivation (hence the extension of "haggard" to mean a wild, wasted, worn look as from sleeplessness) man and bird were broken to

each other. Implicit in this process is the Elizabethan opinion that the schooled bird is the better bird. Petruchio is suggesting Kate's aptitude to such schooling; Hortensio, Bianca's reversion to the wild. As a metaphor for the woman, "haggard" carries a double cultural valence that "shrew" does not.

25. "Scolding Brides and Bridling Scolds," 182.

26. O.E.D. v.2 trans. To wager, stake (e.g. money, one's life, one's head). Quotation ref. 1560: "Stene Robesone weddit ten markis of money aganes the said tar barrell that scho suld nocht marry the saide King of Swane."

27. The phrase is Jan Kott's in "The Gender of Rosalind: Androgyny in Shakespeare's England—and in Gautier's France," *New Theatre Quarterly* 7 (1991): 118.

28. I come to these observations about dangerous extremes, erasure, and role-play after seeing the 1991/92 Cheek by Jowl *As You Like It,* an all-male production that, by self-consciously displaying the gap between (male) actors and (female) characters, reanimated the Elizabethan notion of performance as role-play and released in the audience the pleasurable freedom of watching Rosalind as a role, as a collection of performance strategies, not as a woman, a representative of universalized or psychologized femininity. An all-male company meant, stylistically, that performances were alienated, not personalized. It meant, politically, that women in the audience were permitted to laugh without defensiveness at a play-thing that was itself laughing at "women's" postures and posturing. A reversal of what I am suggesting may have been the 1592 audience's experience of watching *Shrew*—that the play interrogated *male* cultural practices and *male* spectator positions by demonstrating the constructedness of gender roles through role-play as the Cheek by Jowl *As You Like It,* levying upon the same understanding of the constructedness of role, permitted the 1992 audience to interrogate *female* cultural practices and *female* spectator positions that in our contemporary theater require the (female) actor, even in an Elizabethan play, somehow to represent modern feminism. Sarah Lyon, one of the new generation of highly politicized feminist academics, explained it to me while we were trying to analyze our (unexpected) deep delight in the production: "Women have a problem in the audience these days. We want, we *need,* women on stage to be *strong.* If we had seen any woman playing Phebe like that, we would have been *furious.* But because it was a man playing Phebe, we didn't have to be defensive." This *As You Like It* was clearly a game, a "play," and the magic free territory marked out by play allowed this role-play to go to dangerous extremes to permit *women* in the audience to laugh at *women.*

29. Michael Billington, *The Guardian,* 5 May 1978; Irving Wardle, *The Times,* 26 September 1973.

30. All of my quotation of Fiona Shaw comes either from conversations with her in February and March 1988 or from *Drama,* September 1987.

31. When it suited his purposes, Miller put a contemporary spin on his evocation of Elizabethan imagery or abandoned the decorum of that culture entirely: Kate's white smock in 4.3 looked like a hospital gown; Petruchio (fully dressed) offering her food then depriving her of it (while Grumio and Hortensio, likewise fully dressed, looked on) stood in the role of analyst. Fiona Shaw, in conversation with me, observed that Miller in rehearsal talked of Kate as a damaged child: "He thought that she behaves like many children do who are unloved: badly, really younger than she is, under-developed. Until this man comes. And without beating her up he very unviolently disorientates her by not accepting anything she says. Miller says that's what doctors do with badly

behaved children who spew vulgarities—they turn the desk over and the children get a fright. I think he was translating the 'taming' of the shrew into 'therapy,' the realignment of the delinquent. It's just one step further to putting Petruchio in a white coat." Shaw's representation of Miller squares with his own comments on Kate in *Subsequent Performances* where he uses a psychiatrist's vocabulary—"self-image," "unloved," "rejected"—to diagnose "symptoms of unhappiness" (121–22). Reviewing Miller's production in the *TLS* (September 18–24 1987), Katherine Duncan-Jones remarked on program notes that quoted Lawrence Stone on Elizabethan psychology: she saw Miller enlisting "deprivation syndrome" as "an almost invisible underpinning to [his] adjustment of Shakespeare's savagely patriarchal fable of wife-taming to the responses of a contemporary, postfeminist audience." For a critique of Miller's dubious historicizing in his 1980 BBC (video) and in his 1987 Royal Shakespeare Company *Shrew*, see Graham Holderness, *Shakespeare in Performance: The Taming of the Shrew* (Manchester: Manchester University Press, 1989), 111–20.

32. My thinking on looking relationships in the theater is indebted to Laura Mulvey's influential essay, "Visual Pleasure and Narrative Cinema," *Screen* 16 (1975), 6–18; rpt. in *Feminism and Film Theory*, ed. Constance Penley (New York: Routledge, 1988), 57–68. Woman as object-of-the-gaze is now almost a cliché of feminist materialist criticism: see, for example, Jean Howard's "Scripts and/Versus Playhouses," *Renaissance Drama* 20 (1990): 31–49. Katharine Eisaman Maus is much more acute and accessible in "Horns of Dilemma: Jealousy, Gender, and Spectatorship in English Renaissance Drama," *English Literary History* 54 (1987): 561–83. For a brilliant analysis of spectatorly pleasure in *Shrew*, see Barbara Hodgdon, "Katherina Bound." Zeffirelli's film *Shrew* (1966) reverses spectatorship in the way I am suggesting Shaw's performance did. Kate (Elizabeth Taylor) is first an eye, in close-up, framed in the camera frame but also in the narrow aperture of the window shutter she has cracked open. The eye looks at the audience. But as the camera moves, Kate is looking down at Bianca, summoned home at a run into her sister's surveillance from the carnival marketplace where she has been the object of a different gaze: the focus of all male attention, her veiled face was held in close-up to male view and to (licentious) male serenade, the veil finally lifted (and the face exposed naked) by a fish hook "catching" her. The looking back that Fiona Shaw claimed for Kate in 1987, Amanda Harris, the Royal Shakespeare Company's latest Kate, simply handed back in 1992: her Kate looked not at the audience, but at herself. Picking up the pewter plate Petruchio had thrown down, she licked it, then caught her reflection in the mirror surface and gazed at it silently. The critique registered was of herself. She tried to fix her hair.

33. Reviewing the archival video of Miller's production at the Shakespeare Centre Library, I was reminded of what I always know in the theater but forget in the study, that, in defiance of academic reading of whatever ideological persuasion, audiences claim this scene for comedy. They laugh at Petruchio, at, literally, the lunacy of the sun/moon rigmarole, at their own discomfiture in recognizing a comic routine that entraps them in another replay of here we go again. Petruchio's first remark passes off neutrally, for, in a presentational theater, "Good Lord, how bright and goodly shines the moon!" has the same status as "Well, this is the forest of Arden" or "The moon is down." It is only when Kate contradicts him and Petruchio begins again "I say . . ." that the audience understands the time (as in the tailor scene) but, one step ahead of Kate, under-

stands that that's not the real issue. Like all the onstage audiences of Shrew who spectate on the spectacles Petruchio devises, the audience in the theater is just as disconcerted as Kate: indeed, the playing of the play positions the audience to read the play as Kate does, for Petruchio's lunacy contradicts our sense too. The audience is Kated, is shrewed. And the audience's laughter in this scene is directed as much at itself as at Petruchio; it recognizes that the audience, too, once again has been caught out by Petruchio's anarchy. "I say . . ." is a laugh line in the theater. And the laugher of the audience constructs a meaning for the scene that appropriates the playtext to the business of comedy. Laughter does not make the scene "safe" or "normal," but it does make Kate's predicament the audience's predicament. And it makes Lynda Boose's serious observations about women and a shame culture in "Scolding Brides" incommensurate to the playing of this play.

34. If the exercise, surveillance, and management of female speech and silence is one master topic of early modern drama, so the presentation, inspection, and interrogation of the unsuitable male suitor is another. Early on in A Midsummer Night's Dream (and in Shakespeare's career), Lysander (1.1.135–40) itemizes the standard catalog of misalliance that turns the course of true love awry, and comedy after comedy plays out progressively grotesque versions of the parade of Portia's suitors, presenting to prospective brides prospective grooms who are twits, louts, drunkards, monsters, bankrupts, geriatrics, and foreigners. The misalliances of tragedy pick up the same tropes but render them increasingly extreme. From Kyd to Marlowe, Shakespeare to Jonson, Webster to Middleton and Tourneur, the unsuitable suitor of tragedy is the savage, the black, the imbecile, the rapist, the incestuous brother, the psychotic, and the deformed. If As You Like It dramatizes the process by which the unsuitable suitor is made suitable—the education of mad Orlando by that unsuitable suitor par excellence, Ganymede—Othello dramatizes the process in reverse: the marriage of true minds is wrecked by the unsuitable suitor who woos Othello into unholy matrimony, sealed, like that other proxy marriage in the forest of Arden, when the couple kneels to "engage" their words "in the due reverence of a sacred vow." The blasphemous ceremony ends with Iago, bridelike, swearing "I am your own for ever" (3.3.461, 480). Such preoccupation among male playwrights with this issue must, surely, indicate some anxiety about the patriarchal prerogative of making marriages.

35. Theatre Records, 42 (1 and 2 June 1954).

36. Directed by Michael Bogdanov. It opened at the Royal Shakespeare Theatre 4 May 1978; Petruchio, Jonathan Pryce; Kate, Paola Dionisotti.

37. Directed by Jonathan Miller. It opened at the Royal Shakespeare Theatre 8 September 1987; Petruchio, Brian Cox; Kate, Fiona Shaw.

38. Theatre Records, 55 (23 April 1962). Indeed, most reviews across the years fail to mention Bianca at all.

39. As I argue here, Bianca's plot, far from being an irrelevance, is the master text against which Kate's deviant text must be read. A production that loses Bianca loses the point.

40. Directed by Bill Alexander. It opened at the Royal Shakespeare Theatre 1 April 1992; Petruchio, Anton Lesser; Kate, Amanda Harris. All of my quotation of Rebecca Saire comes from conversations with her in September, 1992.

41. Alexander originally devised the Watchers for his Royal Shakespeare Company touring production of Shrew (September 1990–January 1991).

42. All of my quotation of Emily Watson and Catherine Mears comes from conversations with them in September, 1992.

43. I want to thank my colleagues at the University of Warwick, Tony Howard and Martin Wright, for reading drafts of this essay. Miriam Gilbert offered invaluable advice, and Barbara Hodgdon, as always, challenging conversation and support.

A New Watershed?
Robert Lepage's *"Mudsummer"* Night's
Dream

Jay L. Halio

"DEALING with Shakespeare, we're dealing with an avalanche of resources, a box of toys to be taken out . . . . What's so extraordinary about Shakespeare is that this man was so intuitive, he gives us the story of mankind. I think he offers a lot of permission to the actor, the translator, the director. You don't feel in a literal environment when working with Shakespeare, Dante, or authors like that."[1] Indeed not, where Robert Lepage is concerned, as his production of *A Midsummer Night's Dream* at the Royal National Theatre in 1992 abundantly demonstrated. At a stroke, like Peter Brook before him (to whom he was—and is—often compared), he freed the *Dream* from all preconceptions, including those that had eventuated from Brook's production. Lepage gave everyone—actors, designers, audience—a brand new opportunity to do what he believes theater should do—exist in a state of discovery and become creative, not passive or tradition-bound.

Lepage's remarks, quoted here, were delivered to Richard Eyre, Artistic Director of the Royal National Theatre, in May 1992, while the *Dream* was still in rehearsal. They allude to another aspect of his idea of a theater—*play*. For Lepage, theater had become "a profession, a very serious word, but the concept of playing had disappeared from the staging of shows." In his approach, which emphasizes "theatricality," not "theater", he sees himself continuing (or reviving) an approach that Brook used two decades earlier in his *Dream*.[2] As Lepage said to Matt Wolf in another interview, "The basic thing in [Brook's] production

---

In its original form (altered for this collection), this essay formed a chapter in *Shakespeare in Performance: A Midsummer Night's Dream* published by Manchester University Press, U.K., in 1994.

was to get the people to actually *play*. It's not an attitude or approach you only use with the *Dream*: it's something you use in general. All too often people are acting a play, not playing it. They're not having fun with it."[3]

Lest Lepage seem too frivolous, to be trivializing performance, it should be said at once that both he and his company worked very hard in staging the *Dream*—as in all other works he has directed. Rehearsals actually began many months before opening night, starting with a series of workshops on dreams and the *Dream*, during which Lepage asked the performers to bring with them their experiences, dreams, drawings. They had fun doing so and soon began to see connections with others' metaphors. A huge drawing resulted, made out of everyone's impressions; then the company read the play, "and there it was. Suddenly it was full of water and mud and staircases and upside down forests and all sorts of things," Lepage said, adding, "that's I think what people should try to do. . . . you really have to reinvent the whole thing."[4]

Certainly that is what most audiences and critics felt Lepage and his company had done with their *Dream*. The stage setting was as far removed as possible from anything anyone had ever seen, heard, or read about. A large circular pool of water, about 25 mm. deep over an area of 120 square meters, surrounded by a bank of mud (made of Bentonite mixed with lignite and water), dominated the set from the first scene to the last. Around the mud bank was a track of firmer material on which the lovers could run without slipping and sliding, although most of the action of the play took place in or on the water. There was, in fact, so much splashing of water and splattering of mud that plastic mackintoshes were issued to the audience sitting in the first three rows of the stalls. Above the surface of the water at the pool's center hung a single light bulb suspended by a cord.

Why the water and the mud? And if the central episodes of this play occur in a forest, where were the trees? And what about Theseus's court, in which the play begins and ends? Questions to be asked, as of course they repeatedly were.

Part of the answer has already appeared in the description of what happened during Lepage's workshops the preceding December. Michael Levine, the set designer, offered more answers in his discussion with Heather Neill and Lepage shortly before the play opened. For Levine, the mud was "a purely sensual idea" but also a metaphor: "the characters, getting dirtier by the minute, become embroiled in the complications of the plot and, literally, wallow in experience."[5] Although Levine had made some designs before the workshops began, he threw them all out afterwards. He had worked with Lepage before, and together they made a good team, both believing, they said, in the intuitions of the author and the actors. Moreover, they saw in the text of A Midsummer Night's Dream a good many references to floods and tempests, all of which confirmed the intuitions they had come to accept.

The ghosts of Freud and Jung inhabited the production, too, and quotations from Jung, anthropologists, and Freudian psychologists as well as Jan Kott appeared in the program. The first two passages quoted in the program have, I think, the greatest significance. One is from Rupert Brooke's poem "Heaven":

> One may not doubt that, somehow, Good
> Shall come of Water and of Mud;
> And, sure, the reverent eye must see
> A Purpose in Liquidity.[6]

The other, quite different, is from Peter Brook's The Shifting Point:

> People have often asked me "what is the theme of A Midsummer Night's Dream?" There is only one answer to that question, the same as one would give regarding a cup. The quality of a cup is its cupness. I say this by way of introduction, to show that if I lay so much stress on the dangers involved in trying to define the themes of The Dream it is because too many productions, too many attempts at visual interpretation are based on preconceived ideas, as if these had to be illustrated in some way. In my opinion we should first of all try to rediscover the play as a living thing; then we shall be able to analyse our discoveries. Once I have finished working on the play, I can begin to produce my theories.[7]

In staging A Midsummer Night's Dream, Lepage and his company were clearly out to "rediscover the play as a living thing" and, in the process, to find "a purpose in liquidity"—liquidity in the text, which they then translated to the stage. Or, as others have suggested, citing for example, the program's references to primitive tribal customs in Africa, this Dream was meant to take us back to the beginnings of life and to suggest connections between the primitive world and the civilized one—hence the primordial mud, a "violent sexual coupling between an androgynous Puck . . . and a blue-faced fairy" at the start of 3.1, the "group sex" in muddy water (3.1–2), and the "noisy rutting" of Titania and Bottom (4.1).[8]

Mud and water were not the only surprising, not to say unconventional, aspects of this *Dream*. The performance began with a strange creature dressed in scarlet, one breast exposed, crawling crabwise across the stage to the center of the pool directly beneath the light bulb, which was on. When she got there, she reached up and turned it off. Blackout. This was Puck, played by Angela Laurier walking on her hands with her feet over her shoulders. She scurried off the stage during the blackout, and when the lights came up, the action proper of the play began.

Plunged thus into a strange and different world—a world of dreams and fantasies, it would quickly appear—what the audience saw first was a brass bedstead with mattress—the main props used in this production—pushed on stage by the four lovers. Theseus and Hippolyta rode on the bed, followed by Philostrate and Egeus on foot. Philostrate carried a chair and Demetrius's spectacles. The bed was set downstage and the bulb flown out. As Theseus and Hippolyta remained perched at the bedhead, the lovers got into position, lying down at the other end. Their posture clearly suggested that they were asleep; hence, what ensued could reasonably be understood as their collective "dream."[9] Meanwhile, Philostrate set the chair upstage right of the bed and crouched down at one corner of it, Egeus crouching at another. After the initial dialogue between Theseus and Hippolyta, Egeus crossed to the chair and stood on it to make his complaint against Lysander and Hermia, while Philostrate crossed around and, now on the bed also, like any gondolier began poling it counterclockwise around the pool.

Everyone wore white, light clothing—Theseus and Hippolyta in flowing "Moroccan" robes, the lovers in what looked like nighties and pajamas. Eventually, during the trials in the "forest," the latter became splattered with mud and water. If, as Simon Coates (who played Demetrius) remarked, "the play is about people finding out about themselves, reaching their basest level," then the dirtiness became symbolic of that.[10] The bed was doubtless the most versatile sort of prop, representing first Duke Theseus's "court" (such as it was), the meeting place (and later shelter) for the mechanicals, a door, a perch for Oberon and Puck, Titania's bower, and finally the "stage" for enacting "Pyramus and Thisbe." It was variously upended (to provide the "door"), covered with a blanket (for the shelter), and its mattress used as a hiding place for Puck, who burst out of it at the beginning of 2.1.

The fairies, with blue paint on their faces, were dressed in black, further to distinguish them from the mortals. They created the "forest" that they inhabited by placing a number of chairs in the pool. Titania and Oberon appeared as Eastern potentates, although not encumbered with overly sumptuous garb. To enhance the "foreign" aspect, a gamelan orchestra provided the music, very effectively, from each side of the Olivier stage. The lighting further created magical effects: figures were extended simultaneously as reflections in the pool and as liquid shadows on the back wall, evoking dream-like images as the action moved forward.[11] To suggest that this was more nightmare than dream, as many critics did, perhaps understated the case.

And yet it was by no means gloom and doom throughout. Thanks to Puck's antics, Titania's acrobatics, and the mechanicals' humor, the production, despite is darkness, had many light moments. Angela Laurier's Puck nearly stole the show. Like Lepage a French Canadian, but speaking with a pronounced accent, she was trained as an acrobat and contortionist; in fact, she trained the company in acrobatics for two months during rehearsals. Not that many others engaged in the kinds of feats she exhibited, such as climbing onto Bottom's back in 3.1, twisting her body around so that her feet became his ass's ears, or swiftly spinning on a rope, "encircling" the globe to fetch love-in-idleness for Oberon. No, her training of others was mainly so that they could attain the "physical alertness" in performance that was deemed essential.[12]

The actions of Titania, as performed by Sally Dexter, were also in many ways full of wonder. She did not, for example, lie asleep in her bower, but hung above it, upside down, suspended by a rope from the time the fairies finished their lullaby (2.2.24) until, awakened by Bottom's singing, she was "unhooked" and began to woo him (3.1.129).

As played by Timothy Spall and dressed in loud, spiffy clothes, Bottom evoked his share of laughter, especially when he tried to assert that he was not "afraid" (3.1.124) and had trouble getting the word out without braying. With hooves fixed on his hands and arms, which came through ·the trick sleeves of his leather coat, he was "to all intents and purposes on all fours."[13] Like Brook, Lepage had the intermission come at the end of this scene, as the fairies entered and, carrying the bed frame above their heads, bore Bottom in counterclockwise movement around the pool and took him off. Grasping a rope, Titania was slowly lowered to the pool and crawled through the water in pursuit of her love.[14]

Meanwhile, of course, the lovers were engaged in their pursuit of one another, running around the track but eventually ending up in the pool and in the mud, slipping, sliding, splashing themselves and each other. Indre Ove was a sprightly Hermia, thrusting Demetrius into the mud at 3.2.49 and 62, hurling mud in his face after throwing his glasses into it (80), and then exiting defiantly. Angered by Puck's error in anointing the wrong Athenian, Oberon whipped his cloak at her as she tried to crawl away. Hanging on to it at 3.2.96, Puck was then yanked sliding through the water (98), until she was able to wrap the cloak around herself (100) and, falling, crawl off (101).

As these examples show, the production was highly physical, often at the expense of the language in the text, which some critics complained got lost amidst all the shenanigans.[15] Although he wanted to emphasize the visual aspects of the Dream, Lepage did not intend to slight its verse. He believes that theater is "a meeting place,"[16] not only for performers, designers, directors, and audiences, but also for "voice, vibration, and muscle."[17] Here his success was far from assured. That Laurier's accent obscured some of the lines she spoke was a small part of the reason. With so much physical behavior to attend to, both audiences and performers had difficulty concentrating on what was said as well as what was done, or rather how what was done reflected, or enacted, what was said. This is a principal difference between Lepage's Dream and Brook's, whose characters, while not immediately involved in the action, leaned over the parapet of their white box to watch and listen attentively as their colleagues performed.

Lepage nevertheless tried to protect the integrity of the text. Unlike producers in the centuries preceding the twentieth, and like more recent ones, he cut very few lines, mostly from among the courtiers' quips during the performance of "Pyramus and Thisbe." His major omission was the Bergomask that follows the playlet. Thumping and stamping around in the pool of water, which is what the dance on that set required, was obviously uncalled for at that point. Moreover, some very nice touches were added that somewhat softened the effect of the "mud-wrestling" in the central episodes. For example, at 2.1.248 Puck slid down the rope on which he had encircled the earth and, holding the "flower," climbed onto Oberon's shoulder (249), eventually entwining herself around his body during his speech (253). Later, at 4.1.154, Egeus picked Hermia up after pushing Lysander away and cradled her in his arms like a child. At 172 he slowly put her down and exited (179) as the couples embraced (184).[18] The play then moved to "a haunting climax" when the black screens at the rear were raised to reveal the breaking of a new dawn, and glistening water cascaded down from four showers—one for each of the lovers, who were by then very badly in need of them.[19]

The denouement began with a spotlight searching out Bottom, awakening from his slumber and rising (4.1.200–1). In the meantime, the mechanicals on the bed assembled it into a "shelter" and crouched inside it, hidden from view by the blanket as Bottom soliloquized about his "dream." To begin the next scene, the blanket was pulled back, and Starveling lit a match for the fire, around which the others huddled. Snug then came on from stage left, crossed down to the bed, and entered the shelter from the "door" (15). When Bottom entered, he clambered onto the "roof" of the shelter while those inside reacted to his weight "aloft." They then scrambled out and gleefully surrounded their colleague, dismantling the shelter several lines later (45) and exiting.[20]

The last act presented a most unusual and stately procession. Chairs, which the fairies had used to assemble the forest in 2.1, now were put to different use by Philostrate. After Theseus and Hippolyta entered and crossed to center stage, Philostrate came on from stage left and began setting a number of chairs in a row. As he set the fifth one, Hermia entered and stepped gracefully onto the first chair. By the time she reached the third, Lysander was on the second and Helena began getting on the first. Meanwhile, Philostrate continued setting the sixth and then the seventh chair, as Demetrius completed the procession. Having showered off their mud, the lovers were now dainty and dry in fresh clothes quite similar to those they wore in 1.1. Their "primitive" experience—their baptism of passion in mud and water if not fire—now over, they returned to the world of "civilization," to Duke Theseus's court. As Hermia reached the seventh chair, Philostrate went to the head of the line and took the first chair to the end for Hermia to step on. Thus the procession continued for several more minutes until the young couples stepped off the chairs (28) and Philostrate arranged them in two rows, three behind four, and crossed behind the group to begin reading to Theseus the list of entertainments prepared for the nuptial celebrations.[21]

Here Lepage followed the Quarto in giving the lines to Philostrate rather than, as in the Folio, to Egeus, but he departed from both in letting Theseus comment on the various entertainments as Philostrate read them out—a quite reasonable arrangement. By the time Quince appeared with his Prologue, the four young lovers, with Theseus and Hippolyta, were seated, ready to view the play. The comments on Quince's failure to "stand upon points" (118–26) were cut, but as he spoke, the other mechanicals arranged the bed across center stage and Quince got on it. As he introduced each character, they also mounted the "stage." One bit of bawdry (actually in the text but seldom enacted) drew much laughter: At "stones," an Elizabethan term for testicles (5.1.190), Thisbe kissed Wall's groin. Lepage thus rejected the usual way of performing this action, for Wall's "chink" was represented by his legs, not two fingers spread apart. Lepage thereby permitted his audience to see what Shakespeare's audience most likely saw at this point.[22]

By eliminating many of the courtiers' quips as well as the Bergomask, Lepage kept the action moving briskly forward and got laughs from the broad comedy that the play-within-the-play invites, as when Pyramus, to wound his "pap" (297), bared his left nipple and plunged a stage sword into his breast. Both mood and pace changed as midnight began to chime (361). Puck entered with her broom, then Oberon, carrying a flambeau, with Titania on his right arm. Both entering and leaving, Oberon and Titania led a stately procession, except for the fairies' gamboling and planting flowers in the mud. Meanwhile (at 382), the mechanicals upended the bed (head end onto the floor), with the door hinged so that later (at 407) they could back out through it, threading their way amongst the fairies. The young lovers then followed them, also backing through the door (410–14), as the fairies began gathering up the chairs preparing for their exit with Oberon and Titania (416–22). Here Lepage transposed some of the action, placing Theseus's speech, "the iron tongue of midnight" (363–70), after Oberon's departure with Titania and their train (422).

As he announced the midnight hour, Theseus appeared in the doorway. At "to bed" (364) he and Hippolyta backed out through the door, which Philostrate then closed, leaving the stage to Puck, who "swept" him out also. Leaving her broom against the door, Puck slowly did a "normal" handstand, her head looking straight out at the audience as she spoke the epilogue. The promptbook describes her movements: "Slowly she brings her legs over DS [downstage] so that her feet rest near her shoulders. Then she lowers her body to support her weight on her forearms. Finally she 'snaps' her feet behind her armpits and drops onto her chest. Her body is completely doubled but her head and arms remain quite free for movement so that she may rest on her elbows, hands under her chin, head cocked cheerily to one side. Blackout."

As this brief analysis of his production shows, Lepage was directly opposed to literal-minded realism in his Dream, as in much of his other work. Although he finds film "an extraordinarily exciting place to be," he prefers theater, borrowing from film artistic ways of showing things or telling stories. But he feels that for a long time theater has been borrowing only the naturalism from film, and that's wrong.[23] There's more freedom in theater, he says. For him, theater provides a "vertical" relationship as opposed to the horizontal relationship of film, where the camera always moves horizontally—lineally—whether forwards and backwards or backwards and forwards. Theater is high and deep as well as broad. Lepage thus explains the light bulb at the beginning of the Dream, which drew a line vertically "where the theater starts." The theater permits contact "with above, whether it's with a god or not, with your aspirations." The actor on stage, moreover, stands perpendicularly to the audience. Richard Eyre responded to Lepage's comments very positively, agreeing that the "vertical" relationship of theater permits a three-dimensional structure—"three different things happening simultaneously on stage"—whereas in cinema the screen has to be divided, as in Abel Gance's Napoleon, with the result that cinema often has less poetic resonance.[24]

Shakespeare's theater used realism as and when needed, but it was by no means bound to it. Intermingling of the various, incongruous worlds of A Midsummer Night's Dream is but one example of the freedom Elizabethan drama enjoyed. Within the Dream, as Peter Brook saw, the mechanicals themselves stand in mockery of realistic approaches to theater. In an effort to reassure audiences that who they fear may be as literal-minded as themselves, Bottom and Quince agree on a prologue to explain the "death" of Pyramus and a mask to show that Lion is not really a lion (which might frighten the ladies terribly!), but only Snug, the joiner, after all (3.1.8–46). They are also troubled about moonlight and a wall and thus invent devices, unrealistic as they are, to overcome those problems (47–72). Of course, their concerns appear ludicrous, and are intended to seem so, although—amazingly—serious and sophisticated critics, even to-day, reflect such concerns.

Theater professionals often take a pragmatic approach to pro-duction, accepting what "works" as their essential criterion for innovations in set designs, costuming, blocking, character inter-pretation, or anything else involved in a production. "What works," however, tends to disguise by oversimplifying and at times trivializing the essential, theatrical situation. One needs to peer beneath the pragmatism to discover what the director, designer, or actor is really attempting to do, and that is to provide a new way of seeing, hearing, and *experiencing* as much of a Shakespeare play's infinite complexity as possible. To accom-plish this, the theater often resorts to new, hitherto unimag-ined—even unimaginable—ways of presentation, as in Granville-Barker's *Dream*, Brook's, or Lepage's. In those produc-tions, "what works" translates into what illuminates for us things we did not see or hear or feel and therefore did not comprehend as fully in previous productions.

In a quite different context, the American playwright, David Mamet, acutely comments upon "realism" or "truth" and its place in the theater. Citing the Russians Stanislavsky and Vakh-tangov, he argues that in theater "being true" means being true to the "aesthetic integrity" of a play. He explains:

> In general, each facet of every production must be weighed and understood solely on the basis of its interrelationship to the other elements; on its service or lack of service to the meaning, the *action* of the play. . . . Everything which does not put forward the meaning of the play impedes the meaning of the play. To do too much or too little is to mitigate and weaken the meaning. The acting, the design, the direction should all consist only of that bare minimum necessary to put forward the action. Anything else is embellishment.[25]

Shakespeare's plays, and *A Midsummer Night's Dream* in par-ticular, seem to invite a good deal of what Mamet calls "embel-lishment," as we have seen. In spite of their radical departure from traditional set designs that may have called undue attention to themselves, Lepage's production and Brook's earlier one at-tempted to minimize if not eliminate altogether embellishments of the action. To the extent that they succeeded, they helped restore Shakespeare's play to the audience. Utterly unrealistic (if "realism" is equated to literal-mindedness), the productions sought to discern the "aesthetic integrity" of the play and present it to the audience without superfluous or distracting embellishments. Granted, "embellishments" may be highly decorative, enchanting in their own right. But if they do not serve the "meaning of the play," they are unwarranted intrusions. Unfortunately, in an age like ours, when "designer's theater" seems to rival "director's theater," we are apt to find embellishment increasingly subverting (where it does not entirely overwhelm) aesthetic integrity. But as the economics of professional stage production spur the growth of fringe presentations and the work of many "little" theaters, which cannot afford elaborate embellishment, we are apt to see more and more companies like America's Shenandoah Shakespeare Express, which put on excellent productions almost anywhere, with a minimum of costumes, props, or scenery—and often none at all—to the immense delight of their audiences. Emphasizing the language of the plays and and retaining their dramatic structure, the Express has demonstrated time and again—as in its recent production of *A Midsummer Night's Dream* in 1993—that Mamet's thesis is correct.

NOTES

1. Robert Lepage in *Platform Papers*, No. 3: "Directors," Royal National Theatre, n.d. [1993], 29.

2. Ibid., 27, 24.

3. "Fairy Tales," *City Limits*, 9–16 July 1992.

4. Ibid.

5. "Dream and Nightmare Meet," *Times*, 2 July 1992.

6. Rupert Brooke, *The Complete Poems*, 2nd ed. (London: Sidgwick and Jackson, 1942), 132.

7. Peter Brook, *The Shifting Point* (New York: Harper and Row, 1987), 97.

8. George L. Geckle, Review of *A Midsummer Night's Dream, Shakespeare Bulletin* 11, no. 2 (Spring 1993): 28.

9. Ibid., 27.

10. Quoted by Sarah Hemming, "The Water-Down Version," *The Independent*, 1 July 1992.

11. Irving Wardle, *The Independent on Sunday*, 12 July 1992.

12. Sarah Hemming.

13. Promptbook. I am indebted to the Royal National Theatre for the opportunity to consult the promptbook of the production for this essay.

14. Ibid.

15. See, for instance, Geckle, 28, and Malcolm Rutherford's review in the *Financial Times*, 11 July 1992.

16. *Platform Papers*, 26.

17. Quoted by Jane Edwards, "Puck and Muck," *Time Out*, 24 June–1 July 1992, 22.

18. Promptbook.

19. Ljubima Woods, *Midweek*, 23 July 1992.

20. Promptbook.

21. Ibid.

22. See Thomas Clayton, "'Fie What a Question's That If Thou Wert Near a Lewd Interpreter': The Wall Scene in *A Midsummer Night's Dream*," *Shakespeare Studies* 7 (1974): 111.

23. *Platform Papers*, 24–25.

24. Ibid., 37.

25. David Mamet, "Realism," in *Writing in Restaurants* (New York: Viking Penguin, 1986), 130, 132.

Teaching Shakespeare's Early Comedies

RALPH ALAN COHEN

Teaching one of Shakespeare's early comedies is a harder task than teaching *King Lear* or *Hamlet*. Students come to the famous tragedies with two expectations that help the teacher: they expect the tragedies to be deep, which makes it simpler for a teacher to avouch their depth; and they expect the tragedies *not* to be funny, so any humor a teacher shows them is a bonus. Unfortunately for the teacher, students approach the comedies with the reverse expectations: their expectation that the comedies will *not* have depth makes a teacher's word to the contrary look to them like "reading in," and their expectation that the comedies *will* be funny puts teachers in the position of explaining the jokes—always a losing proposition for comedy. Tragedies benefit and comedies suffer, moreover, from the misconceptions that students have about teachers: to wit, that teachers are old, serious, and wise and know more than students about what's tragic but less than students about what's funny. The aim of this essay is to help the teachers of *The Comedy of Errors*, *The Taming of the Shrew*, and *Love's Labor's Lost* overcome these odds against them.

Each of these three plays represents—almost in the extreme—a specific problem in teaching Shakespeare and, particularly, in teaching his comedies. *The Comedy of Errors* is certainly one of Shakespeare's "thinnest" plays and lends itself poorly to any demonstration of depth in theme or character. Students can easily conclude by it that Shakespeare's plays are plot contrivances that are "not about anything." By contrast, *Shrew* boasts two fascinating characters and insistent thematic material, the long and short of which appears to be that women should be subservient to men. On the basis of *Shrew*, students could decide that Shakespeare is a DWEM (Dead White European Male) and irrelevant for the modern reader. *Love's Labor's Lost* appears to be the flipside of *Errors*, all words and no plot. Perhaps more quickly than any other of his plays, it can convince students that Shakespeare writes about people with whom they have nothing in common and does so in a language that does not belong to them. These three plays—one seemingly all old plot, one seemingly all old ideas, and one seemingly all old words—provide quite different challenges for teachers who would overcome the natural resistance of students to Shakespeare.

THE UNBEARABLE LIGHTNESS OF *THE COMEDY OF ERRORS*

Written as early as 1590, *The Comedy of Errors* may be Shakespeare's first play and is almost certainly his first comedy. The signs of its early place in Shakespeare's works are many, but students will be quick to find the main one: the play appears to be primarily its elaborately contrived plot. Shakespeare has combined two plays, *The Menæchmi* and *Amphitruo*, by the Roman playwright Plautus, and squared the complications by giving each of the separated twins (Antipholus of Syracuse and Antipholus of Ephesus) in his source a separated twin servant (Dromio of Syracuse and Dromio of Ephesus). The central joke of the play is that the man and servant from Syracuse, newly arrived in Ephesus, keep being mistaken for their twin brothers who, unknown to them, live in the city.

However implausible students may find this main conceit, they are likely to be impressed with the way Shakespeare handles the logistical problem of having four characters interact with an entire community without letting the brothers in either set meet one another until the end of the play. (Little wonder this juggling act is Shakespeare's shortest play). A beginning playwright, ambitious to show his stuff, doubtless found a temptation in this elaborate problem of plotting, and Shakespeare's uncharacteristic obedience to the classical unities of time, place, and person further suggests that his attraction to the project was partly theoretical.

The primary evidence, however, that the play is early or that Shakespeare's main interest in this material was structural, is the thinness of the play's characters, who by comparison with the characters found elsewhere in Shakespeare's work, will help teach the meaning of "flat" and "round" characters. Antipholus of Ephesus may be more lighthearted than his brother, and Dromio of Syracuse may be a bit more clever and more mischievous than his twin, but they, like every other character in the play—with one exception—rarely rise above the stereotypes nec-

essary to the plot. That rather remarkable exception to this gener-
alization about *The Comedy of Errors* is Adriana, the jealous
wife of Antipholus of Ephesus, and it is here that teachers have
a particularly good chance of engaging their students.

By convention and the requirements of this plot, Adriana's
role should be the unreasonable, shrewish wife whose unfair
treatment of her husband has driven him from the home. But
even through the comic jangle of the rhymed lines (another sign
of the early Shakespeare, eager to show off his skills), we can
hear an Adriana too human to be pigeonholed by type. Have your
students look for those moments when Adriana's personhood
overtakes her type. When, for example, she worries about her
age, she rather troublingly asks, "What ruins are in me that can
be found, / By him not ruin'd?" (2.1.96–97). It may be funny
when she confronts the wrong Antipholus, a man who has never
seen her before, with her accusations of infidelity, but her general
argument against adultery stands out against the stream of
comedy:

> For if we two be one, and thou play false,
> I do digest the poison of thy flesh,
> Being strumpeted by thy contagion.
>
> (2.2.142–44)

Othello could not have stated any more beautifully the meta-
physical pharmaceutics of sexual infidelity.

Adriana simply refuses to behave as a stereotype; she retains
her distinctive voice to the end of the play. When the Abbess,
who is clearly operating as the adjudicator of the play's conflicts,
blames Adriana for her husband's supposed madness and insists
on keeping him in the abbey, a cipher would have stood aside in
humiliation. Adriana, however, will not yield her rights or
duties:

> I will not hence, and leave my husband here;
> And ill it doth beseem your holiness
> To separate the husband and the wife.
>
> (5.1.109–11)

Even though the Abbess, as the play's emblem of long suffering
and wise matriarchy, might expect the automatic sympathy of
an audience, Shakespeare gives Adriana a surprisingly real and
moving declaration. Here and elsewhere, students can readily
see that Adriana's character provides a stark contrast to the cari-

catures in the play around her. They may be all the more amused to see the little reward that Shakespeare gives this character at the conclusion: he allows her the pleasure of a little secret from her husband, who must wonder just what sort of dessert his twin brother might have had at "dinner" with Adriana.

Just as Adriana is a hint of characters to come (Kate, Beatrice, Portia), the play has in it the seeds of themes and images to come. Here teachers may show their students the separated family, the interrupted banquet, and multiple male-female relationships (Adriana-Antipholus of Ephesus, Luciana-Antipholus of Syracuse, and Nell-Dromio) used as foils for one another. Here also is the theme of searching for one's identity. In Shakespeare's mature works, his main characters—Richard II, Benedick, Hal, Hamlet, Othello, Lear, Macbeth, Antony—learn to know themselves. In Errors that theme works both figuratively and literally: the search of Antipholus and Dromio of Syracuse for their twins forces on all four characters the question of identity ("Am I Dromio?") and of self knowledge. Students might look for those places in the text where each of these characters brings up the matter of identity. They might discuss the different ways that each Antipholus deals with the confusion. Antipholus of Syracuse, for example, seeks for supernatural explanations, while his twin of Ephesus sees conspiracy everywhere.

Perhaps most rewarding, in The Comedy of Errors Shakespeare explores his favorite theme of reality and illusion through the idea of identical twins. Teachers can help students see how questions of staging are inextricable from this theme by examining with them the difficulties of staging a play about two sets of twins. Since it is hardly possible that two such sets of twins made up four of the main actors in Shakespeare's company, we must assume that the company found some way to represent the Antipholi and the Dromios without casting real twins. Using this issue as a point of departure about the nature of the theater, teachers can have students do what every production of the play must do—solve the twin problem.

The search for a solution can go in two directions:

(1) Making the four players look like two set of twins. Cast people from the class who look alike. Make certain the class discusses the reason for their decisions about hair coloring, height, weight, sex, and so on. Try to link those decisions to the text. With the four people in front of the class, move to a discussion of ways of disguising their "untwinness." This approach should lead the class naturally to an enjoyable and entertaining

exploration of the possibilities for making the characters into twins with movement, voice, makeup, and costume.

(2) *Ignoring the look-alike problem altogether.* One way to deal with the question of twins is as a challenge to the audience's imagination. Contrast with the ideal of look-alikes the effect of casting four characters who look nothing at all alike; a teacher may even wish to make a joke about their "twinship" by using males and females, blacks and whites, or tall and short actors as mismatched twins. What sort of effect does that kind of casting choice have on the play? What does it say about reality and illusion? In this way, a discussion of the central production challenge of the play leads directly to a core thematic issue. *Errors* is lightweight by comparison to Shakespeare's other works, but teachers can turn its very lightness to their advantage by showing students the few real nuggets in Shakespeare's stew.

THE POLITICAL ELASTICITY OF *THE TAMING OF THE SHREW*

Written early in his career, perhaps as early as 1593, *The Taming of the Shrew* has many of the classic farcical elements of *The Comedy of Errors*, but it is, in Shakespearean terms, a great leap forward. In the light of that earlier play, you can almost see Shakespeare turn his attention from plot and structure to character and theme. Accordingly, the structure of *The Taming of the Shrew* is episodic, and the plot has almost a perfunctory feel about it, while the play is peopled with much more interesting and unpredictable characters. For example, Petruchio's servant, Grumio, bears some likeness to such classical tricky servants as the Dromios, but in his cranky-affectionate relationship with his master and his fellow servant, he is an original. On the stage, *Shrew* has always been one of Shakespeare's most popular plays, and now the woman's movement has made it one of his most controversial as well.

The play appears to support male domination of women, just as *The Merchant of Venice* appears to support anti-Semitism, just as *Henry V* appears to support militarism, just as *The Tempest* appears to support colonialism. Some of your most thoughtful students will reasonably conclude that Shakespeare is out of date and that his lack of political awareness is proof that he is of an age and not for all times. In the context of today's politics, *The Taming of the Shrew* certainly looks like an obsolete piece of male chauvinism. But this play, like all of Shakespeare's plays, fits into other contexts and leaves room for other views. To help students see the elasticity of the play's politics, teachers might have them look at it from some of those other contexts by asking them, for example, to judge Kate's statement that a woman owes her husband the duty that "the subject owes a prince" (5.2.155) in the light of the fact that the play was performed first for an audience whose prince was Elizabeth I—a woman who had reigned for some thirty-five years. If students are familiar with Shakespeare's other comedies, they then might consider its author's attitude toward women in the light of other female characters such as Portia, Rosalind, and Beatrice.

Most important, students should consider the play in terms of the additional context that Shakespeare himself provided: the Induction. In this strange prefix to the play, an English Lord comes across Christopher Sly, a drunk tinker passed out in the road, takes him home, bathes him, dresses him, and tries to persuade him that he himself is a lord and has been out of his mind for fifteen years. This odd introduction to a play set in Padua is odder still because once Sly has watched two scenes of the play, he disappears wholly from the work.

The inescapable question to put to students is "What do these two scenes about a practical joke on a drunken Englishman have to do with the ensuing story of Kate and Petruchio?" Then point out to them that in both stories the following happens: (1) The power structures of society (in the Induction, the English nobility; in Shrew proper, the paternalistic system we all take for granted) contrive to persuade someone to accept a reality at odds with their own. (2) By appearing to submit to that reality both "victims" believe that they can secure food, clothing, shelter, sex, and social status (for Sly, the wealth, wife, and position of a lord; for Kate, the material, sexual, and social benefits of being Petruchio's wife). (3) Although both characters give a speech that satisfies the powers that they have imposed their realities on the "victim" (Sly's "Upon my life, I am a lord indeed" [Ind. 2.72]; Kate's "Then vail your stomachs, for it is no boot,/And place your hands below your husband's foot;/In token of which duty, if he please, /My hand is ready, may it do him ease" [5.2.176–79]), neither their societies nor the audience can ever know for certain whether the "victims" believe what they say or are only getting the last laugh.

At the heart of that last possibility is the sanctity of the private self, the self that can say one thing and mean another, and Petruchio, the character who is the supposed tool of a paternalistic society, is also the high priest of the private self and, by extension, of the privacy of married love. Petruchio is the second key for your students to the largeness of the play. Though productions and editions of the play portray him as a bully with a whip, nowhere in the text is there evidence that Petruchio ever hits anyone. True, at his first appearance, he and Grumio have a comic quarrel, and the stage direction reads, "He wrings [Grumio] by the ears" (sd.1.2.17), but Hortensio makes it clear that such altercations are part of the friendship between Petruchio and his "ancient, trusty, pleasant servant Grumio" (47). And true as well that when Kate hits Petruchio at their first encounter, he says, "I swear I'll cuff you, if you strike again" (2.1.220), but she takes his warning to heart, and the subject does not come up again.

Shakespeare's Petruchio is no brute; he is a brilliant improviser whose basic strategy in "taming" Kate and in assuring his individuality (and hers) is to make believe, to say the thing that is not. He reveals precisely this approach to the audience about his dealings with Kate—"If she do bid me pack, I'll give her thanks,/ As though she bid me stay by her a week" (2.1.177–78)— but he does the same thing with the society that has been tormenting her. He lies to them continually: he tells them that she and he have agreed to be married the next Sunday and that she hung about his neck and kissed him; he pretends there is some reason for his outrageous dress on his wedding day; he assures them that his business will not let him stay for the feast; and he pretends that he is rescuing her from some sort of assault when he abducts her from the festivities. When he is not simply lying to them, he is telling them to mind their own business:

If she and I be pleas'd, what's that to you?   (2.1.303)

Tedious it were to tell, and harsh to hear—
Sufficeth I am come to keep my word.   (3.2.105–06)

...what a fool am I to chat with you,
When I should bid good morrow to my bride.   (3.2.121–22)

...if you knew my business,
You would entreat me rather go than stay.   (3.2.191–92)

Be mad or merry, or go hang yourselves.   (3.2.226)

The contempt Petruchio has for Kate's status-conscious and paternalistic society is a much overlooked point of the play and one that students will enjoy. Petruchio may let Baptista and the others see him as a shrew tamer, but he is in fact teaching her how to survive as an individual in a conformist world of Baptistas, Biancas, and Gremios. Previously Kate has fought for her integrity by playing exactly the role they have dictated, that of shrew, but Petruchio shows her how easy—and profitable—it is to pretend a belief in other realities. He demonstrates his own contempt for appearance by his attitude to dress—his bizarre wedding outfit ("To me she's married, not unto my clothes" [3.2.117]), the soiling of her wedding clothes, his destruction of the dress for her sister's wedding (". . . Tis the mind that makes the body rich" [4.3.172])—and he teaches her from the moment they meet ("hearing thy mildness prais'd in every town" [2.1.191]) that one's speech and reality need not be connected. This lesson gets more and more sophisticated. He tells her it is seven in the morning, when she knows it is two in the afternoon. Having challenged the evidence of a clock (which could, after all, be rigged), he contradicts the evidence of the sun that shines incontrovertibly above them. He tells her the sun is the moon and insists she agree to that proposition. Here is the crux of his lesson: whatever she says will not change the reality—the sun will shine still. At that moment she finally understands, for when he tells her to greet an old man as if he were a young woman, she goes Petruchio one better and plays the game more skillfully than he: "Young budding virgin," she begins, and concludes with congratulations for "the man whom favorable stars / Allots thee for his lovely bedfellow" (4.5.37–41).

The example of Sly in the Induction, Petruchio's own example and his lessons about make-believe, and her evident love for him are the contexts in which Kate gives that final troublesome speech. We cannot know whether or not she believes what she says; only she knows, and that may be Shakespeare's point. Read thus, the play is not about man against woman, but about the individual against society, about the final inviolability of self. When Petruchio and Kate go offstage "to bed," they leave behind a bewildered Padua. Though Hortensio tries to draw the play to an easy conclusion by saying that Petruchio "hast tamed a curst shrow" (5.2.188), Shakespeare does not make his the last word, but instead has Lucentio make the much more ambiguous observation that "'Tis a wonder, by your leave, she will be tam'd so" (5.2.189).

In other words, through discussion and suggestion teachers can present to their students a reading in which Shakespeare subverts not only the phallocentric assumptions of the play, but also the very title he has given it. Until teachers show it to them, however, students will be suspicious that they are merely imposing a politically correct interpretation on male-chauvinist material. Suggesting such a reading to students is one thing; showing them how it might work is another. The class should, therefore, stage that final scene.

To do that, a teacher will need to find a student who can act reasonably well and spend about an hour working out of class with him or her on Kate's final speech. Try three readings: totally serious, totally ironic (perhaps with a Southern accent), and totally in league and in love with Petruchio (the reading that comes out of my comments above). Petruchio has only the last line, but Kate should use him as a prop whenever she likes.

In the first reading, have the actress do the speech seriously, without reference at all to Kate's character earlier in the play-- as though she were the most fervent adherent of a patriarchal faith—a fundamentalist Christian, Muslim, or Jew. The effect can be chilling. Ask the students what they think of it. Chances are they will object that it makes no sense at all in terms of Petruchio's interest in Kate. From his first altercation with Grumio, it is clear that he is a man who enjoys a good fight, and after the ferocity of their first encounter, he calls their battle a "chat" and tells Kate that he is "a husband for your turn." For such a man, the submissive fawning of a wife who follows the precepts of Kate's speech would be death by boredom.

In the second reading, the actress can do the speech as it is done in most recent productions, as a Kate who does not believe a word of her speech. Her message to Bianca and the Widow (a teacher can situate two other women on the "stage" to stand in as Bianca and the widow) is "wink, wink, nudge, nudge: don't believe a word of this." Such a reading show a Katherine who has simply assumed Bianca's methods of dealing with men: flatter them by pretending to love and obey them.

If both these versions of the speech seem at odds with the rest of the play, the solution may lay outside a "true or false" approach. But where? To answer that question, the actress might ask herself not how she feels about her speech, but how she feels about her husband. Have her focus entirely on him, as if the speech is their little joke on the "regular" couples who have bet against them, and her main intent is to surprise him with how well he has taught her the fun and profit of make-believe. This exercise is likely to show students that Shakespeare's play entrusts its meaning to the actors who play it, and, on that basis, they may conclude that at the heart of the play is Petruchio's game of improvisation, that its truth is an actor's truth—contingent on the moment.

TEACHING IRONY IN *LOVE'S LABOR'S LOST*

In many ways, *Love's Labor's Lost* confirms all the worst fears students may have about Shakespeare. To start with, little actually happens in the plot of the play: four noblemen, led by the King of Navarre, swear oaths of study and abstinence, and, when four ladies, led by the Princess of France, come for a visit, they break those oaths by falling in love and writing poetry; meanwhile, an assortment of underclass characters join together to put on a masque; the masque goes unfinished and the four couples part unmarried. End of play. In no other of Shakespeare's plays does so little actually transpire—no action, no violence, no sex, no weddings, and no major changes in anyone's situation. Whereas *The Comedy of Errors* juggles the constant conflicts created by two sets of twins and ends with a wedding and the reunion of a family, *Love's Labor's Lost* contains nearly no narrative excitement at all. And while *The Taming of the Shrew* sets forth a timeless battle of the sexes between two appealing and interesting characters, *Love's Labor's Lost* gives us a contest between men and women in which the men are unappealing and helpless nitwits. Worst of all, for those who come to Shakespeare fearing his language, *Love's Labor's Lost* is stuffed with all the difficulties they could ever have expected: ornate speeches that are long on words and short on matter, Elizabethan vernacular, poetical flourishes, classical allusions, and even jokes in Latin. Shakespeare could hardly have designed a play less likely than *Love's Labor's Lost* to overcome a student's conditioned reflex against his work. And for that very reason, the teacher who shows students how *Love's Labor's Lost* speaks to them, and even for them, will have given them a tool that opens much else in Shakespeare and works as well with any work of literature. That tool in the case of *Love's Labor's Lost* is irony.

If students were to consider what they think Shakespeare felt about the plot, the characters, and the language in this play, chances are they will assume one of two things: either Shake-

speare, as some sort of superbrain, could see and hear something
in the action and speech of these characters that regular people
cannot see and hear, or Shakespeare and his audience of four
hundred years ago were all dweebs of some sort and behaved
and sounded like the people in this play. But how would they
feel about the play if they saw that Shakespeare stands apart
from the characters he created, that he may even have written
the play to make fun of such characters and their language, and
that the entire play subverts the very things that they—the students—would themselves attack? In other words, how would
they feel about *Love's Labor's Lost* is they knew that the play
was poking fun at what they poke fun at when they think of
"Shakespeare"?

Love's Labor's Lost is full of people who abuse language: they
speak too much, they put the form of what they say over the
content, and they reach for obscure words and syntax. Students
have little trouble seeing the absurd linguistic excesses of Holofernes, Nathaniel, and Don Armado. Holofernes, a schoolteacher,
provides an easily recognizable target as someone who must always be finding a difficult way to say a thing. "The deer is dead"
thus becomes:

> The deer was (as you know) *sanquis* in blood, ripe as the pomewater,
> who now hangeth like a jewel in the ear of *coelo*, the sky, the welkin,
> the heaven, and anon falleth like a crab on the face of *terra*, the soil,
> the land, the earth.
>
> (4.2.3–7)

Holofernes's need to show off his Latin is so clear it may obscure
the pretentious inflation of the speech as a whole. Holofernes's
comparison of the death of a deer to the fall of an apple (the
pomewater) is too elaborate. The apple becomes an earring in
the ear of the sky that falls on the face of the earth like a "crab."
"Crab" here certainly means "crab apple," and the image of a
deer falling on the face of the earth like a crab apple is preposterous enough, but the eulogy for the deer suffers even more if the
meaning of "crab" as "crustacean" leaks into the image.

And of course Nathaniel, the curate, mimics the flaws of his
admired friend:

> I did converse this quondam day with a companion of the King's,
> who is intituled, nominated, or called, Don Adriano de Armado.
>
> (5.1.6–8)

Thus does Nathaniel introduce the third of the obviously comic overspeakers, the "vain, ridiculous, and thrasonical" (5.1.12) Spanish braggadocio. The comedy of this character's language is manifest: like Holofernes and Nathaniel, he never settles for one word when a dozen will serve—"I do affect the very ground (which is base) where her shoe (which is baser) guided by her foot (which is basest) doth tread" (1.2.167–69). He carries to excess such rhetorical flourishes as the apostrophe: "Adieu, valour, rust, rapier, be still, drum, for your manager is in love; yea, he loveth. . . . Devise, wit, write, pen, for I am for whole volumes in folio" (181–85). The comedy of such language needs little more support from a teacher than a clear line reading.

But while students may assume that they can laugh at the play's clowns, their conditioned reflex to Shakespeare as serious and as "other" inhibits their laughter at the play's "heroes." For that reason they may have trouble seeing that the preposterous language in the subplot is not just a matter of comic relief from the serious business of the play, but rather a vantage point from which to view the male characters of the main plot. The four noblemen—Navarre, Dumain, Longaville, and Berowne—share with the verbose clowns a tendency to abuse speech by caring more for how they say things than for what they say. Like Holofernes and Don Armado, they speak too much, and their obsession with style over content obscures their meaning and, in the end, debases not only language but themselves.

Look, for example, at the King of Navarre's speech at the very opening of the play. If we read that speech without the understanding that Shakespeare can stand apart from his characters, we might accept at face value the King's project—an academy devoted to learning and one that, as we find out, allows no conversation with women, no meals, and hardly any sleep. For an audience or readers to take such a project seriously, they must set aside everything that they know about human nature, and the problem is that students are likely to assume that, when they read Shakespeare, they're supposed to do just that—set aside all they know about themselves. But showing them how Shakespeare sets up the speech as a huge joke shows them that what they know about themselves matters.

Navarre doesn't sound like he's proposing a study group; he sounds like he's leading an army into the most heroic military action ever undertaken:

> Let fame, that all hunt after in their lives,
> Live regist'red upon our brazen tombs,

And then grace us in the disgrace of death;
When spite of cormorant devouring Time,
Th'endeavor of this present breath may buy
That honour which shall bate his scythe's keen edge,
And make us heirs of all eternity.
Therefore, brave conquerors—

(1.1.1–8)

And at this point an audience could reasonably expect to hear
Navarre say, "once more into the breach, dear friends" and rush
with his three fellows into battle. What Navarre says instead is
that the "brave conquerors" have sworn to make their court a
"little academe." That is, when we hear the irony of this heroic
language ending with the proposition that four young men lock
themselves in an ivory tower, we can enjoy the fact that Shakespeare has made a joke. The playwright has cast into a humorous
light the main project of the plot, and his evident sense of its
foolishness will precisely match that of the students. Introducing
them in this way to the irony in the work will let them see that
Shakespeare is on their side against the action of his own play.
Thus repositioned, they can view the story of *Love's Labor's Lost*
free from the burden of Shakespeare as adversary.

Consider Berowne's response to the King's opening. Berowne
is the realist among these four, the man most likely to sniff out
pretension and to speak his mind; he thinks the King's plan is
silly, and this is how he says so:

So much, dear liege, I have already sworn,
But there are other strict observances:
As not to see a woman in that term,
Which I hope well is not enrolled there;
And one day in a week to touch no food,
And but one meal on every day beside,
The which I hope is not enrolled there;
And then to sleep but three hours in the night,
And not be seen to wink of all the day—
When I was wont to think no harm all night,
And make a dark night too of half the day—
Which I hope well is not enrolled there.
O, these are barren tasks, too hard to keep,
Not to see ladies, study, fast, not sleep.

(34–48)

Unlike his comic counterparts, Berowne can handle language;
where Holofernes or Don Armado would bungle a figure of

speech or rhetorical flourish, Berowne passes them off smoothly. If it is read aloud, students are likely to admire it as they would a well-written poem: it has rhymes, it keeps its meter, it is better than they could do. Berowne's speech is excellent in the way that students expect "literature" to be excellent—words used in cleverer ways than normal—and that is precisely the response that innoculates them against a more critical view.

As charming and as playful as the speech may be, it reveals Berowne's infatuation with language for language's sake. His own first words virtually concede that he has nothing to add to the speeches of Dumain and Longaville, who have already sworn to join the King: "I can but say their protestation over." He then adds that in any case he has "already sworn." That said, he should say no more, but of course, he has much more to say. His refrain—"which I hope is not enrolled there"—is vain in both meanings of the word: as a thrice-repeated rhetorical strategy, it suggests the vanity of the speaker (as does his interruptive boast about sleeping late), but Berowne's hope is also "in vain," since all the conditions that he has complained about *are* enrolled in the agreement. How odd, then, that Berowne should "hope" that the restrictions before his eyes in the document he is holding in his hand are *not* in the document. The king thinks it odd as well and reminds Berowne that he has given his oath, to which Berowne protests that, "I only swore to study with Your Grace, / And stay here in your court for three years' space" (51–52). When Longaville objects, "You swore to that Berowne, and to the rest" (53), Berowne answers rather flippantly, "By yea and nay, sir, then I swore in jest" (54).

Berowne's first exchanges should reveal to students a man who likes to play with words, who first denies an oath and then claims to have sworn in jest. In his attitude toward that oath, we can see the logical extension of these nobles' attitude toward language. Valuing form over content, they all become forsworn. Language for these men has come unstuck from meaning, and by noticing that the words of even the best of these noblemen have much in common with the language of the so-called "comic" figures, students not only find themselves on Shakespeare's side, but they also find their way into the core of the play.

To notice the irony that there are similarities between the noblemen and the clowns is to begin to see much else. We can glimpse, for example, the hypocrisy of the four noblemen when they mock the content and the style of Don Armado's letter— "How low soever the matter, I hope in God for high words," jokes

Berowne (1.1.192–93). Sensing their hypocrisy, we may even be a little uncomfortable when the aristocrats subject this letter written only to Navarre to pubic ridicule. Feeling that discomfort, we may take more satisfaction when—in Act Four—the private writing of the four lords (their sonnets to the ladies) becomes in turn the object of public sport.[1] Understanding, moreover, that the four lords are more than a little infatuated with themselves and their words, we may be suspicious when we hear Berowne's overlong apology for "perjury" and his flowery renunciation of "speeches penned" of "taffeta phrases" and of "spruce affectation" (5.2.394–409). And when we hear his promise to speak more plainly in the future—

> Henceforth my wooing mind shall be express'd
> In russet yeas and honest kersey noes.
> And to begin, wench, so God help me law!
> My love to thee is sound, sans crack or flaw.
>
> (5.2.412–15)

—we may anticipate Rosaline's quick response to the French affectation that betrays him: "Sans 'sans,' I pray you" (416).

Finally, the same ironic distance that levels the aristocrats with their comic counterparts helps us to view more critically the scorn Navarre and his cronies heap on the masque of the "Nine Worthies." This unfinished "show" at the end of Shakespeare's play, like "Pyramus and Thisbe" in *A Midsummer Night's Dream*, relies for its comedy on the absurd theatrics of amateurs who wish to offer entertainment to their superiors. In *Dream*, Bottom's irrepressible enthusiasm for the project and the formal demands of the occasion preserve the show from the discourteous trio of grooms, but in *Love's Labor's Lost*, the four gentlemen—intent on showing off for one another and the visiting ladies—heckle the show to a close. In *Dream*, we may almost ignore the onstage audience and their annoying commentary, but in *Love's Labor's Lost*, the lords' relentless rudeness ruins the proferred interlude and forces us to think about the interaction on the stage. Shakespeare, who always had to concern himself with the number of available actors in his plays, must have taken some delight in the mathematics of this scene and the commentary that it makes on the four nobles. Costard, Moth, Holofernes, Nathaniel, and Don Armado try to stage the Nine Worthies with five actors, but what we watch is a more disturbing show about nine men that might be entitled "the Five Worthies and the Four Unworthies."

To get at the complexity of this moment and its satirical quality, a teacher can stage the scene (from the entrance of Costard as Pompey to the exit of the Worthies) in the classroom with a "blocked reading." Arrange the members of the class who will be the "real" audience three-quarters around an imaginary platform (to simulate the groundlings in an Elizabethan theatre); in front of their desks situate the nine students who represent the audience within the play (four lords, four ladies, and Boyet); and then have the five others come out to play the clowns at the center of the semicircle created by the two concentric audiences. In this way the class reproduces the physical arrangement of audience and players at the Theatre where Shakespeare's Company first staged the play, and the students may much more readily understand how that configuration makes the "real" audience an extension of the action is the play. The "production" may be elaborate or simple, but with students in this configuration a simple reading of the lines will allow their teacher to ask some telling questions: How does the physical arrangement of "real" audience and "play" audience connect the two? Do the members of the "real" audience begin to feel irritation with the audience of aristocrats who will not let the show go on? Which of the gallants leads the heckling? What part does Boyet play in the proceedings? Why is the King relatively quiet? How are we to take the Princess's encouraging comments ("Proceed, good Alexander" [567]; "Stand aside, good Pompey" [587]; "Alas, poor Maccabaeus, how hath he been baited" [631]; "Speak, brave Hector, we are much delighted" [665])? What is the effect of the silence of the other women?

What emerges from such questions is a growing sense of the callousness of the "gentlemen" and the humanity of the "clowns." When the aristocrats torment Holofernes by pretending to confuse Judas Maccabee with Judas Iscariot and then descend to the even more puerile name game of calling him "Jud-as[s]," Holfernes rightly protests, "This is not generous, not gentle, not humble" (629). Later, after a thorough humiliation by his noble hosts, Don Armado exits with this speech:

For mine own part, I breathe free breath. I have seen the day of wrong through the little hole of discretion, and I will right myself like a soldier.

(722–24)

The speech is remarkable. The initial butt of the play asserts his freedom, sees his faults, and determines to improve himself. He says all this, moreover, in a speech which is relatively straight to the point. The man that our putative heroes mocked at the beginning of the play for his language ends the play by rising above them. Unlike the aristocrats, Don Armado has seen himself as others see him.

Irony is what provides access to this reading of the play, a reading that does not require students to admire either the actions or the language of the play's protagonists. That ironic view makes it no surprise that the four women decline the proposals of men. That ironic view endears the play's clowns to an audience. That ironic view puts Shakespeare on the students' side against the very affectations and attitudes that they may once have condemned as "Shakespearean."

NOTE

1. I have had much success with an exercise in which students "grade" the four poems the noblemen have written to the ladies. The teacher simply makes copies of each of the poems (leaving off the name of the lord who wrote it) and has students present readings of each. The class then questions such things as the logic, the rhyme, the syntax, the clarity, and the mood of each poem. Which is the best poem? Which is the worst? Then the teacher reveals the names of each author and asks how the substance and style of each poem relate to the character who wrote it.

Index

245